INHUMAN

AN VOL. 1: GENESIS. Contains material originally published in magazine form as INHUMAN #1-6. First printing 2014. ISBN# 978-0-7851-8577-2. Published by MARVEL WORLDWIDE, INC., a subsidiary of MARVEL ˙AINMENT, LLC. OFFICE OF PUBLICATION: 135 West 50th Street, New York, NY 10020. Copyright © 2014 Marvel Characters, Inc. All rights reserved. All characters featured in this issue and the distinctive names ˙nesses thereof, and all related indicia are trademarks of Marvel Characters, Inc. No similarity between any of the names, characters, persons, and/or institutions in this magazine with those of any living or dead or institution is intended, and any such similarity which may exist is purely coincidental. **Printed in Canada.** ALAN FINE, EVP - Office of the President, Marvel Worldwide, Inc. and EVP & CMO Marvel Characters ˙N BUCKLEY, Publisher & President - Print, Animation & Digital Divisions; JOE QUESADA, Chief Creative Officer; TOM BREVOORT, SVP of Publishing; DAVID BOGART, SVP of Operations & Procurement, Publishing; BULSKI, SVP of Creator & Content Development; DAVID GABRIEL, SVP Print, Sales & Marketing; JIM O'KEEFE, VP of Operations & Logistics; DAN CARR, Executive Director of Publishing Technology; SUSAN CRESPI, ˙ Operations Manager; ALEX MORALES, Publishing Operations Manager; STAN LEE, Chairman Emeritus. For information regarding advertising in Marvel Comics or on Marvel.com, please contact Niza Disla, ˙ of Marvel Partnerships, at ndisla@marvel.com. For Marvel subscription inquiries, please call 800-217-9158. **Manufactured between 10/3/2014 and 11/10/2014 by SOLISCO PRINTERS, SCOTT, QC, CANADA.**

7 6 5 4 3 2 1

WRITER
CHARLES SOULE
ARTISTS
JOE MADUREIRA (#1-3) &
RYAN STEGMAN (#4-6)

COLORIST
MARTE GRACIA

LETTERER
VC'S CLAYTON COWLES

COVER ART
JOE MADUREIRA & MARTE GRACIA (#1-3) AND
RYAN STEGMAN & MARTE GRACIA (#4-6)

ASSISTANT EDITOR
DEVIN LEWIS

EDITOR
NICK LOWE

INHUMANS CREATED BY STAN LEE & JACK KIRBY

COLLECTION EDITOR:
SARAH BRUNSTAD
ASSOCIATE MANAGING EDITOR:
ALEX STARBUCK
EDITORS, SPECIAL PROJECTS:
JENNIFER GRÜNWALD & MARK D. BEAZLEY
SENIOR EDITOR, SPECIAL PROJECTS:
JEFF YOUNGQUIST
BOOK DESIGNER:
NELSON RIBEIRO

SVP PRINT, SALES & MARKETING:
DAVID GABRIEL
EDITOR IN CHIEF:
AXEL ALONSO
CHIEF CREATIVE OFFICER:
JOE QUESADA
PUBLISHER:
DAN BUCKLEY
EXECUTIVE PRODUCER:
ALAN FINE

MILLIONS OF YEARS AGO, WHEN HUMANKIND WAS IN ITS INFANCY, AN ALIEN CIVILIZATION CALLED THE KREE EXPERIMENTED ON ANCIENT HOMO SAPIENS. THE EXPERIMENTS CREATED A NEW RACE WHO CALLED THEMSELVES INHUMANS, AN EVOLUTIONARY LEAP OVER THEIR CAVE-DWELLING BRETHREN.

WHEN ONE OF THESE INHUMANS DISCOVERED A CHEMICAL CALLED TERRIGEN THAT UNLOCKED SECRET SUPER-POWERS BURIED IN THEIR DNA BY THE KREE, IT FRAGMENTED INHUMAN SOCIETY. SOME INHUMANS STAYED IN THEIR HOME CITY OF ATTILAN, SOME MIXED IN WITH REGULAR HUMANS AND SOME JUST DISAPPEARED...

THOUSANDS OF YEARS LATER, BLACK BOLT, THE KING OF THE ATTILAN INHUMANS, DETONATED A TERRIGEN BOMB TO SAVE THE WORLD FROM AN INCREDIBLE THREAT. THIS TERRIGEN BOMB DESTROYED BLACK BOLT'S CITY AND CREATED A CLOUD OF TERRIGEN MIST THAT HAS BEEN FLOWING AROUND THE WORLD ACTIVATING THE DNA OF HUMANS THAT HAD NO IDEA THEY WERE PART OF A SECRET HISTORY OR THAT THEY WERE...

INHUMAN

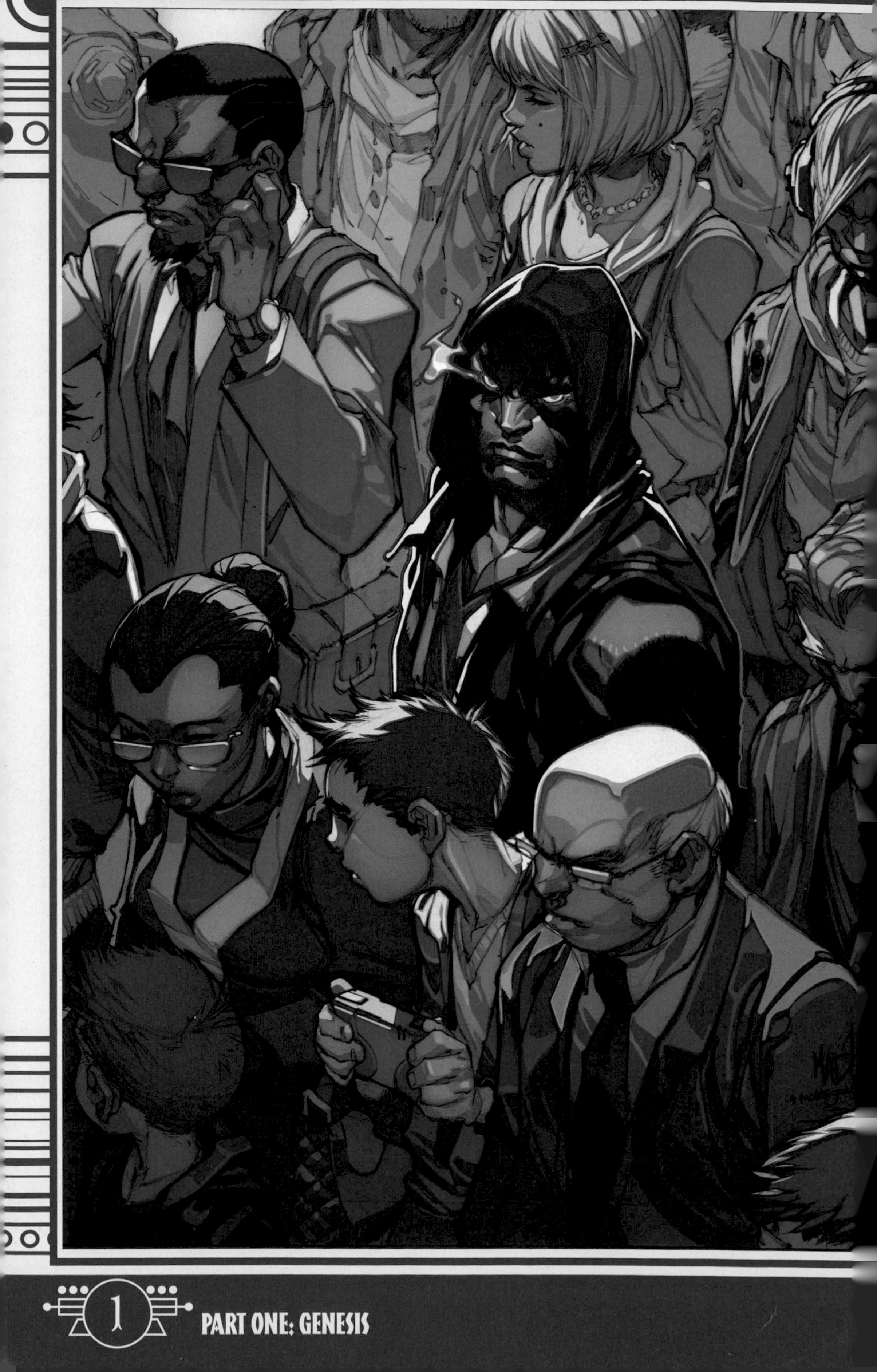

1

PART ONE: GENESIS

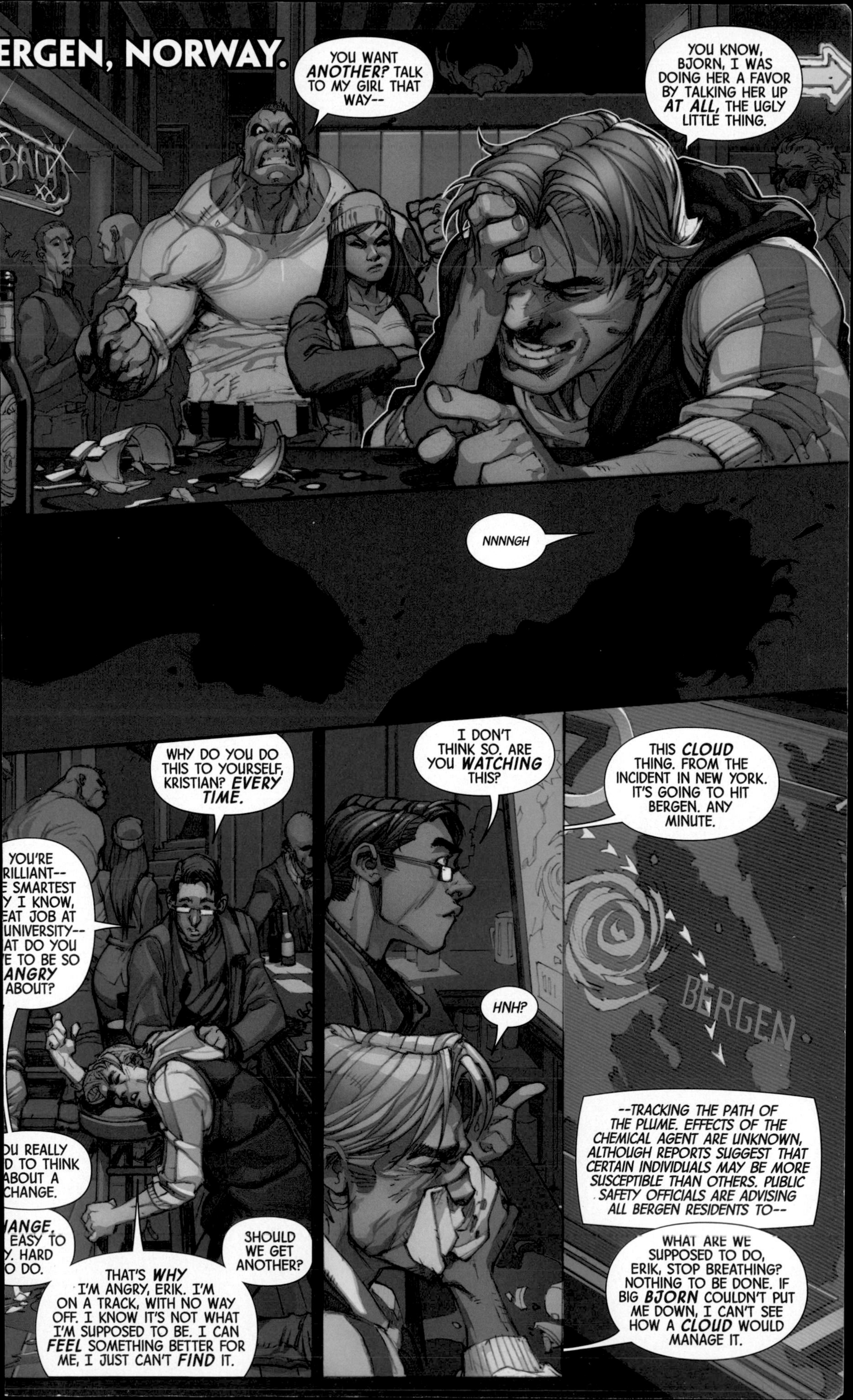
ERGEN, NORWAY.
YOU WANT ANOTHER? TALK TO MY GIRL THAT WAY--
YOU KNOW, BJORN, I WAS DOING HER A FAVOR BY TALKING HER UP AT ALL, THE UGLY LITTLE THING.
NNNNGH
WHY DO YOU DO THIS TO YOURSELF, KRISTIAN? EVERY TIME.
YOU'RE RILLIANT-- E SMARTEST Y I KNOW, EAT JOB AT UNIVERSITY-- AT DO YOU E TO BE SO ANGRY ABOUT?
OU REALLY D TO THINK ABOUT A CHANGE.
ANGE. EASY TO Y. HARD O DO.
THAT'S WHY I'M ANGRY, ERIK. I'M ON A TRACK, WITH NO WAY OFF. I KNOW IT'S NOT WHAT I'M SUPPOSED TO BE. I CAN FEEL SOMETHING BETTER FOR ME, I JUST CAN'T FIND IT.
SHOULD WE GET ANOTHER?
I DON'T THINK SO. ARE YOU WATCHING THIS?
HNH?
THIS CLOUD THING. FROM THE INCIDENT IN NEW YORK. IT'S GOING TO HIT BERGEN. ANY MINUTE.
BERGEN
--TRACKING THE PATH OF THE PLUME. EFFECTS OF THE CHEMICAL AGENT ARE UNKNOWN, ALTHOUGH REPORTS SUGGEST THAT CERTAIN INDIVIDUALS MAY BE MORE SUSCEPTIBLE THAN OTHERS. PUBLIC SAFETY OFFICIALS ARE ADVISING ALL BERGEN RESIDENTS TO--
WHAT ARE WE SUPPOSED TO DO, ERIK, STOP BREATHING? NOTHING TO BE DONE. IF BIG BJORN COULDN'T PUT ME DOWN, I CAN'T SEE HOW A CLOUD WOULD MANAGE IT.

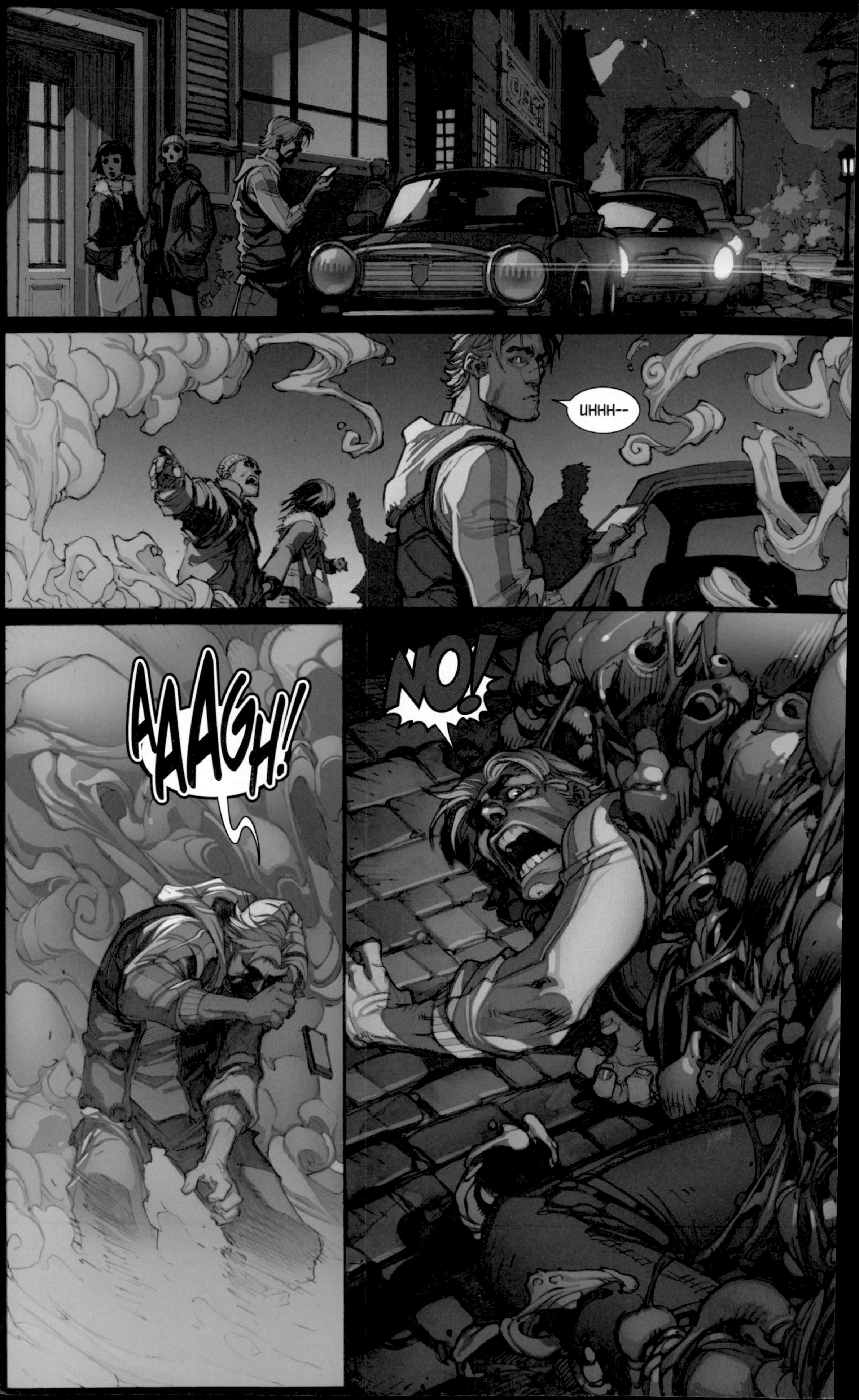
UHHH--
AAAGH!
NO!

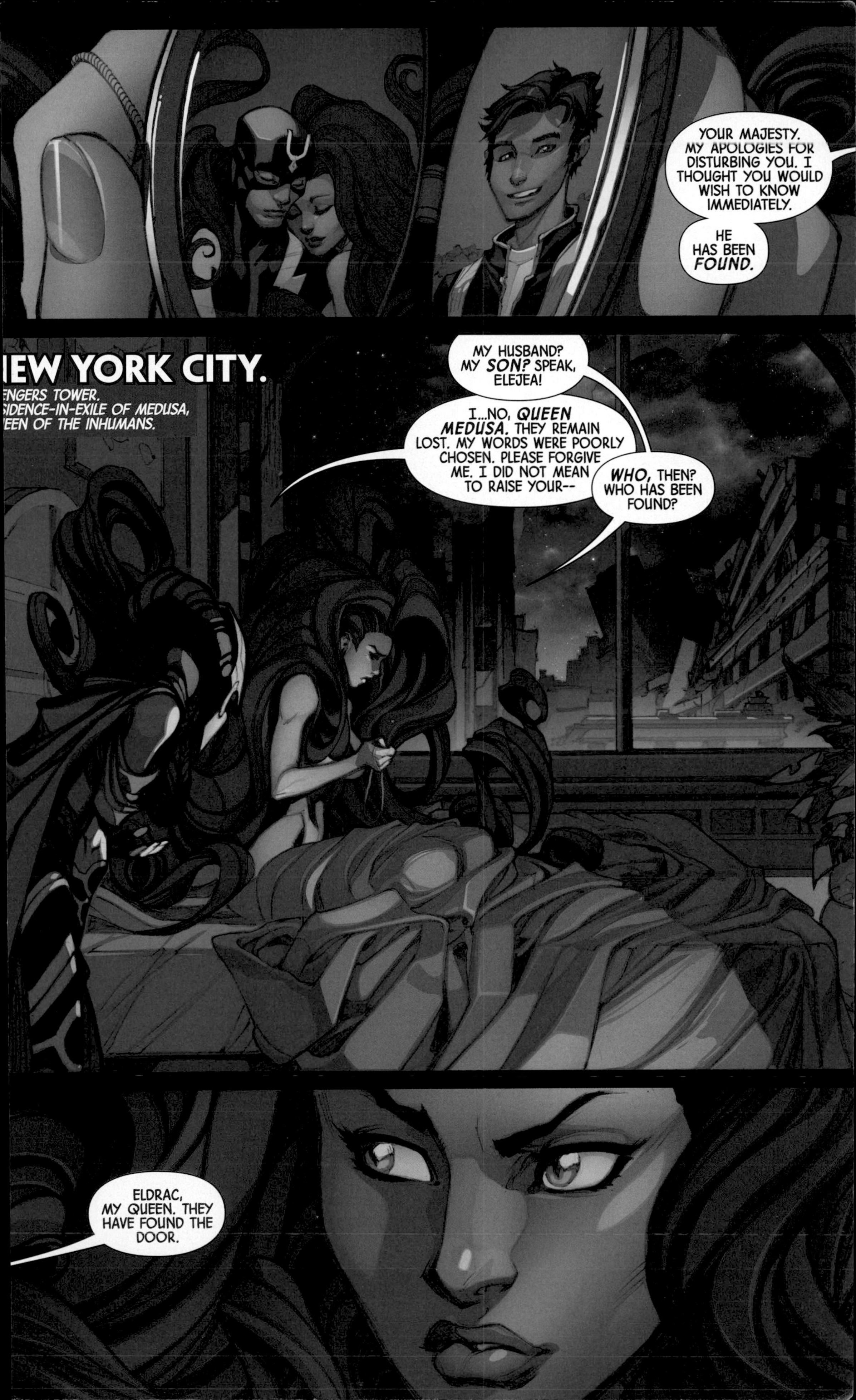

YOUR MAJESTY. MY APOLOGIES FOR DISTURBING YOU. I THOUGHT YOU WOULD WISH TO KNOW IMMEDIATELY.
HE HAS BEEN FOUND.
IEW YORK CITY.
ENGERS TOWER.
SIDENCE-IN-EXILE OF MEDUSA,
JEEN OF THE INHUMANS.
MY HUSBAND? MY SON? SPEAK, ELEJEA!
I...NO, QUEEN MEDUSA. THEY REMAIN LOST. MY WORDS WERE POORLY CHOSEN. PLEASE FORGIVE ME. I DID NOT MEAN TO RAISE YOUR--
WHO, THEN? WHO HAS BEEN FOUND?
ELDRAC, MY QUEEN. THEY HAVE FOUND THE DOOR.

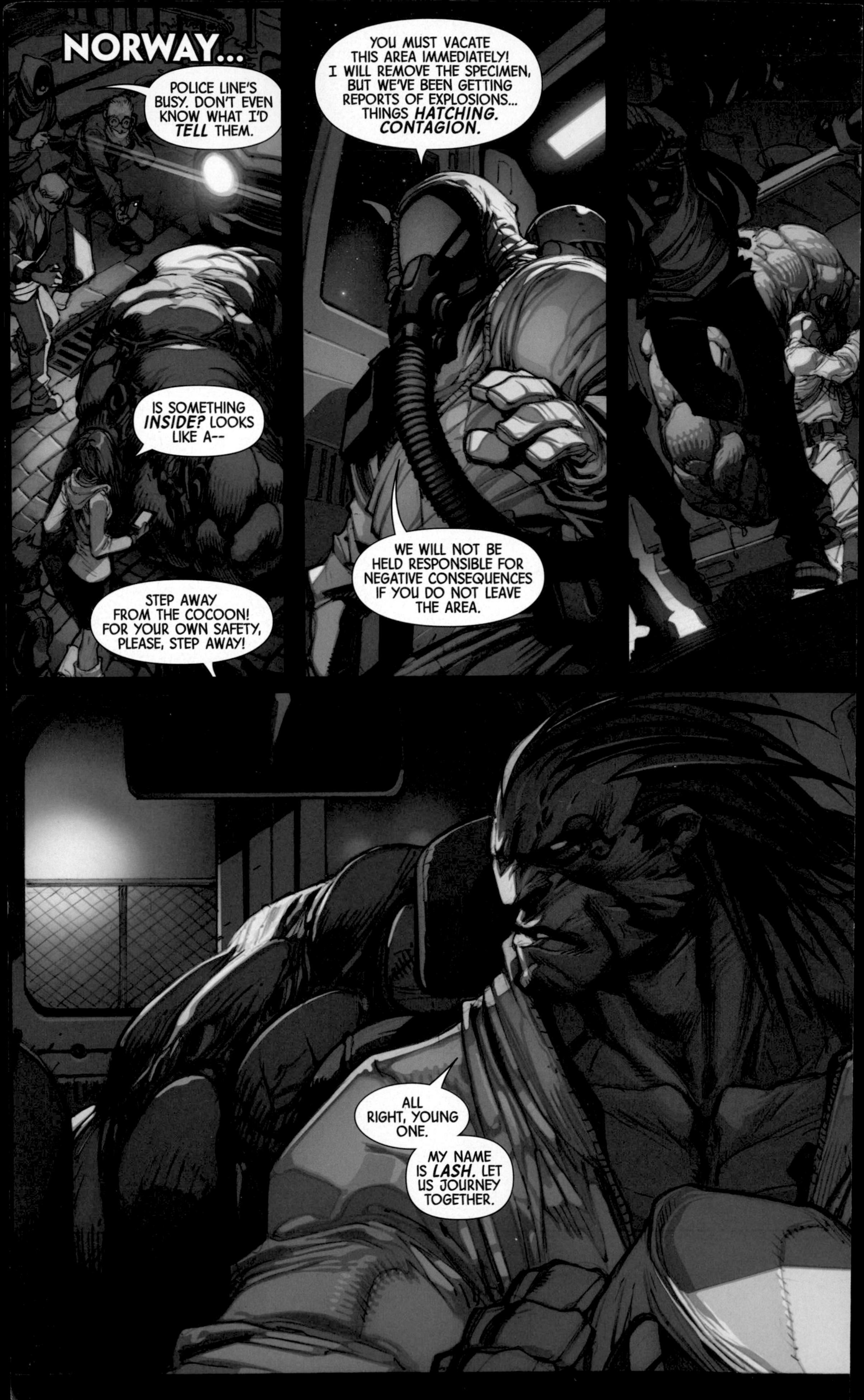
NORWAY...
POLICE LINE'S BUSY. DON'T EVEN KNOW WHAT I'D TELL THEM.
IS SOMETHING INSIDE? LOOKS LIKE A--
STEP AWAY FROM THE COCOON! FOR YOUR OWN SAFETY, PLEASE, STEP AWAY!
YOU MUST VACATE THIS AREA IMMEDIATELY! I WILL REMOVE THE SPECIMEN, BUT WE'VE BEEN GETTING REPORTS OF EXPLOSIONS... THINGS HATCHING. CONTAGION.
WE WILL NOT BE HELD RESPONSIBLE FOR NEGATIVE CONSEQUENCES IF YOU DO NOT LEAVE THE AREA.
ALL RIGHT, YOUNG ONE.
MY NAME IS LASH. LET US JOURNEY TOGETHER.

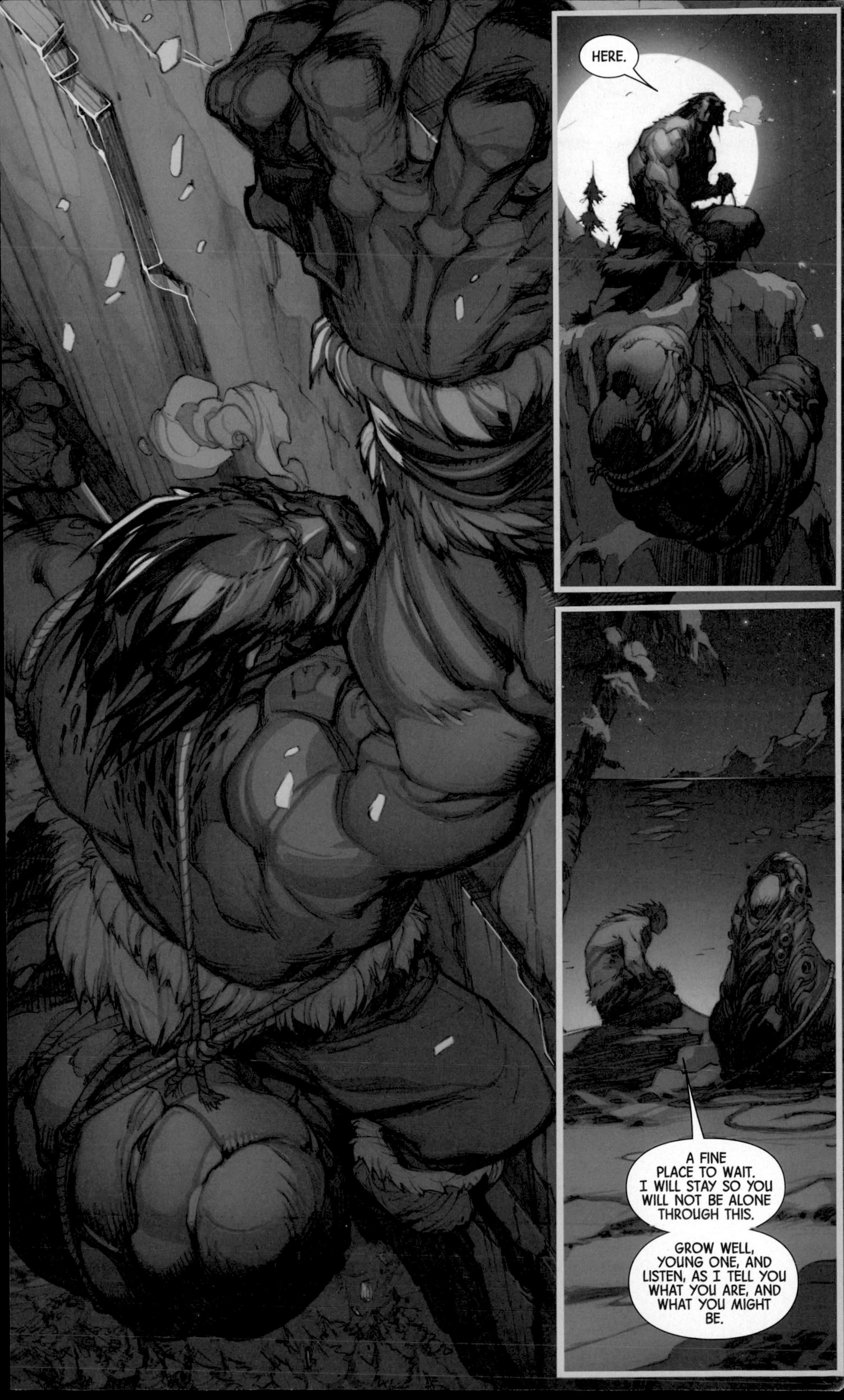
HERE.
A FINE PLACE TO WAIT. I WILL STAY SO YOU WILL NOT BE ALONE THROUGH THIS.
GROW WELL, YOUNG ONE, AND LISTEN, AS I TELL YOU WHAT YOU ARE, AND WHAT YOU MIGHT BE.

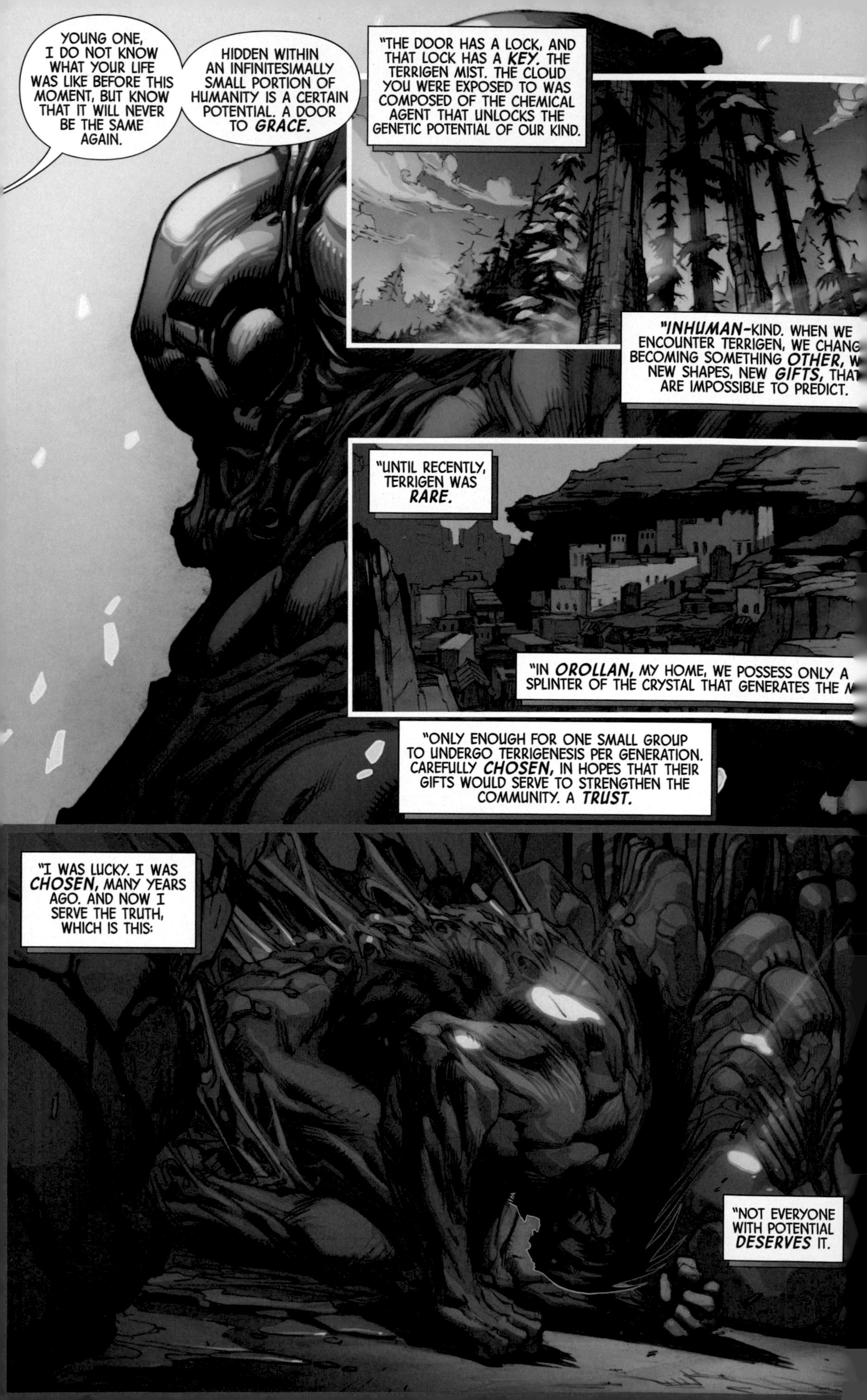
YOUNG ONE, I DO NOT KNOW WHAT YOUR LIFE WAS LIKE BEFORE THIS MOMENT, BUT KNOW THAT IT WILL NEVER BE THE SAME AGAIN.
HIDDEN WITHIN AN INFINITESIMALLY SMALL PORTION OF HUMANITY IS A CERTAIN POTENTIAL. A DOOR TO GRACE.
"THE DOOR HAS A LOCK, AND THAT LOCK HAS A KEY. THE TERRIGEN MIST. THE CLOUD YOU WERE EXPOSED TO WAS COMPOSED OF THE CHEMICAL AGENT THAT UNLOCKS THE GENETIC POTENTIAL OF OUR KIND.
"INHUMAN-KIND. WHEN WE ENCOUNTER TERRIGEN, WE CHANG BECOMING SOMETHING OTHER, W NEW SHAPES, NEW GIFTS, THAT ARE IMPOSSIBLE TO PREDICT.
"UNTIL RECENTLY, TERRIGEN WAS RARE.
"IN OROLLAN, MY HOME, WE POSSESS ONLY A SPLINTER OF THE CRYSTAL THAT GENERATES THE
"ONLY ENOUGH FOR ONE SMALL GROUP TO UNDERGO TERRIGENESIS PER GENERATION. CAREFULLY CHOSEN, IN HOPES THAT THEIR GIFTS WOULD SERVE TO STRENGTHEN THE COMMUNITY. A TRUST.
"I WAS LUCKY. I WAS CHOSEN, MANY YEARS AGO. AND NOW I SERVE THE TRUTH, WHICH IS THIS:
"NOT EVERYONE WITH POTENTIAL DESERVES IT.

"MOST OF THE TERRIGEN IN [EXIS]TENCE WAS HELD CAPTIVE BY [ONE] OF OUR PEOPLE, ONE WHO CALLED HIMSELF A KING.

"BLACK BOLT WAS HIS NAME.

"HE WAS PROFLIGATE [W]ITH THIS GREAT TREASURE, [ALLO]WING ALL OF HIS SUBJECTS [TO] EXPERIENCE TERRIGENESIS, [W]ITH NO REGARD FOR THE SACRED TRUTHS.

"BLACK BOLT HELD HIMSELF SEPARATE, IN HIS FLOATING CITY-- ATTILAN. HE WAS NOT MY KING.

"NO KING OF MINE WOULD DO SUCH THINGS.

"HE PAID THE PRICE FOR HIS TRANSGRESSIONS, AS ALL TRANSGRESSORS EVENTUALLY DO.

"BUT HIS DEATH RELEASED THE TERRIGEN INTO THE WORLD. NO CONTROLS, NO TRUTH TO IT. IT IS EVERYWHERE, AND ANYWHERE.

"ALL ACROSS THE WORLD, PEOPLE ARE LEARNING THE TRUTH OF WHAT THEY ARE. AS YOU DID. YOU ARE ONE OF US. INHUMAN.

"I BELIEVE THIS MAY BE WHAT BLACK BOLT WANTED. HE WAS THINKING ONLY OF HOW MANY INHUMANS THERE COULD BE."

I THINK ONLY OF HOW MANY INHUMANS THERE SHOULD BE.

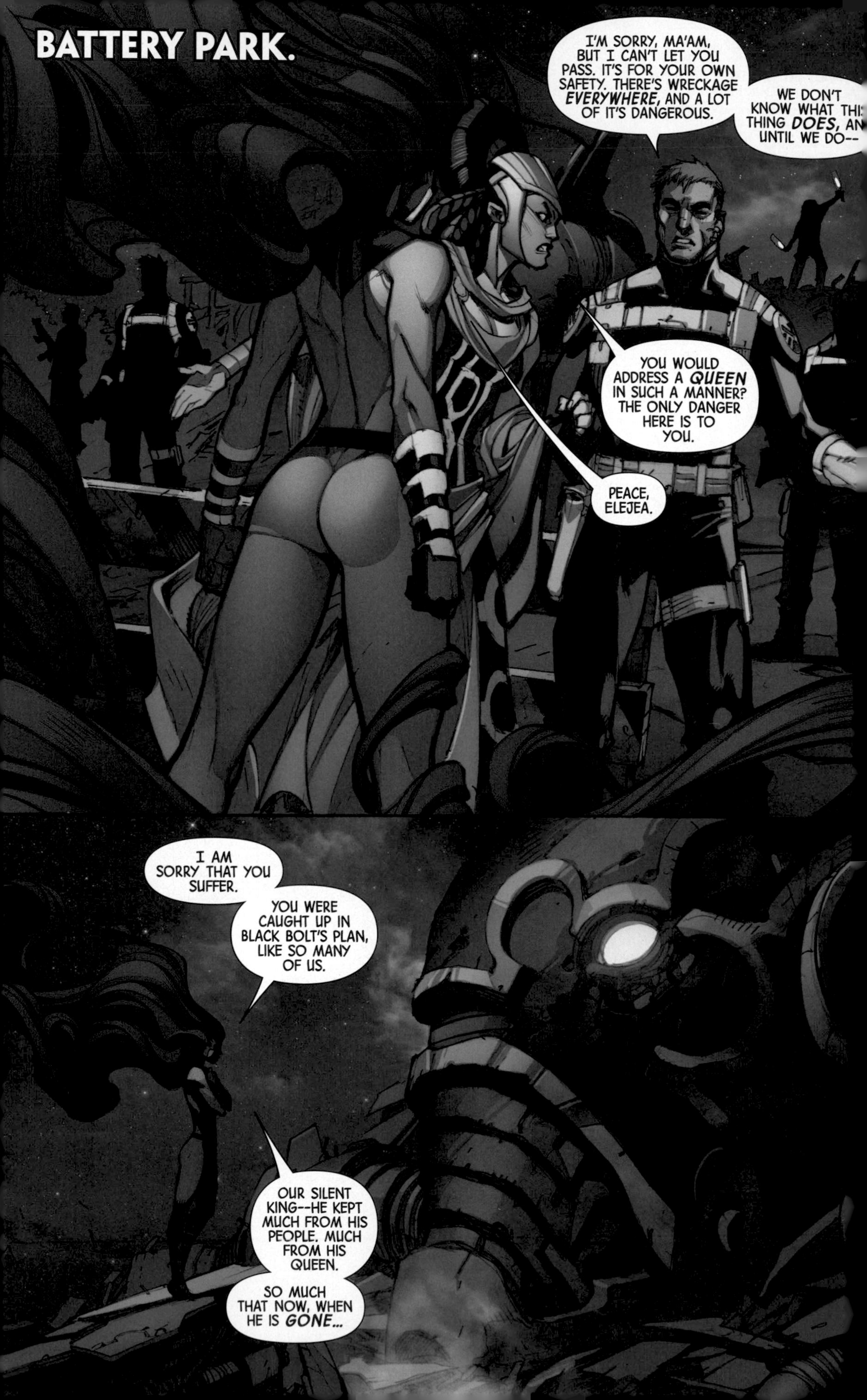
BATTERY PARK.
I'M SORRY, MA'AM, BUT I CAN'T LET YOU PASS. IT'S FOR YOUR OWN SAFETY. THERE'S WRECKAGE EVERYWHERE, AND A LOT OF IT'S DANGEROUS.
WE DON'T KNOW WHAT THIS THING DOES, AN UNTIL WE DO--
YOU WOULD ADDRESS A QUEEN IN SUCH A MANNER? THE ONLY DANGER HERE IS TO YOU.
PEACE, ELEJEA.
I AM SORRY THAT YOU SUFFER.
YOU WERE CAUGHT UP IN BLACK BOLT'S PLAN, LIKE SO MANY OF US.
OUR SILENT KING--HE KEPT MUCH FROM HIS PEOPLE. MUCH FROM HIS QUEEN.
SO MUCH THAT NOW, WHEN HE IS GONE...

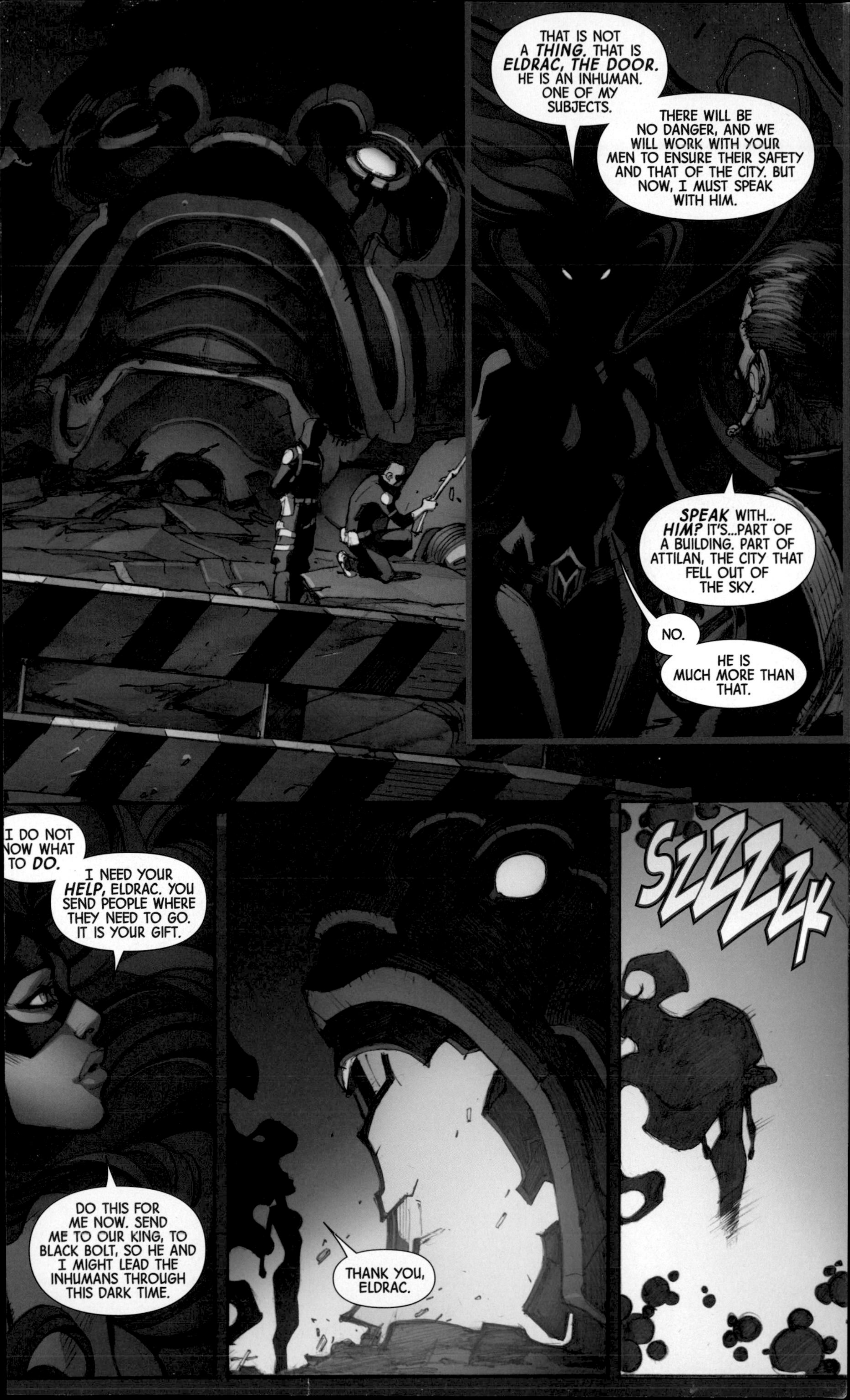
THAT IS NOT A THING. THAT IS ELDRAC, THE DOOR. HE IS AN INHUMAN. ONE OF MY SUBJECTS.
THERE WILL BE NO DANGER, AND WE WILL WORK WITH YOUR MEN TO ENSURE THEIR SAFETY AND THAT OF THE CITY. BUT NOW, I MUST SPEAK WITH HIM.
SPEAK WITH... HIM? IT'S...PART OF A BUILDING. PART OF ATTILAN, THE CITY THAT FELL OUT OF THE SKY.
NO.
HE IS MUCH MORE THAN THAT.
I DO NOT NOW WHAT TO DO.
I NEED YOUR HELP, ELDRAC. YOU SEND PEOPLE WHERE THEY NEED TO GO. IT IS YOUR GIFT.
DO THIS FOR ME NOW. SEND ME TO OUR KING, TO BLACK BOLT, SO HE AND I MIGHT LEAD THE INHUMANS THROUGH THIS DARK TIME.
THANK YOU, ELDRAC.
SZZZZK

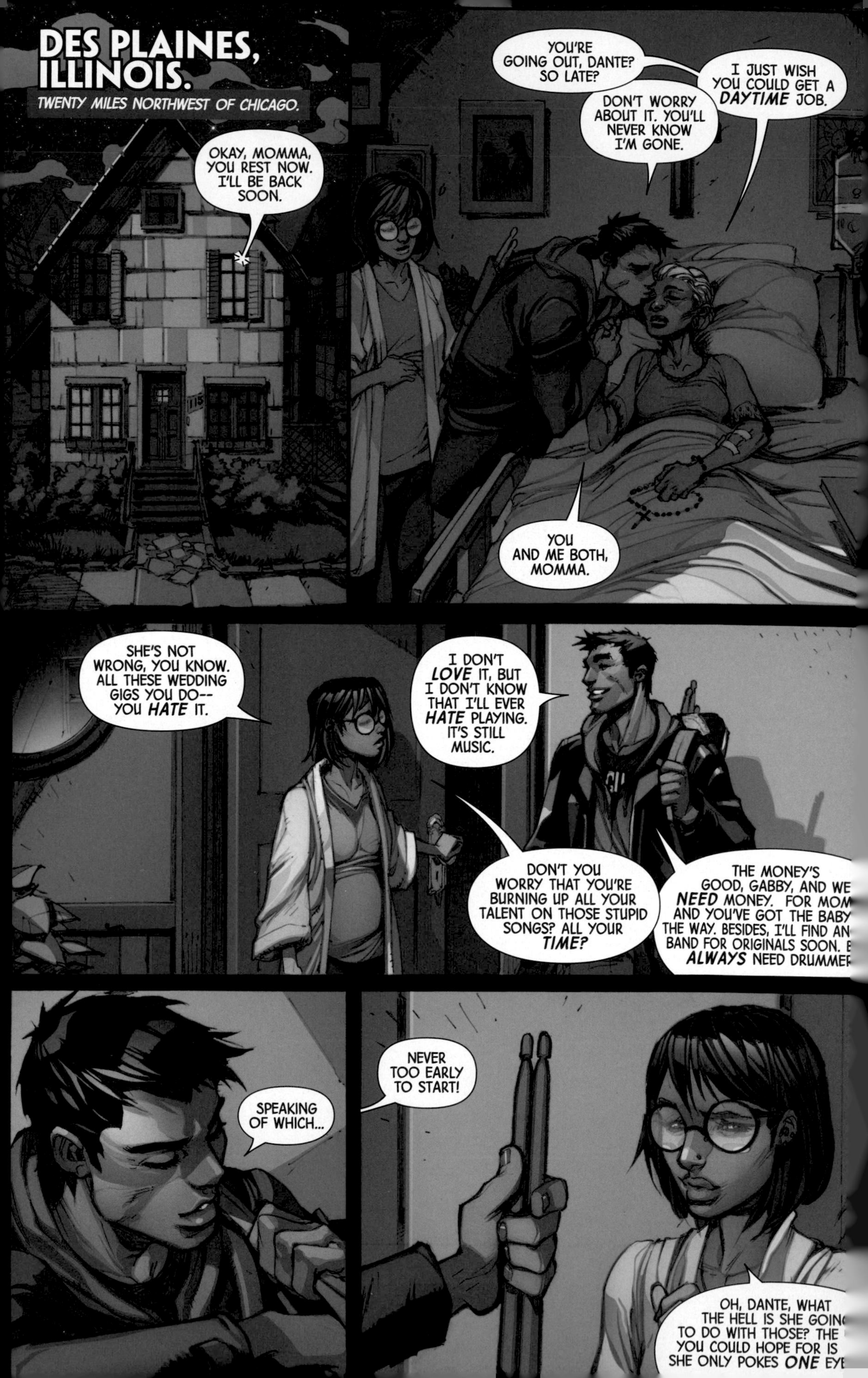
DES PLAINES, ILLINOIS.
TWENTY MILES NORTHWEST OF CHICAGO.
OKAY, MOMMA, YOU REST NOW. I'LL BE BACK SOON.
YOU'RE GOING OUT, DANTE? SO LATE?
DON'T WORRY ABOUT IT. YOU'LL NEVER KNOW I'M GONE.
I JUST WISH YOU COULD GET A DAYTIME JOB.
YOU AND ME BOTH, MOMMA.
SHE'S NOT WRONG, YOU KNOW. ALL THESE WEDDING GIGS YOU DO-- YOU HATE IT.
I DON'T LOVE IT, BUT I DON'T KNOW THAT I'LL EVER HATE PLAYING. IT'S STILL MUSIC.
DON'T YOU WORRY THAT YOU'RE BURNING UP ALL YOUR TALENT ON THOSE STUPID SONGS? ALL YOUR TIME?
THE MONEY'S GOOD, GABBY, AND WE NEED MONEY. FOR MOM AND YOU'VE GOT THE BABY THE WAY. BESIDES, I'LL FIND AN BAND FOR ORIGINALS SOON. ALWAYS NEED DRUMMER
SPEAKING OF WHICH...
NEVER TOO EARLY TO START!
OH, DANTE, WHAT THE HELL IS SHE GOIN TO DO WITH THOSE? THE YOU COULD HOPE FOR IS SHE ONLY POKES ONE EYE

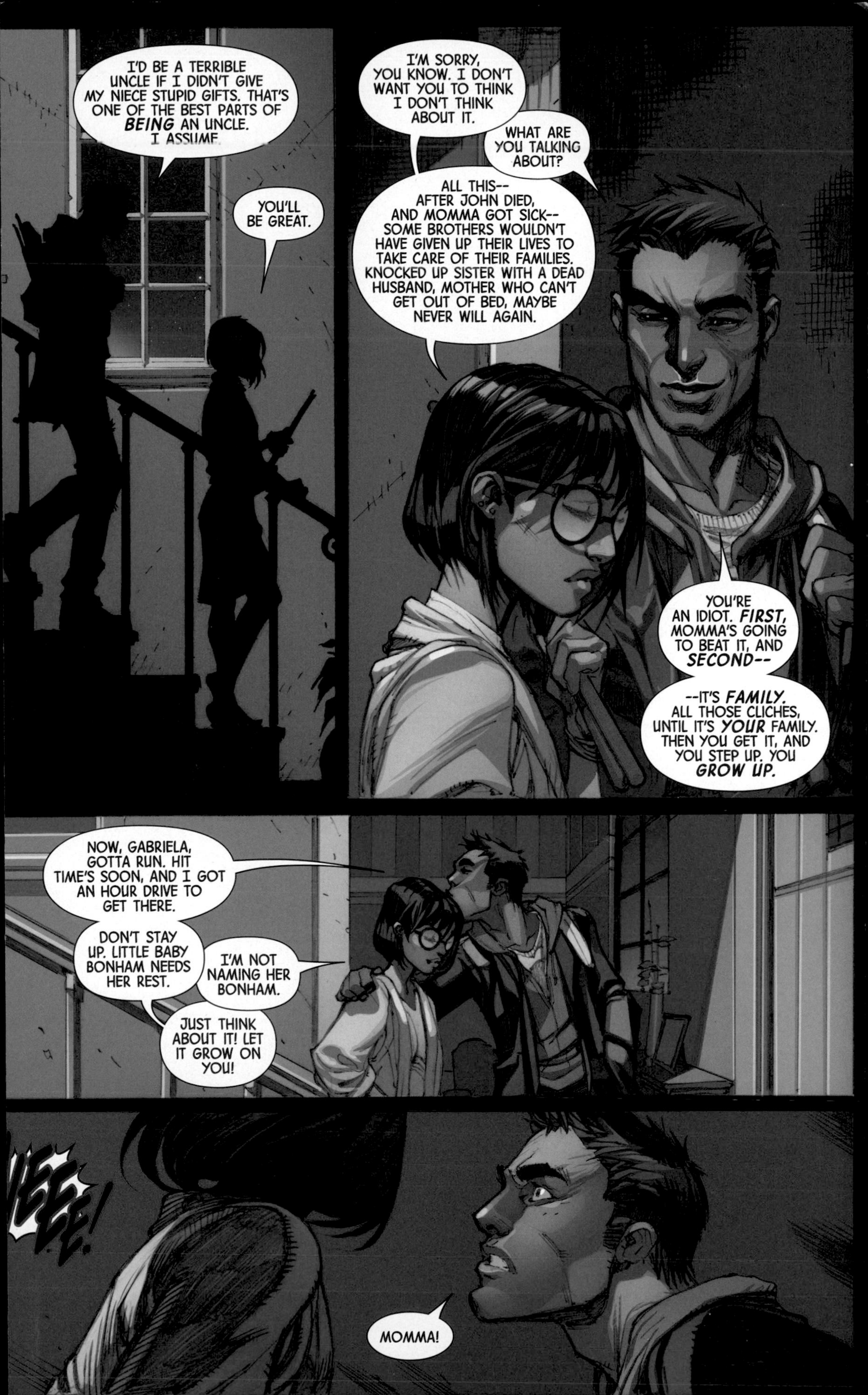
I'D BE A TERRIBLE UNCLE IF I DIDN'T GIVE MY NIECE STUPID GIFTS. THAT'S ONE OF THE BEST PARTS OF BEING AN UNCLE. I ASSUME.
YOU'LL BE GREAT.
I'M SORRY, YOU KNOW. I DON'T WANT YOU TO THINK I DON'T THINK ABOUT IT.
WHAT ARE YOU TALKING ABOUT?
ALL THIS-- AFTER JOHN DIED, AND MOMMA GOT SICK-- SOME BROTHERS WOULDN'T HAVE GIVEN UP THEIR LIVES TO TAKE CARE OF THEIR FAMILIES. KNOCKED UP SISTER WITH A DEAD HUSBAND, MOTHER WHO CAN'T GET OUT OF BED, MAYBE NEVER WILL AGAIN.
YOU'RE AN IDIOT. FIRST, MOMMA'S GOING TO BEAT IT, AND SECOND--
--IT'S FAMILY. ALL THOSE CLICHES, UNTIL IT'S YOUR FAMILY. THEN YOU GET IT, AND YOU STEP UP. YOU GROW UP.
NOW, GABRIELA, GOTTA RUN. HIT TIME'S SOON, AND I GOT AN HOUR DRIVE TO GET THERE.
DON'T STAY UP. LITTLE BABY BONHAM NEEDS HER REST.
I'M NOT NAMING HER BONHAM.
JUST THINK ABOUT IT! LET IT GROW ON YOU!
MOMMA!

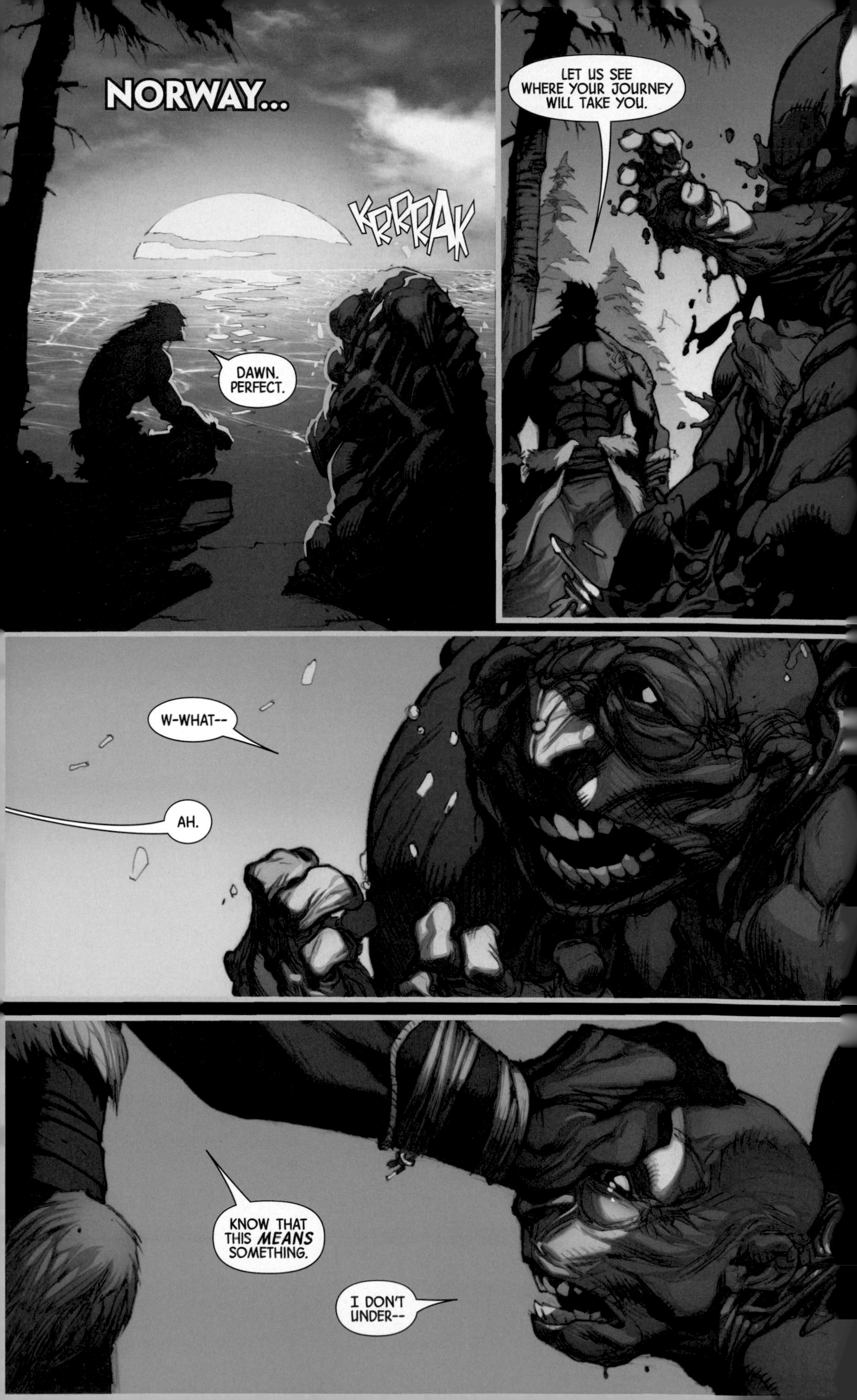
NORWAY...
KRRRAK
DAWN. PERFECT.
LET US SEE WHERE YOUR JOURNEY WILL TAKE YOU.
W-WHAT--
AH.
KNOW THAT THIS *MEANS* SOMETHING.
I DON'T UNDER--

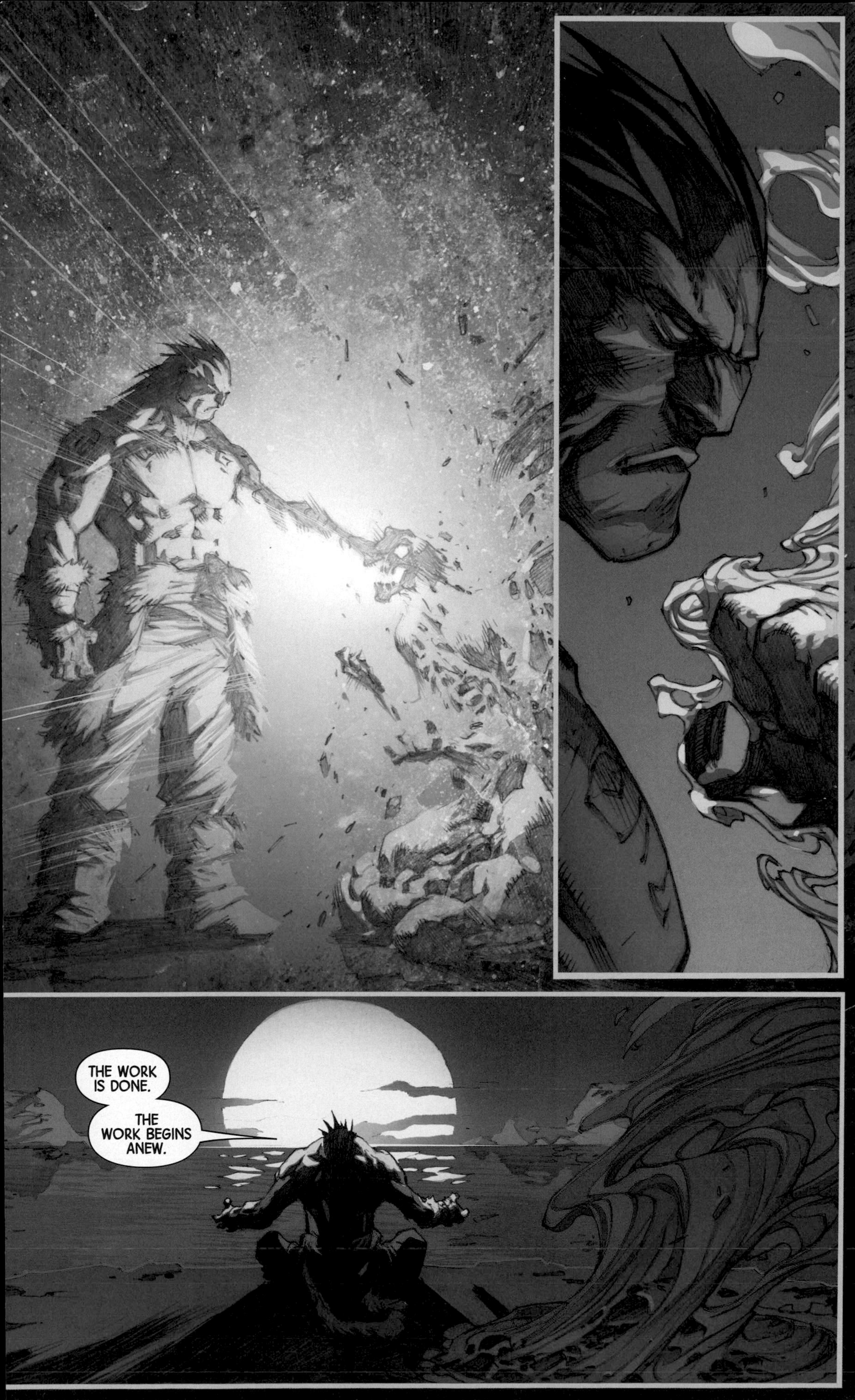
THE WORK IS DONE.
THE WORK BEGINS ANEW.

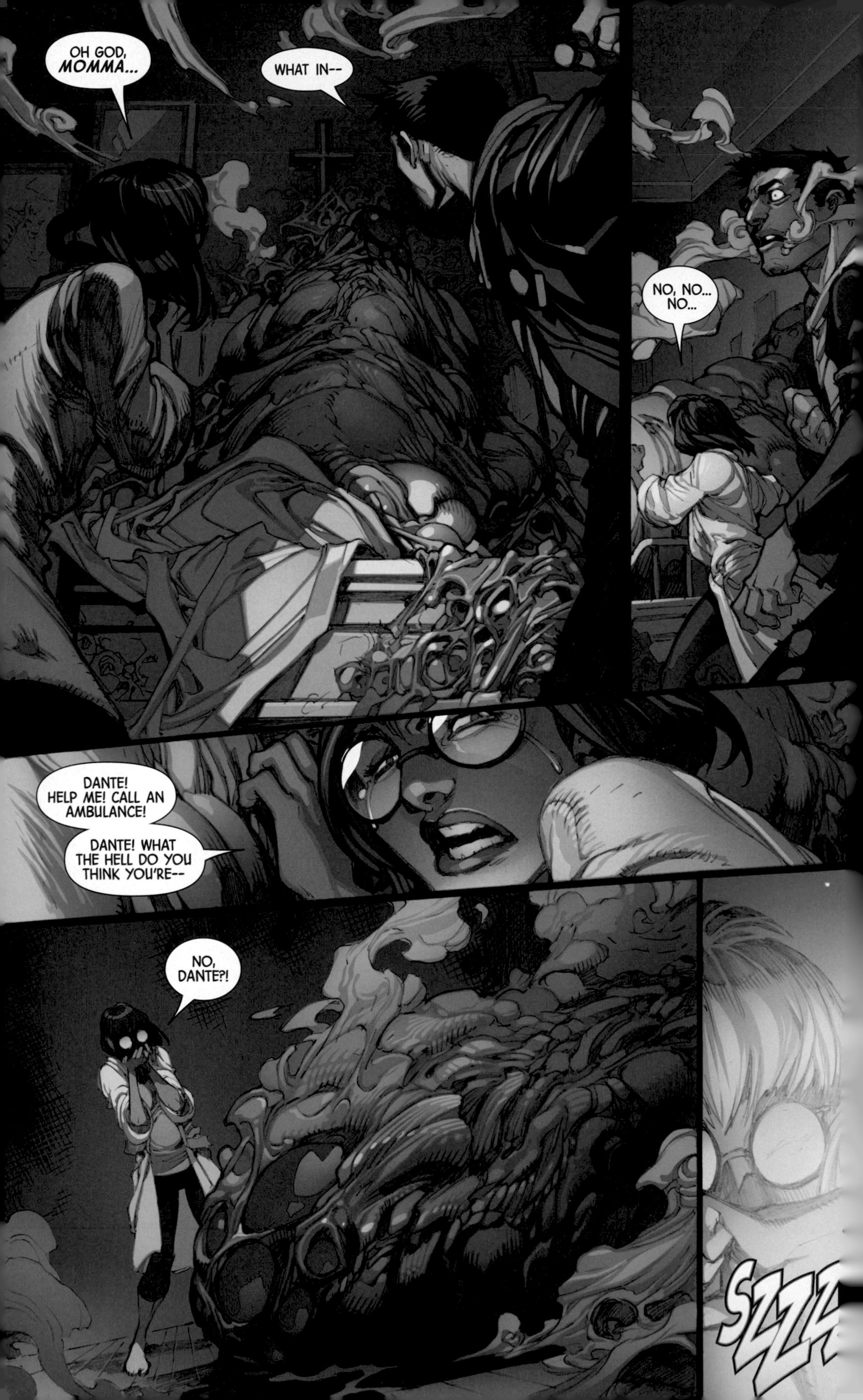
OH GOD, MOMMA...
WHAT IN--
NO, NO... NO...
DANTE! HELP ME! CALL AN AMBULANCE!
DANTE! WHAT THE HELL DO YOU THINK YOU'RE--
NO, DANTE?!
SZZZ

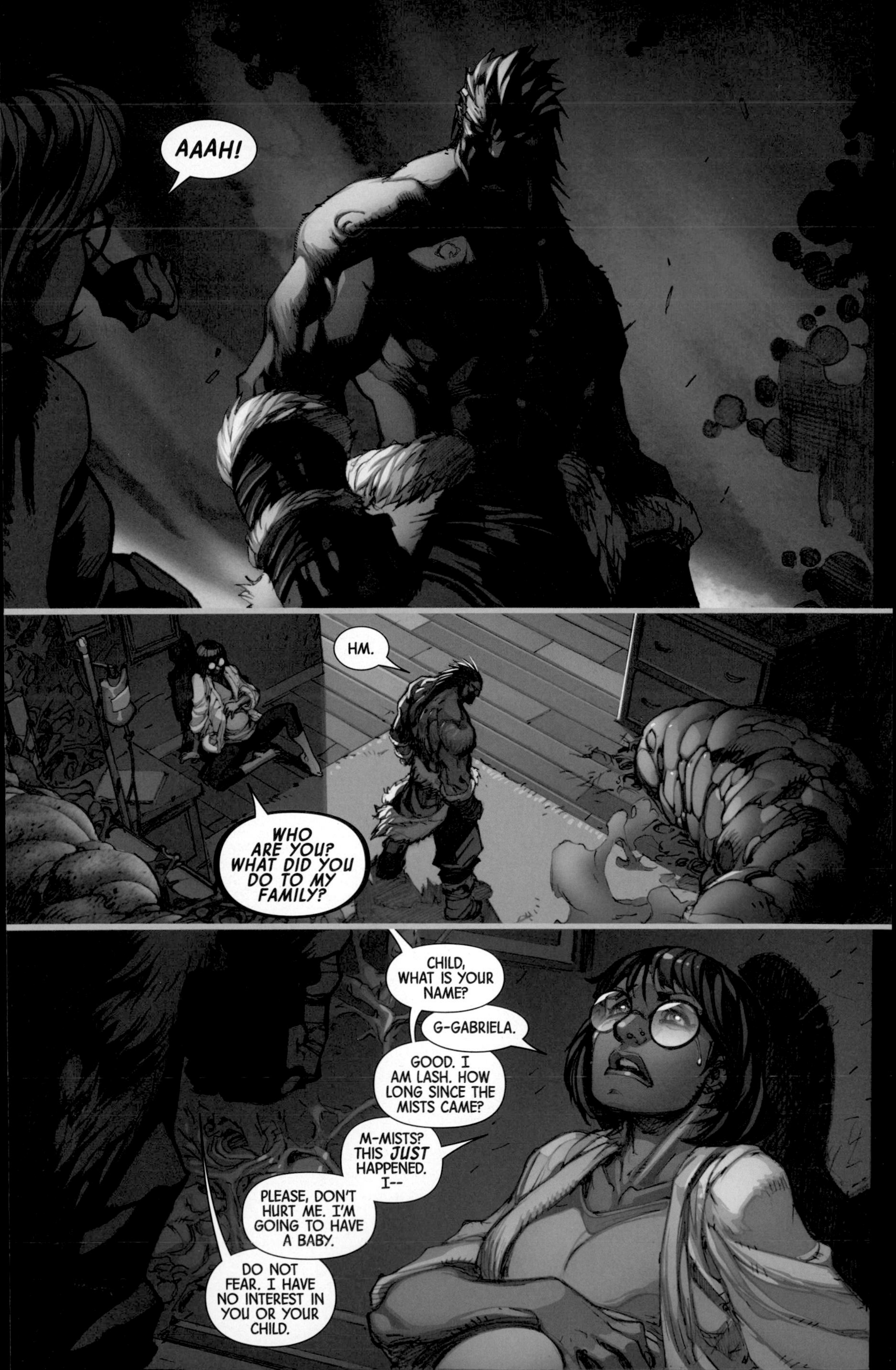
AAAH!
HM.
WHO ARE YOU? WHAT DID YOU DO TO MY FAMILY?
CHILD, WHAT IS YOUR NAME?
G-GABRIELA.
GOOD. I AM LASH. HOW LONG SINCE THE MISTS CAME?
M-MISTS? THIS JUST HAPPENED. I--
PLEASE, DON'T HURT ME. I'M GOING TO HAVE A BABY.
DO NOT FEAR. I HAVE NO INTEREST IN YOU OR YOUR CHILD.

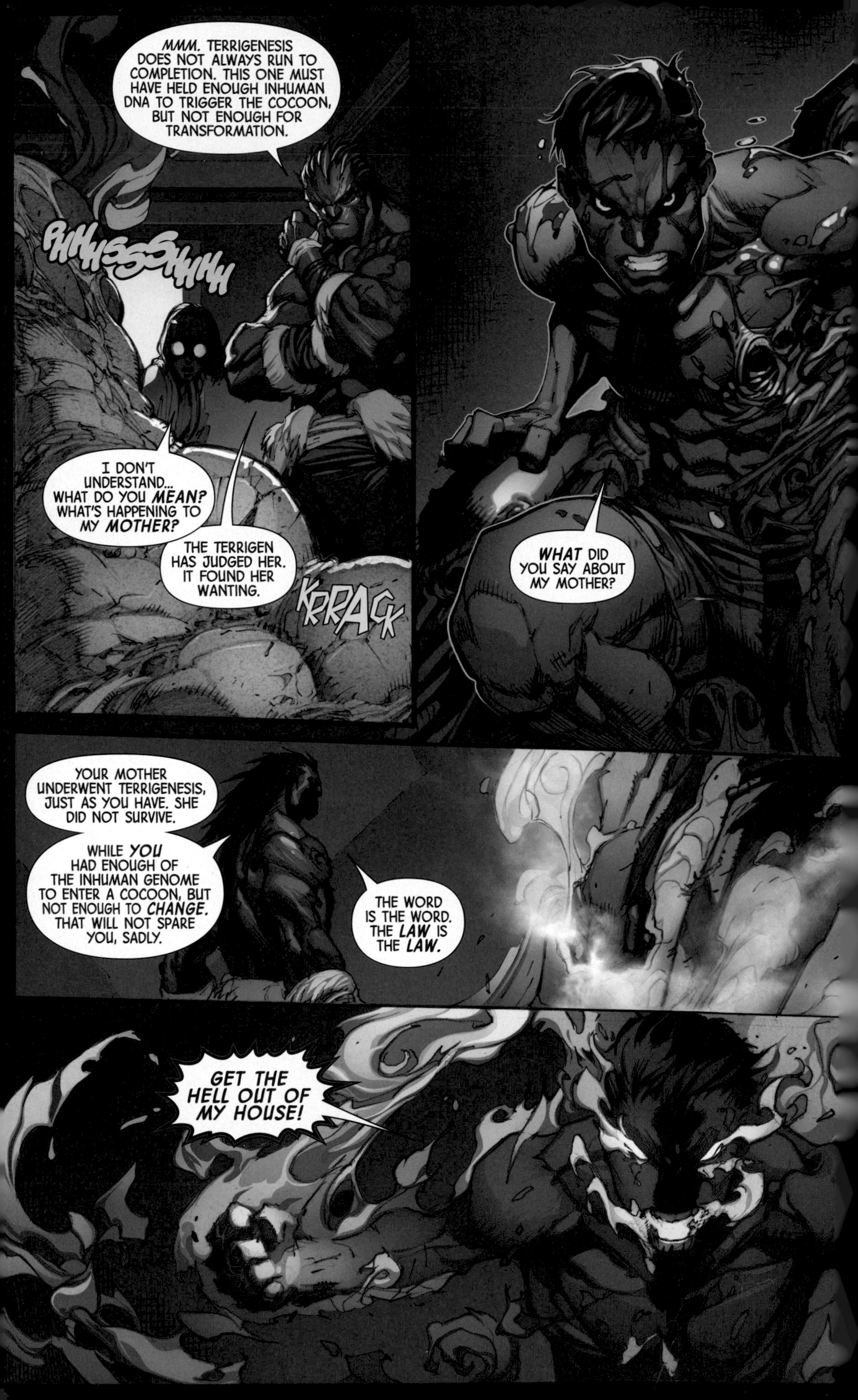
MMM. TERRIGENESIS DOES NOT ALWAYS RUN TO COMPLETION. THIS ONE MUST HAVE HELD ENOUGH INHUMAN DNA TO TRIGGER THE COCOON, BUT NOT ENOUGH FOR TRANSFORMATION.
PHHSSSHHHH
I DON'T UNDERSTAND... WHAT DO YOU MEAN? WHAT'S HAPPENING TO MY MOTHER?
THE TERRIGEN HAS JUDGED HER. IT FOUND HER WANTING.
KRRACK
WHAT DID YOU SAY ABOUT MY MOTHER?
YOUR MOTHER UNDERWENT TERRIGENESIS, JUST AS YOU HAVE. SHE DID NOT SURVIVE.
WHILE YOU HAD ENOUGH OF THE INHUMAN GENOME TO ENTER A COCOON, BUT NOT ENOUGH TO CHANGE. THAT WILL NOT SPARE YOU, SADLY.
THE WORD IS THE WORD. THE LAW IS THE LAW.
GET THE HELL OUT OF MY HOUSE!

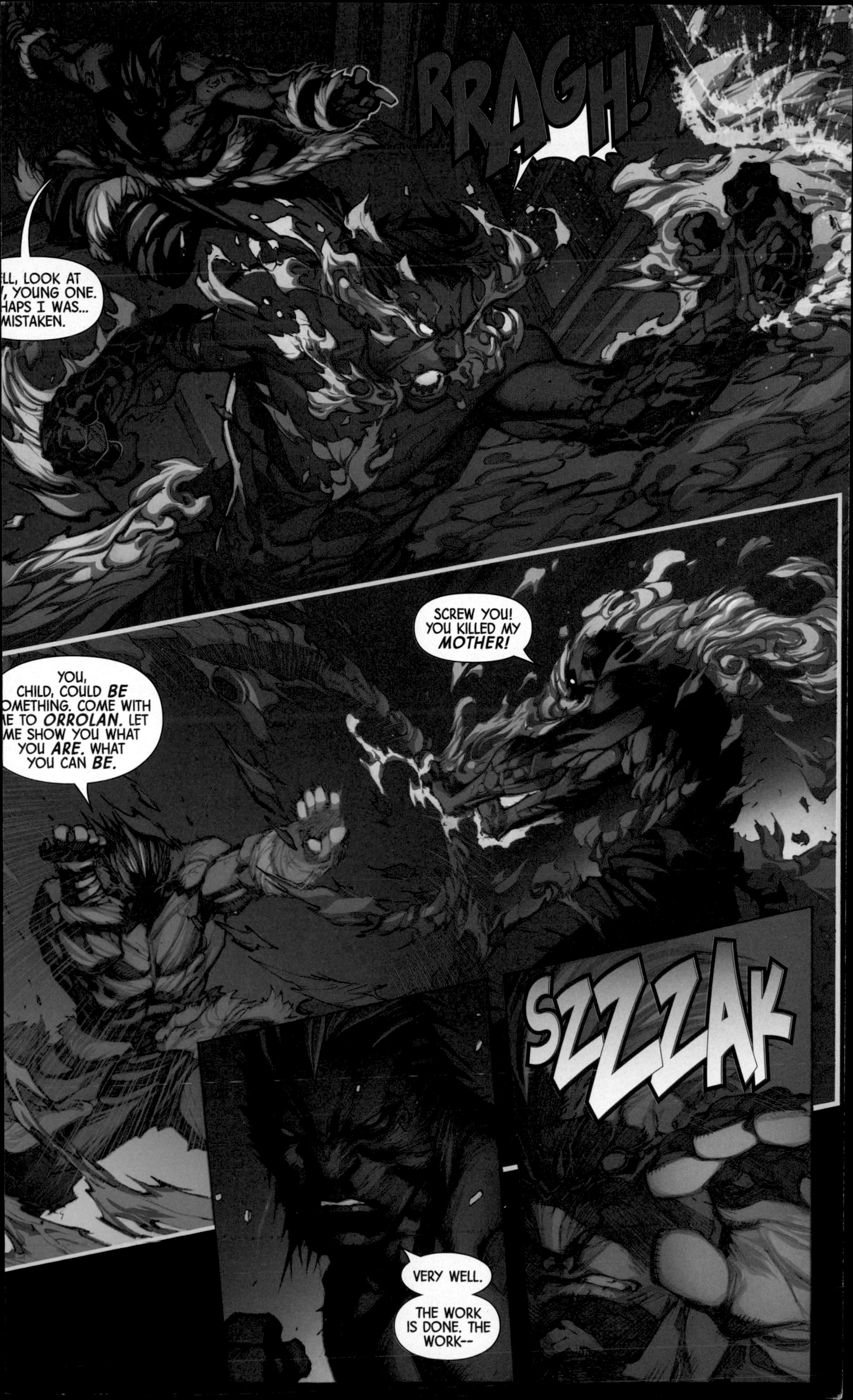
RRAGH!
LL, LOOK AT , YOUNG ONE. HAPS I WAS... MISTAKEN.
YOU, CHILD, COULD BE OMETHING. COME WITH E TO ORROLAN. LET ME SHOW YOU WHAT YOU ARE. WHAT YOU CAN BE.
SCREW YOU! YOU KILLED MY MOTHER!
SZZZAK
VERY WELL.
THE WORK IS DONE. THE WORK--

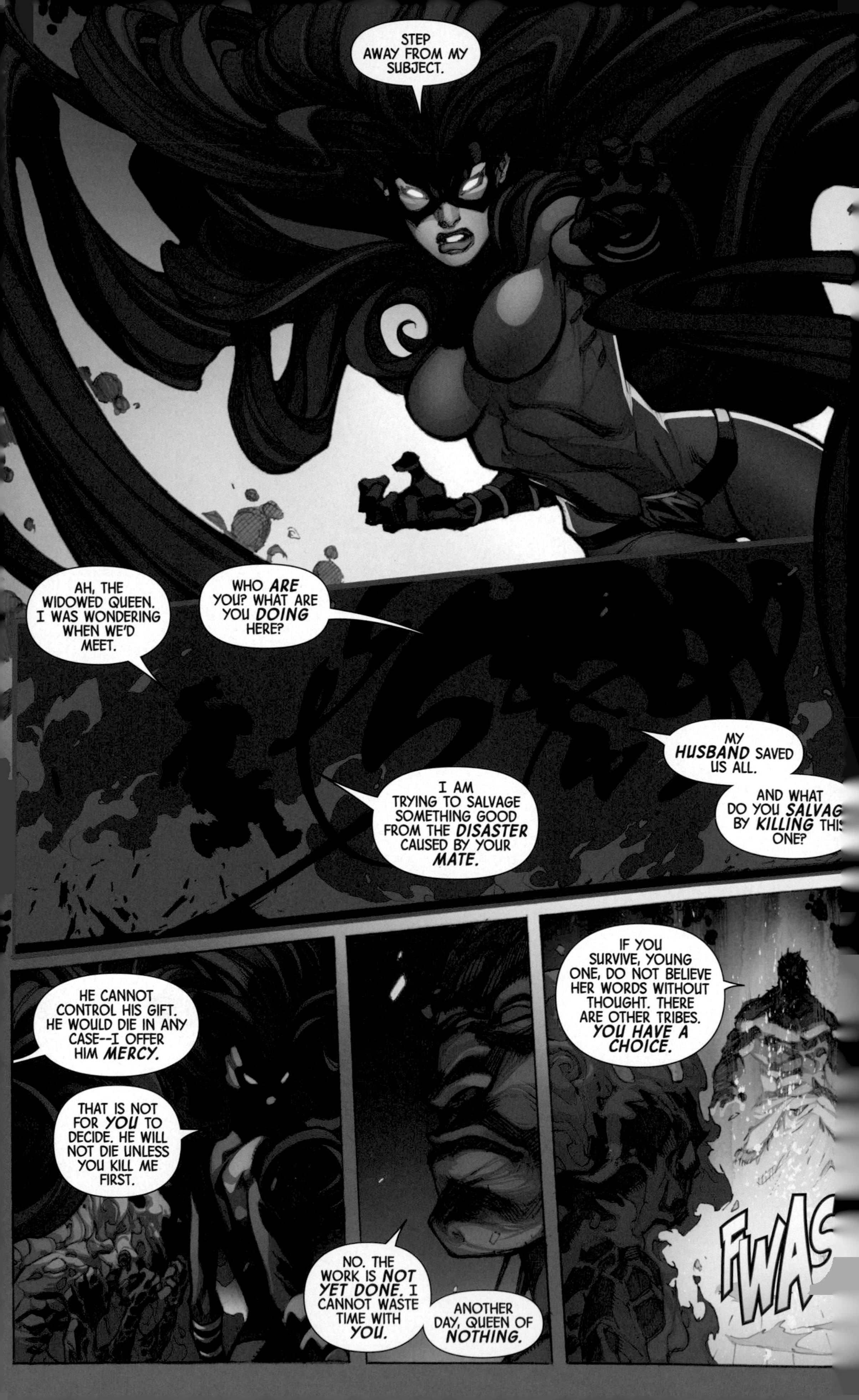
STEP AWAY FROM MY SUBJECT.
AH, THE WIDOWED QUEEN. I WAS WONDERING WHEN WE'D MEET.
WHO ARE YOU? WHAT ARE YOU DOING HERE?
I AM TRYING TO SALVAGE SOMETHING GOOD FROM THE DISASTER CAUSED BY YOUR MATE.
MY HUSBAND SAVED US ALL.
AND WHAT DO YOU SALVAG BY KILLING THIS ONE?
HE CANNOT CONTROL HIS GIFT. HE WOULD DIE IN ANY CASE--I OFFER HIM MERCY.
THAT IS NOT FOR YOU TO DECIDE. HE WILL NOT DIE UNLESS YOU KILL ME FIRST.
NO. THE WORK IS NOT YET DONE. I CANNOT WASTE TIME WITH YOU.
ANOTHER DAY, QUEEN OF NOTHING.
IF YOU SURVIVE, YOUNG ONE, DO NOT BELIEVE HER WORDS WITHOUT THOUGHT. THERE ARE OTHER TRIBES. YOU HAVE A CHOICE.
FWAS

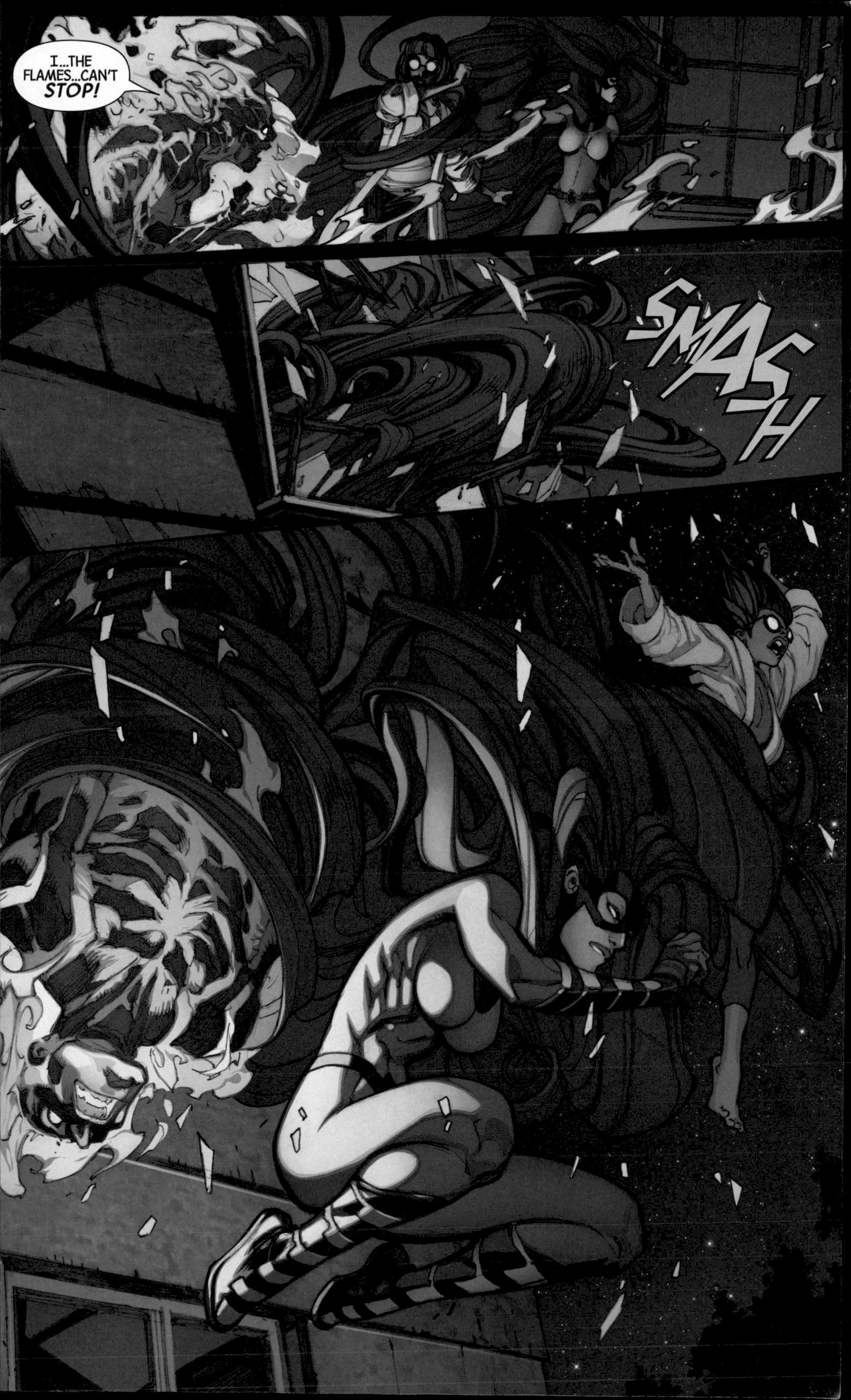
I...THE FLAMES...CAN'T STOP!
SMASH

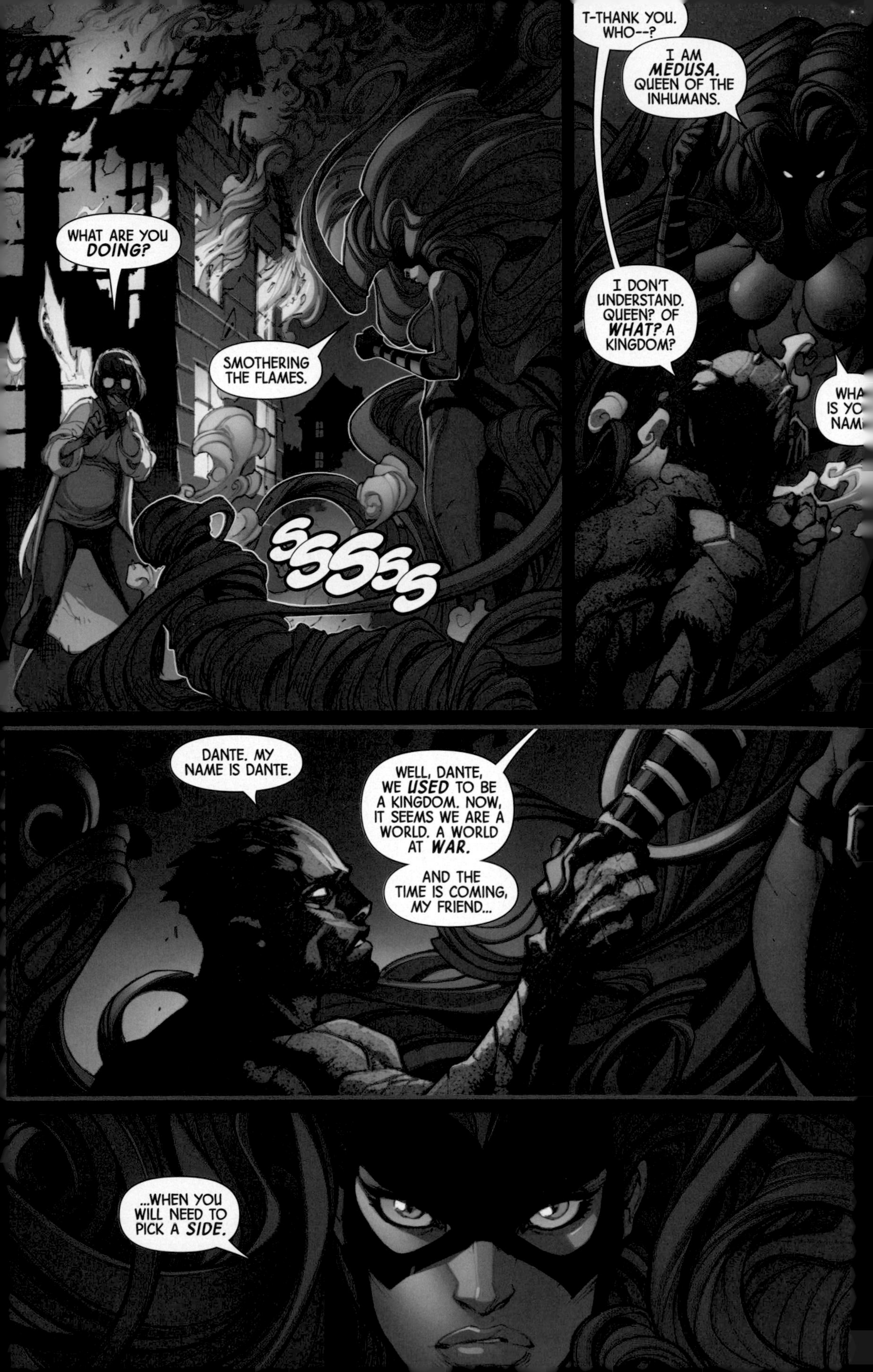
WHAT ARE YOU DOING?
SMOTHERING THE FLAMES.
SSSSSS
T-THANK YOU. WHO--?
I AM MEDUSA. QUEEN OF THE INHUMANS.
I DON'T UNDERSTAND. QUEEN? OF WHAT? A KINGDOM?
DANTE. MY NAME IS DANTE.
WELL, DANTE, WE USED TO BE A KINGDOM. NOW, IT SEEMS WE ARE A WORLD. A WORLD AT WAR.
AND THE TIME IS COMING, MY FRIEND...
...WHEN YOU WILL NEED TO PICK A SIDE.

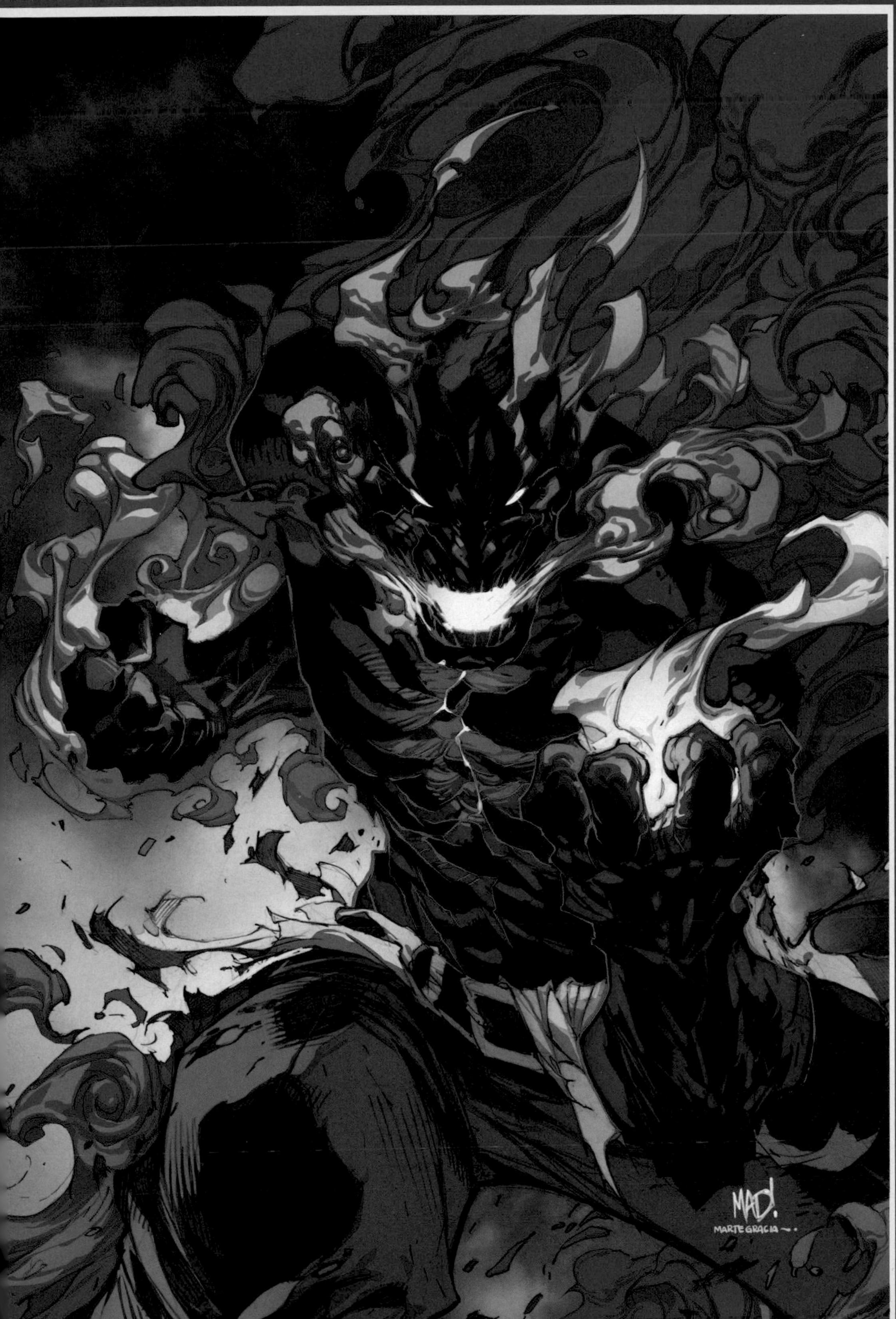
MAD!
MARTEGRACIA

PART TWO: THE QUEEN IN THE SKY

2

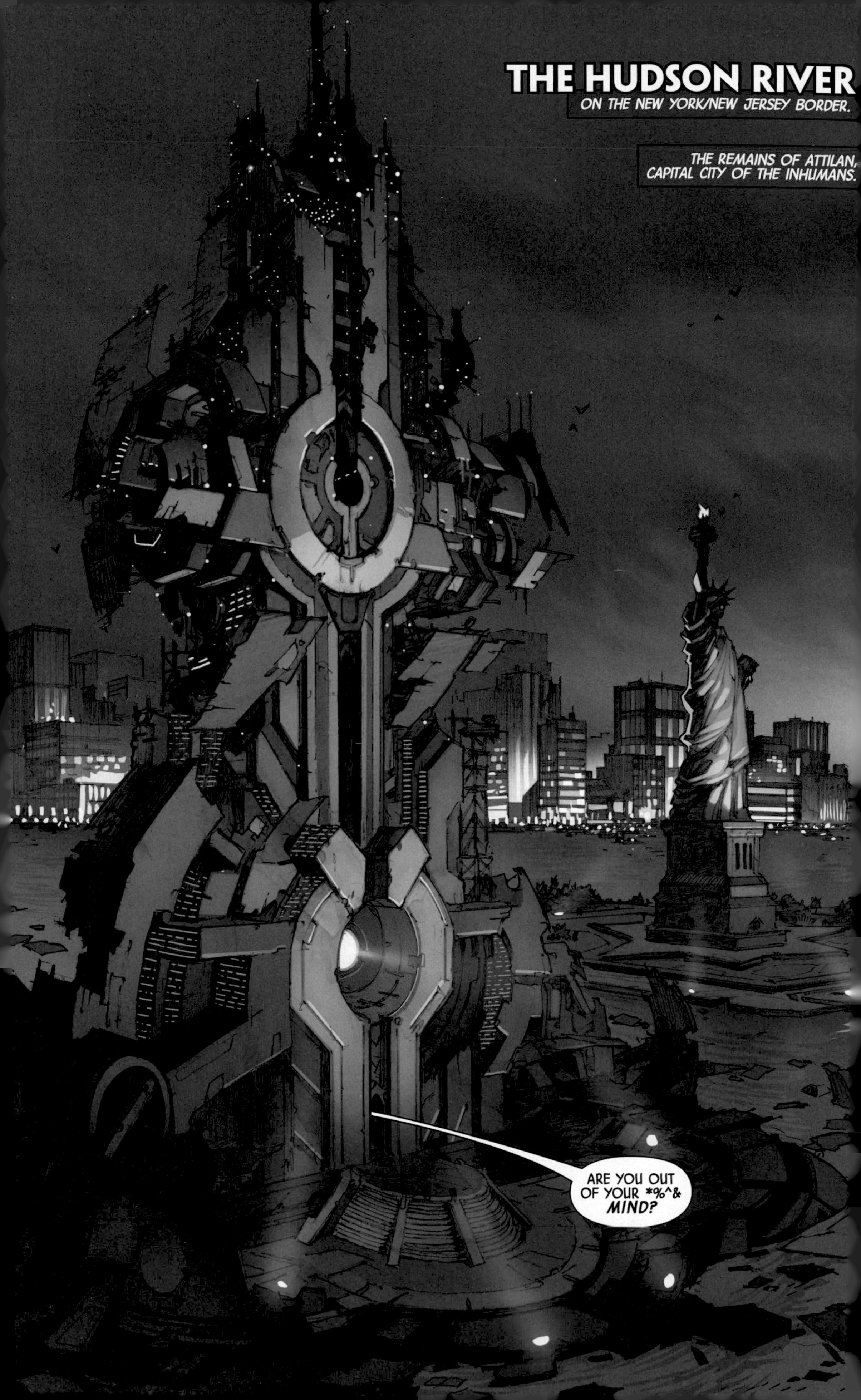

THE HUDSON RIVER
ON THE NEW YORK/NEW JERSEY BORDER.
THE REMAINS OF ATTILAN, CAPITAL CITY OF THE INHUMANS.
ARE YOU OUT OF YOUR *%^& MIND?

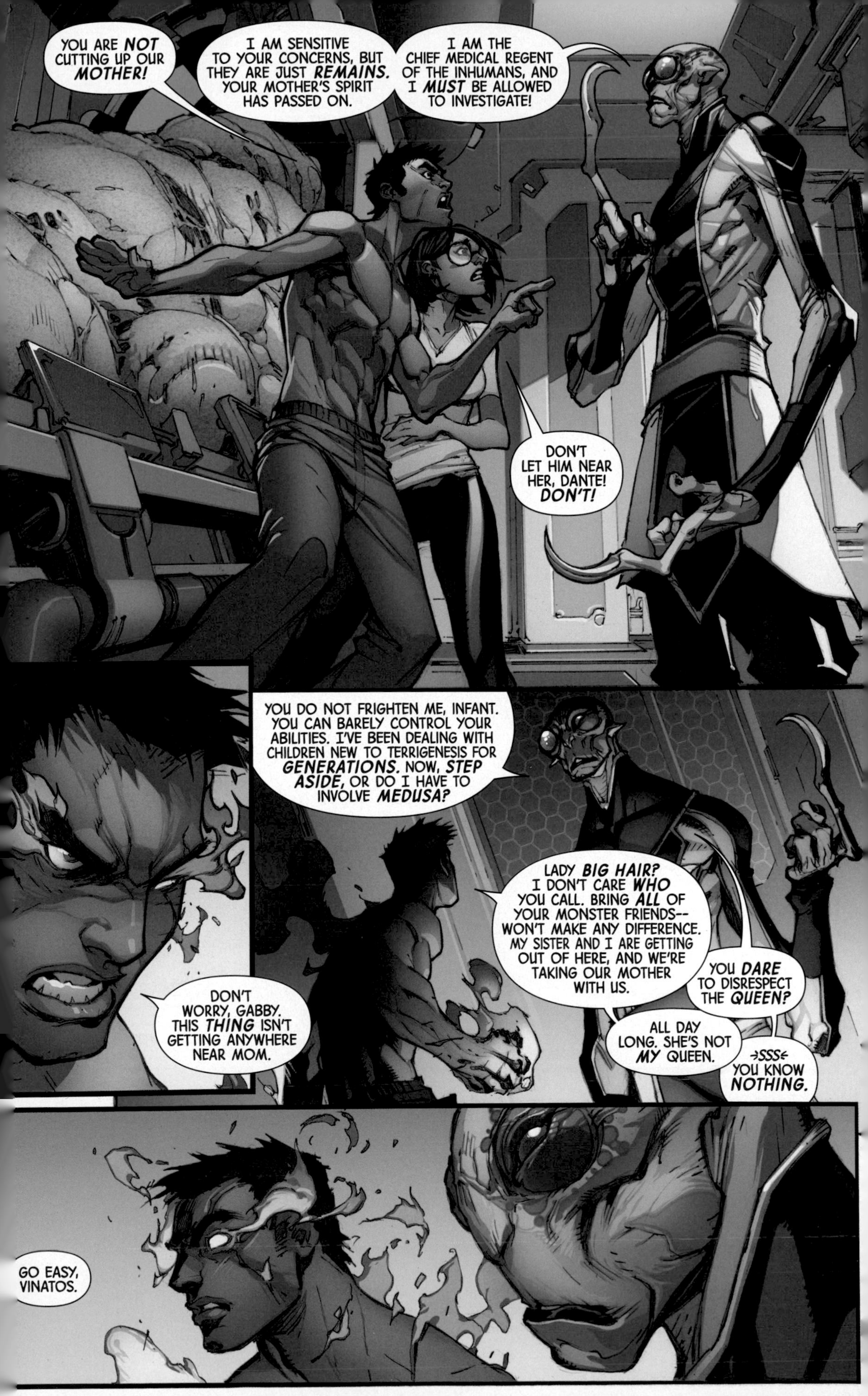
YOU ARE NOT CUTTING UP OUR MOTHER!
I AM SENSITIVE TO YOUR CONCERNS, BUT THEY ARE JUST REMAINS. YOUR MOTHER'S SPIRIT HAS PASSED ON.
I AM THE CHIEF MEDICAL REGENT OF THE INHUMANS, AND I MUST BE ALLOWED TO INVESTIGATE!
DON'T LET HIM NEAR HER, DANTE! DON'T!
DON'T WORRY, GABBY. THIS THING ISN'T GETTING ANYWHERE NEAR MOM.
YOU DO NOT FRIGHTEN ME, INFANT. YOU CAN BARELY CONTROL YOUR ABILITIES. I'VE BEEN DEALING WITH CHILDREN NEW TO TERRIGENESIS FOR GENERATIONS. NOW, STEP ASIDE, OR DO I HAVE TO INVOLVE MEDUSA?
LADY BIG HAIR? I DON'T CARE WHO YOU CALL. BRING ALL OF YOUR MONSTER FRIENDS-- WON'T MAKE ANY DIFFERENCE. MY SISTER AND I ARE GETTING OUT OF HERE, AND WE'RE TAKING OUR MOTHER WITH US.
YOU DARE TO DISRESPECT THE QUEEN?
ALL DAY LONG. SHE'S NOT MY QUEEN.
→SSS← YOU KNOW NOTHING.
GO EASY, VINATOS.

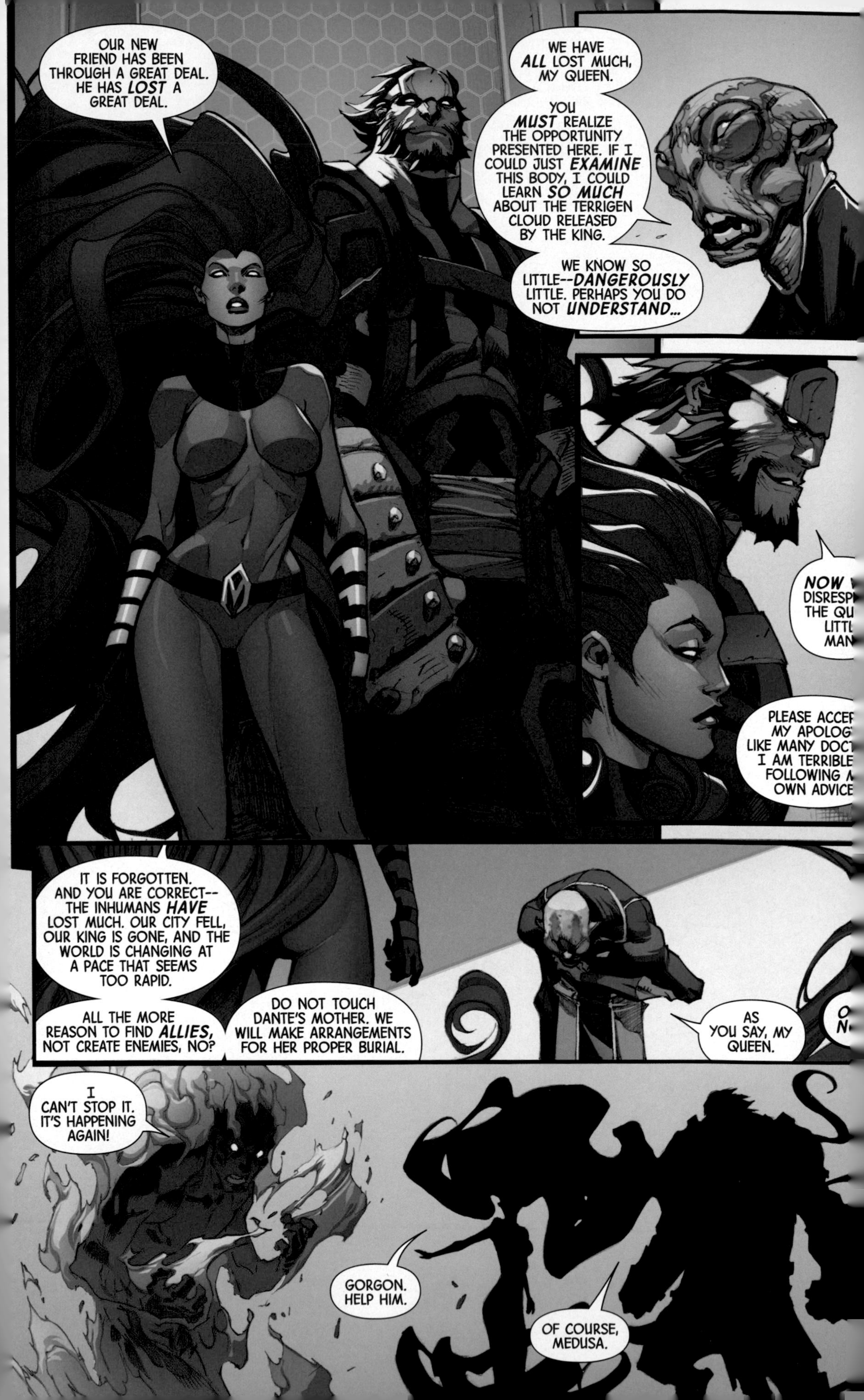
OUR NEW FRIEND HAS BEEN THROUGH A GREAT DEAL. HE HAS LOST A GREAT DEAL.
WE HAVE ALL LOST MUCH, MY QUEEN.
YOU MUST REALIZE THE OPPORTUNITY PRESENTED HERE. IF I COULD JUST EXAMINE THIS BODY, I COULD LEARN SO MUCH ABOUT THE TERRIGEN CLOUD RELEASED BY THE KING.
WE KNOW SO LITTLE--DANGEROUSLY LITTLE. PERHAPS YOU DO NOT UNDERSTAND...
NOW DISRESP THE QU LITTL MAN
PLEASE ACCEP MY APOLOG LIKE MANY DOCT I AM TERRIBLE FOLLOWING OWN ADVICE
IT IS FORGOTTEN. AND YOU ARE CORRECT-- THE INHUMANS HAVE LOST MUCH. OUR CITY FELL, OUR KING IS GONE, AND THE WORLD IS CHANGING AT A PACE THAT SEEMS TOO RAPID.
ALL THE MORE REASON TO FIND ALLIES, NOT CREATE ENEMIES, NO?
DO NOT TOUCH DANTE'S MOTHER. WE WILL MAKE ARRANGEMENTS FOR HER PROPER BURIAL.
AS YOU SAY, MY QUEEN.
I CAN'T STOP IT. IT'S HAPPENING AGAIN!
GORGON. HELP HIM.
OF COURSE, MEDUSA.

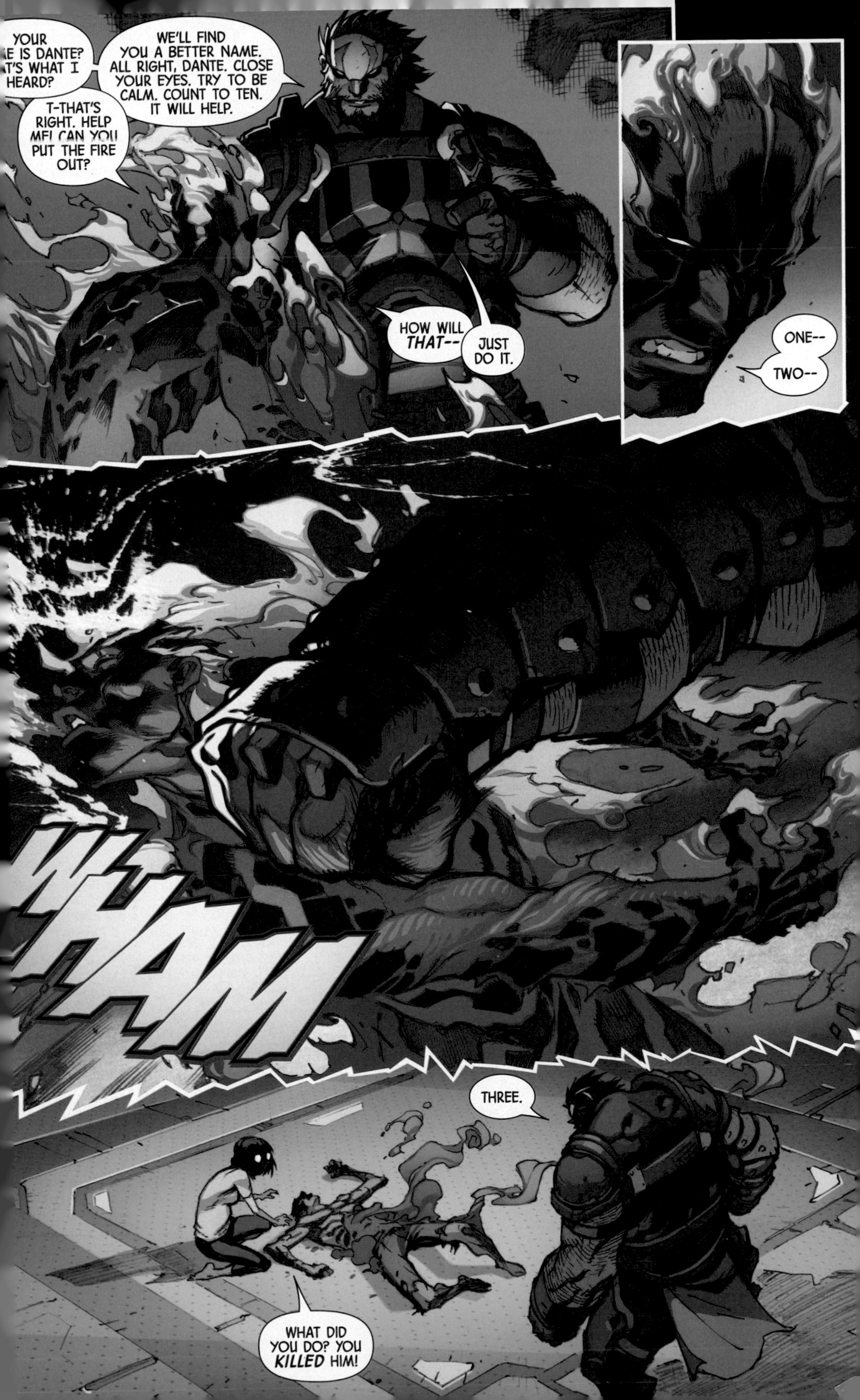

YOUR E IS DANTE? T'S WHAT I HEARD?
WE'LL FIND YOU A BETTER NAME. ALL RIGHT, DANTE. CLOSE YOUR EYES. TRY TO BE CALM. COUNT TO TEN. IT WILL HELP.
T-THAT'S RIGHT. HELP ME! CAN YOU PUT THE FIRE OUT?
HOW WILL *THAT*--
JUST DO IT.
ONE--
TWO--
WHAM
THREE.
WHAT DID YOU DO? YOU *KILLED* HIM!

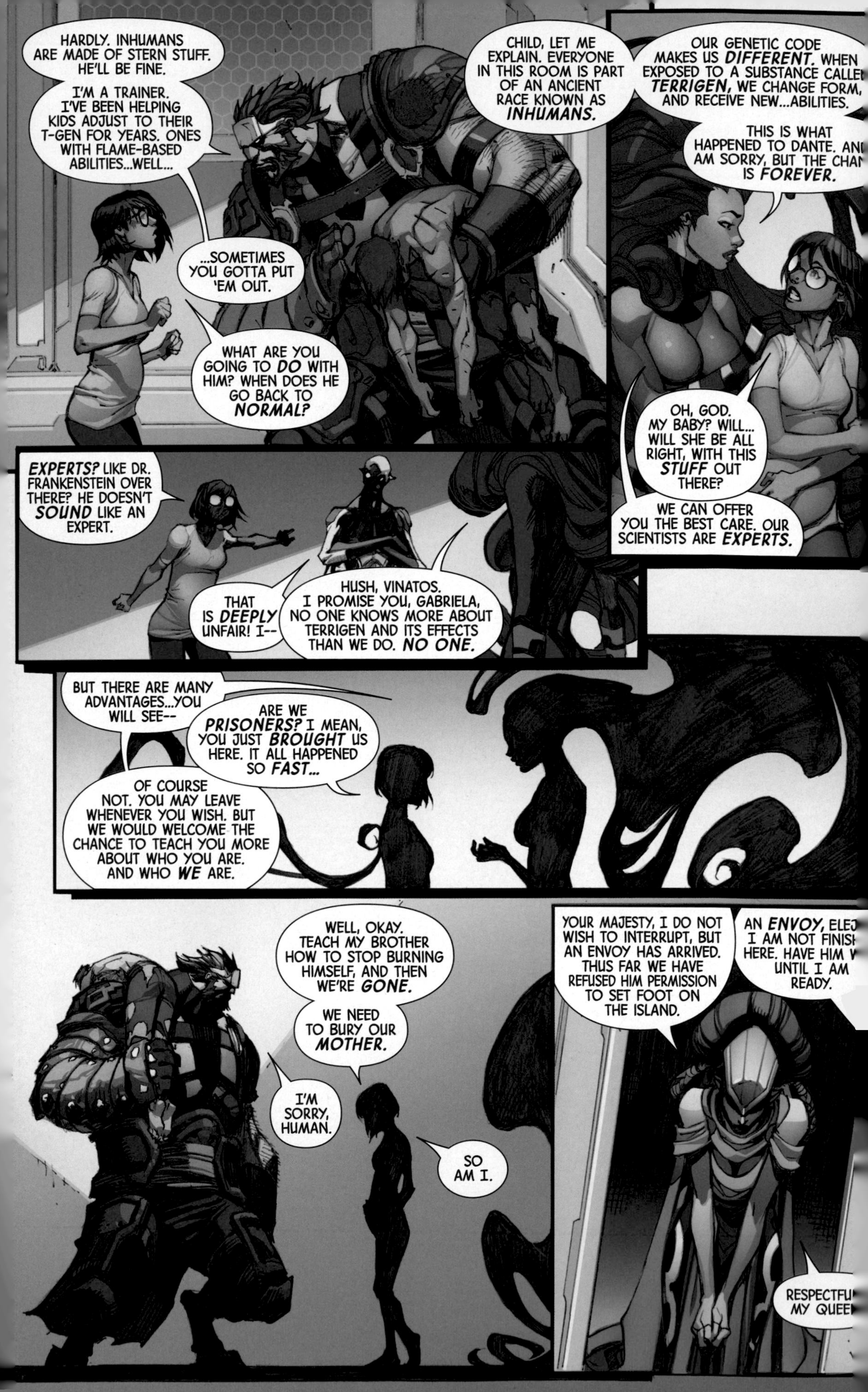
HARDLY. INHUMANS ARE MADE OF STERN STUFF. HE'LL BE FINE.
I'M A TRAINER. I'VE BEEN HELPING KIDS ADJUST TO THEIR T-GEN FOR YEARS. ONES WITH FLAME-BASED ABILITIES...WELL...
...SOMETIMES YOU GOTTA PUT 'EM OUT.
WHAT ARE YOU GOING TO DO WITH HIM? WHEN DOES HE GO BACK TO NORMAL?
CHILD, LET ME EXPLAIN. EVERYONE IN THIS ROOM IS PART OF AN ANCIENT RACE KNOWN AS INHUMANS.
OUR GENETIC CODE MAKES US DIFFERENT. WHEN EXPOSED TO A SUBSTANCE CALLE TERRIGEN, WE CHANGE FORM, AND RECEIVE NEW...ABILITIES.
THIS IS WHAT HAPPENED TO DANTE. AN AM SORRY, BUT THE CHA IS FOREVER.
OH, GOD. MY BABY? WILL... WILL SHE BE ALL RIGHT, WITH THIS STUFF OUT THERE?
WE CAN OFFER YOU THE BEST CARE. OUR SCIENTISTS ARE EXPERTS.
EXPERTS? LIKE DR. FRANKENSTEIN OVER THERE? HE DOESN'T SOUND LIKE AN EXPERT.
THAT IS DEEPLY UNFAIR! I--
HUSH, VINATOS. I PROMISE YOU, GABRIELA, NO ONE KNOWS MORE ABOUT TERRIGEN AND ITS EFFECTS THAN WE DO. NO ONE.
BUT THERE ARE MANY ADVANTAGES...YOU WILL SEE--
ARE WE PRISONERS? I MEAN, YOU JUST BROUGHT US HERE. IT ALL HAPPENED SO FAST...
OF COURSE NOT. YOU MAY LEAVE WHENEVER YOU WISH. BUT WE WOULD WELCOME THE CHANCE TO TEACH YOU MORE ABOUT WHO YOU ARE. AND WHO WE ARE.
WELL, OKAY. TEACH MY BROTHER HOW TO STOP BURNING HIMSELF, AND THEN WE'RE GONE.
WE NEED TO BURY OUR MOTHER.
I'M SORRY, HUMAN.
SO AM I.
YOUR MAJESTY, I DO NOT WISH TO INTERRUPT, BUT AN ENVOY HAS ARRIVED. THUS FAR WE HAVE REFUSED HIM PERMISSION TO SET FOOT ON THE ISLAND.
AN ENVOY, ELE I AM NOT FINIS HERE. HAVE HIM UNTIL I AM READY.
RESPECTFU MY QUEE

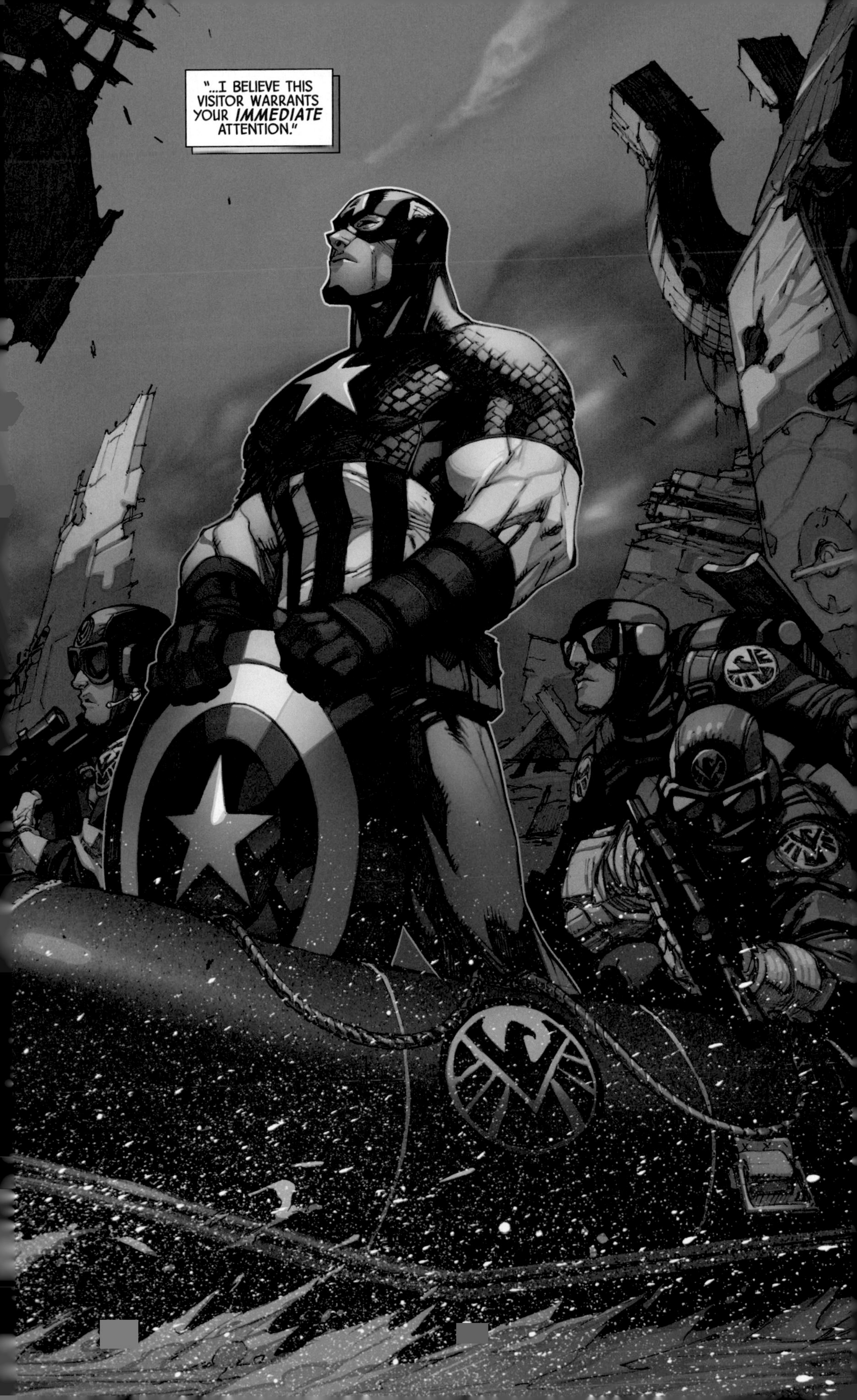
"...I BELIEVE THIS VISITOR WARRANTS YOUR *IMMEDIATE* ATTENTION."

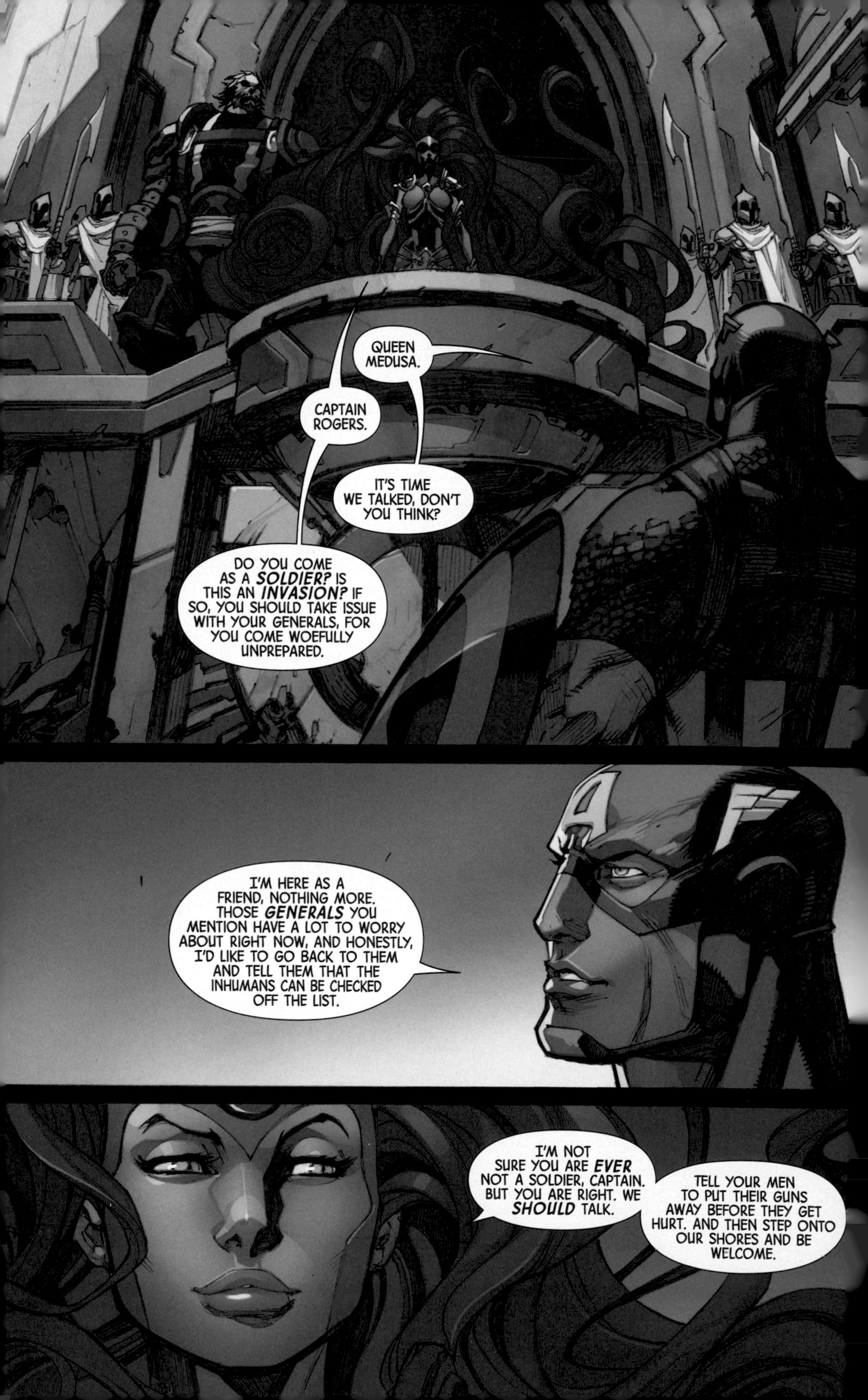
QUEEN MEDUSA.
CAPTAIN ROGERS.
IT'S TIME WE TALKED, DON'T YOU THINK?
DO YOU COME AS A SOLDIER? IS THIS AN INVASION? IF SO, YOU SHOULD TAKE ISSUE WITH YOUR GENERALS, FOR YOU COME WOEFULLY UNPREPARED.
I'M HERE AS A FRIEND, NOTHING MORE. THOSE GENERALS YOU MENTION HAVE A LOT TO WORRY ABOUT RIGHT NOW, AND HONESTLY, I'D LIKE TO GO BACK TO THEM AND TELL THEM THAT THE INHUMANS CAN BE CHECKED OFF THE LIST.
I'M NOT SURE YOU ARE EVER NOT A SOLDIER, CAPTAIN. BUT YOU ARE RIGHT. WE SHOULD TALK.
TELL YOUR MEN TO PUT THEIR GUNS AWAY BEFORE THEY GET HURT. AND THEN STEP ONTO OUR SHORES AND BE WELCOME.

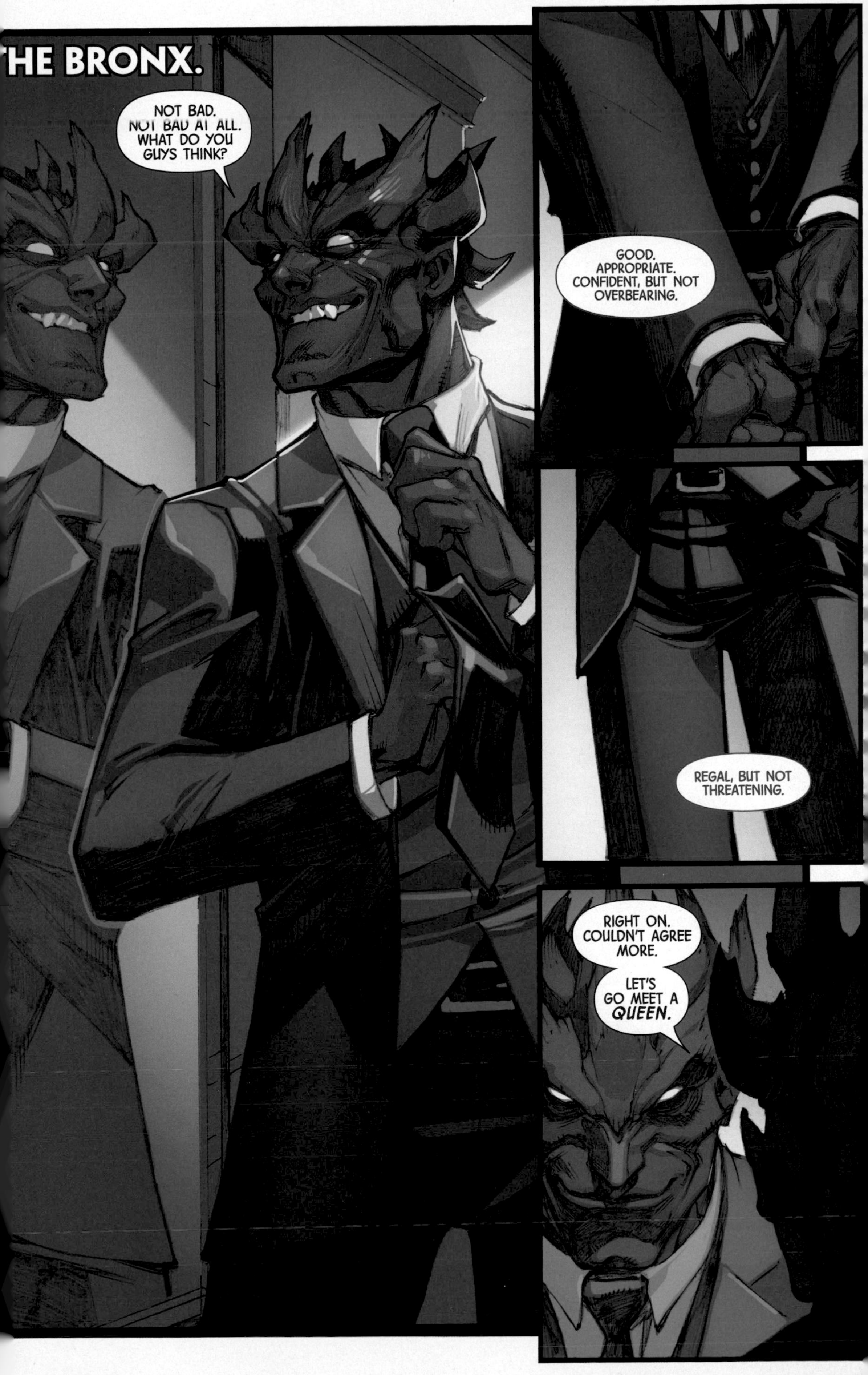
THE BRONX.
NOT BAD. NOT BAD AT ALL. WHAT DO YOU GUYS THINK?
GOOD. APPROPRIATE. CONFIDENT, BUT NOT OVERBEARING.
REGAL, BUT NOT THREATENING.
RIGHT ON. COULDN'T AGREE MORE.
LET'S GO MEET A QUEEN.

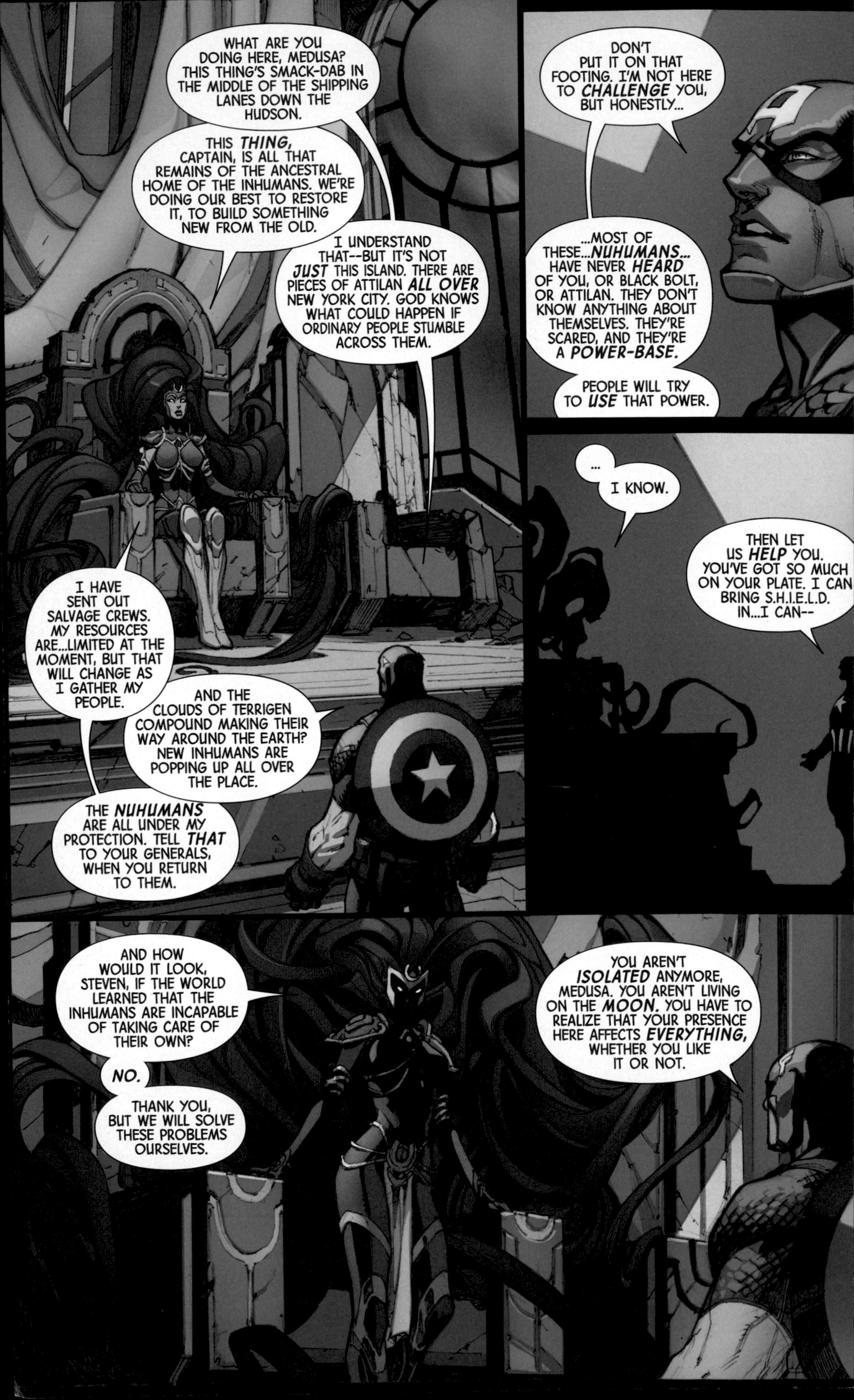
WHAT ARE YOU DOING HERE, MEDUSA? THIS THING'S SMACK-DAB IN THE MIDDLE OF THE SHIPPING LANES DOWN THE HUDSON.
THIS THING, CAPTAIN, IS ALL THAT REMAINS OF THE ANCESTRAL HOME OF THE INHUMANS. WE'RE DOING OUR BEST TO RESTORE IT, TO BUILD SOMETHING NEW FROM THE OLD.
I UNDERSTAND THAT--BUT IT'S NOT JUST THIS ISLAND. THERE ARE PIECES OF ATTILAN ALL OVER NEW YORK CITY. GOD KNOWS WHAT COULD HAPPEN IF ORDINARY PEOPLE STUMBLE ACROSS THEM.
I HAVE SENT OUT SALVAGE CREWS. MY RESOURCES ARE...LIMITED AT THE MOMENT, BUT THAT WILL CHANGE AS I GATHER MY PEOPLE.
AND THE CLOUDS OF TERRIGEN COMPOUND MAKING THEIR WAY AROUND THE EARTH? NEW INHUMANS ARE POPPING UP ALL OVER THE PLACE.
THE NUHUMANS ARE ALL UNDER MY PROTECTION. TELL THAT TO YOUR GENERALS, WHEN YOU RETURN TO THEM.
DON'T PUT IT ON THAT FOOTING. I'M NOT HERE TO CHALLENGE YOU, BUT HONESTLY...
...MOST OF THESE...NUHUMANS... HAVE NEVER HEARD OF YOU, OR BLACK BOLT, OR ATTILAN. THEY DON'T KNOW ANYTHING ABOUT THEMSELVES. THEY'RE SCARED, AND THEY'RE A POWER-BASE.
PEOPLE WILL TRY TO USE THAT POWER.
...
I KNOW.
THEN LET US HELP YOU. YOU'VE GOT SO MUCH ON YOUR PLATE. I CAN BRING S.H.I.E.L.D. IN...I CAN--
AND HOW WOULD IT LOOK, STEVEN, IF THE WORLD LEARNED THAT THE INHUMANS ARE INCAPABLE OF TAKING CARE OF THEIR OWN?
NO.
THANK YOU, BUT WE WILL SOLVE THESE PROBLEMS OURSELVES.
YOU AREN'T ISOLATED ANYMORE, MEDUSA. YOU AREN'T LIVING ON THE MOON. YOU HAVE TO REALIZE THAT YOUR PRESENCE HERE AFFECTS EVERYTHING, WHETHER YOU LIKE IT OR NOT.

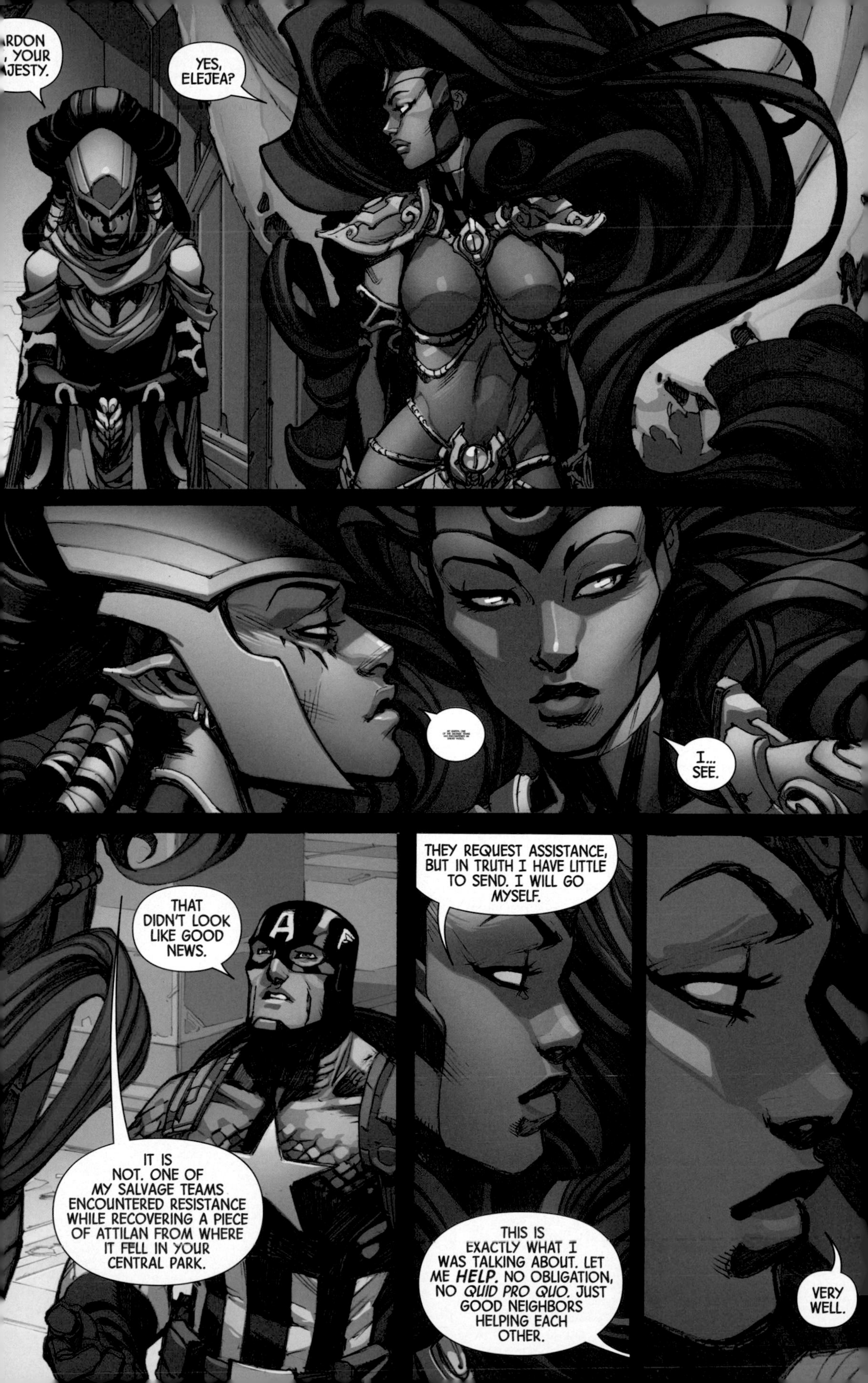
RDON
, YOUR
JESTY.
YES, ELEJEA?
I... SEE.
THAT DIDN'T LOOK LIKE GOOD NEWS.
IT IS NOT. ONE OF MY SALVAGE TEAMS ENCOUNTERED RESISTANCE WHILE RECOVERING A PIECE OF ATTILAN FROM WHERE IT FELL IN YOUR CENTRAL PARK.
THEY REQUEST ASSISTANCE, BUT IN TRUTH I HAVE LITTLE TO SEND. I WILL GO MYSELF.
THIS IS EXACTLY WHAT I WAS TALKING ABOUT. LET ME *HELP.* NO OBLIGATION, NO *QUID PRO QUO.* JUST GOOD NEIGHBORS HELPING EACH OTHER.
VERY WELL.

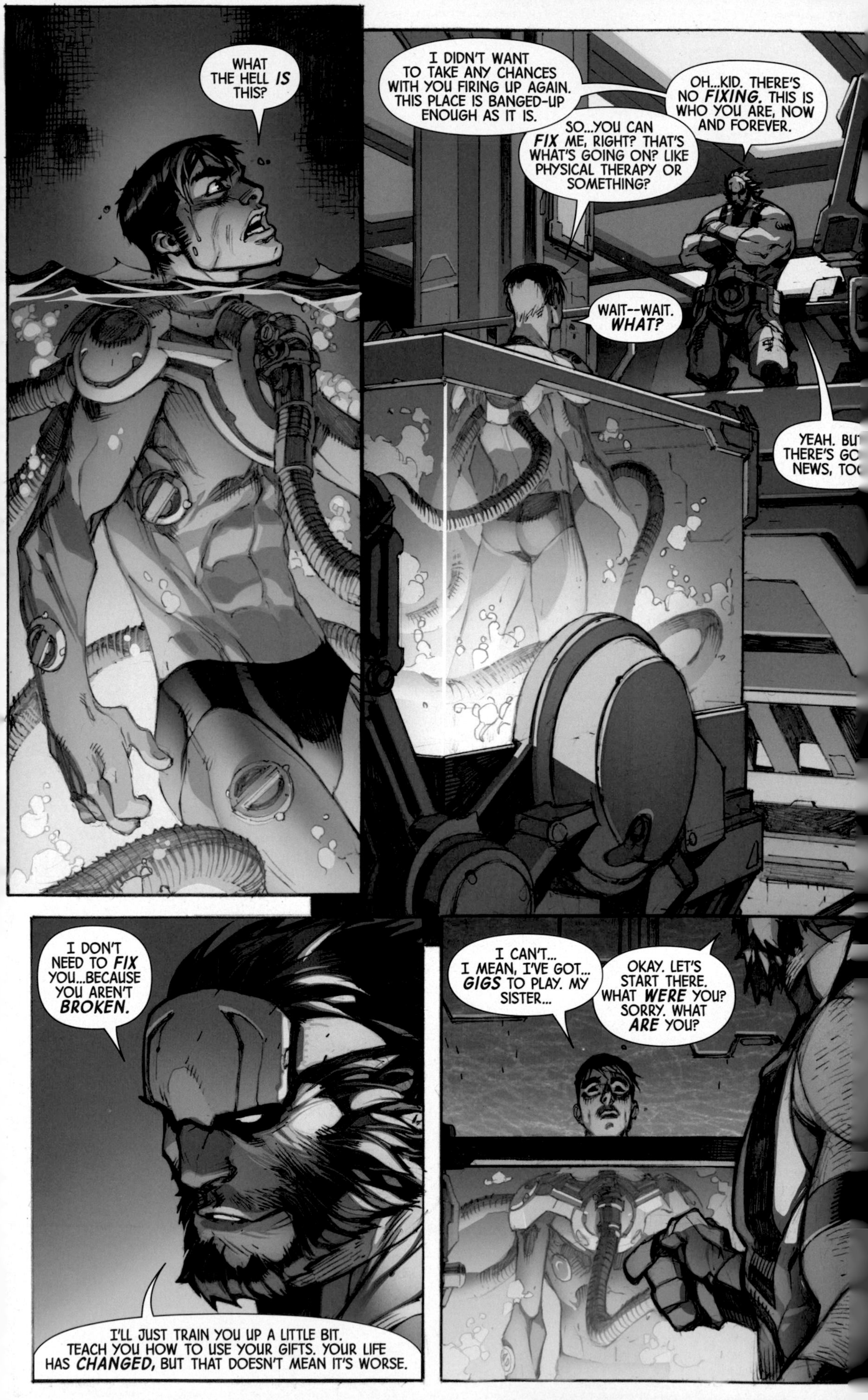

WHAT THE HELL *IS* THIS?
I DIDN'T WANT TO TAKE ANY CHANCES WITH YOU FIRING UP AGAIN. THIS PLACE IS BANGED-UP ENOUGH AS IT IS.
SO...YOU CAN *FIX* ME, RIGHT? THAT'S WHAT'S GOING ON? LIKE PHYSICAL THERAPY OR SOMETHING?
OH...KID. THERE'S NO *FIXING.* THIS IS WHO YOU ARE, NOW AND FOREVER.
WAIT--WAIT. *WHAT?*
YEAH. BU THERE'S GO NEWS, TO
I DON'T NEED TO *FIX* YOU...BECAUSE YOU AREN'T *BROKEN.*
I'LL JUST TRAIN YOU UP A LITTLE BIT. TEACH YOU HOW TO USE YOUR GIFTS. YOUR LIFE HAS *CHANGED,* BUT THAT DOESN'T MEAN IT'S WORSE.
I CAN'T... I MEAN, I'VE GOT... *GIGS* TO PLAY. MY SISTER...
OKAY. LET'S START THERE. WHAT *WERE* YOU? SORRY. WHAT *ARE* YOU?

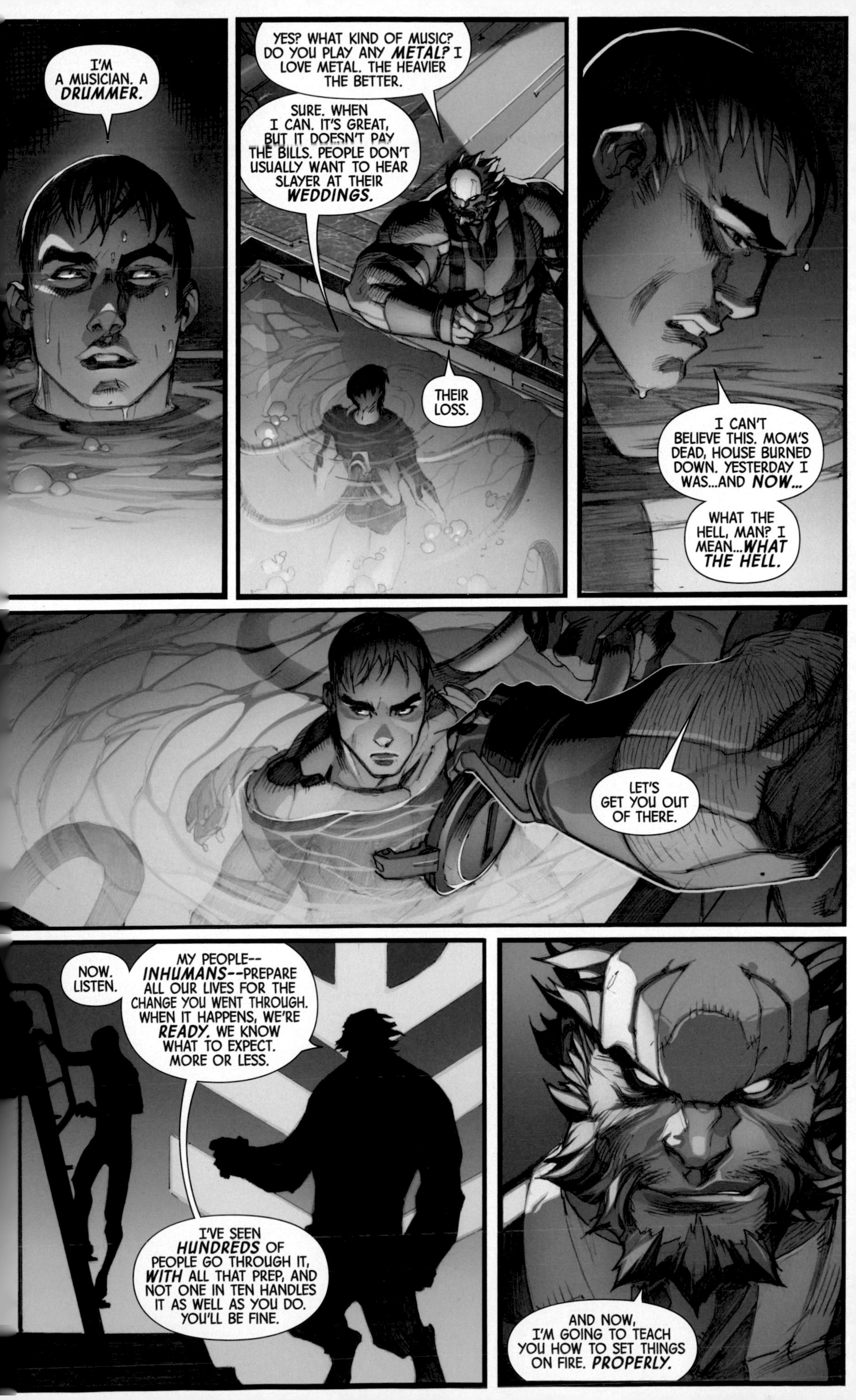
I'M A MUSICIAN. A DRUMMER.
YES? WHAT KIND OF MUSIC? DO YOU PLAY ANY METAL? I LOVE METAL. THE HEAVIER THE BETTER.
SURE. WHEN I CAN. IT'S GREAT, BUT IT DOESN'T PAY THE BILLS. PEOPLE DON'T USUALLY WANT TO HEAR SLAYER AT THEIR WEDDINGS.
THEIR LOSS.
I CAN'T BELIEVE THIS. MOM'S DEAD, HOUSE BURNED DOWN. YESTERDAY I WAS...AND NOW...
WHAT THE HELL, MAN? I MEAN...WHAT THE HELL.
LET'S GET YOU OUT OF THERE.
NOW. LISTEN.
MY PEOPLE--INHUMANS--PREPARE ALL OUR LIVES FOR THE CHANGE YOU WENT THROUGH. WHEN IT HAPPENS, WE'RE READY. WE KNOW WHAT TO EXPECT. MORE OR LESS.
I'VE SEEN HUNDREDS OF PEOPLE GO THROUGH IT, WITH ALL THAT PREP, AND NOT ONE IN TEN HANDLES IT AS WELL AS YOU DO. YOU'LL BE FINE.
AND NOW, I'M GOING TO TEACH YOU HOW TO SET THINGS ON FIRE. PROPERLY.

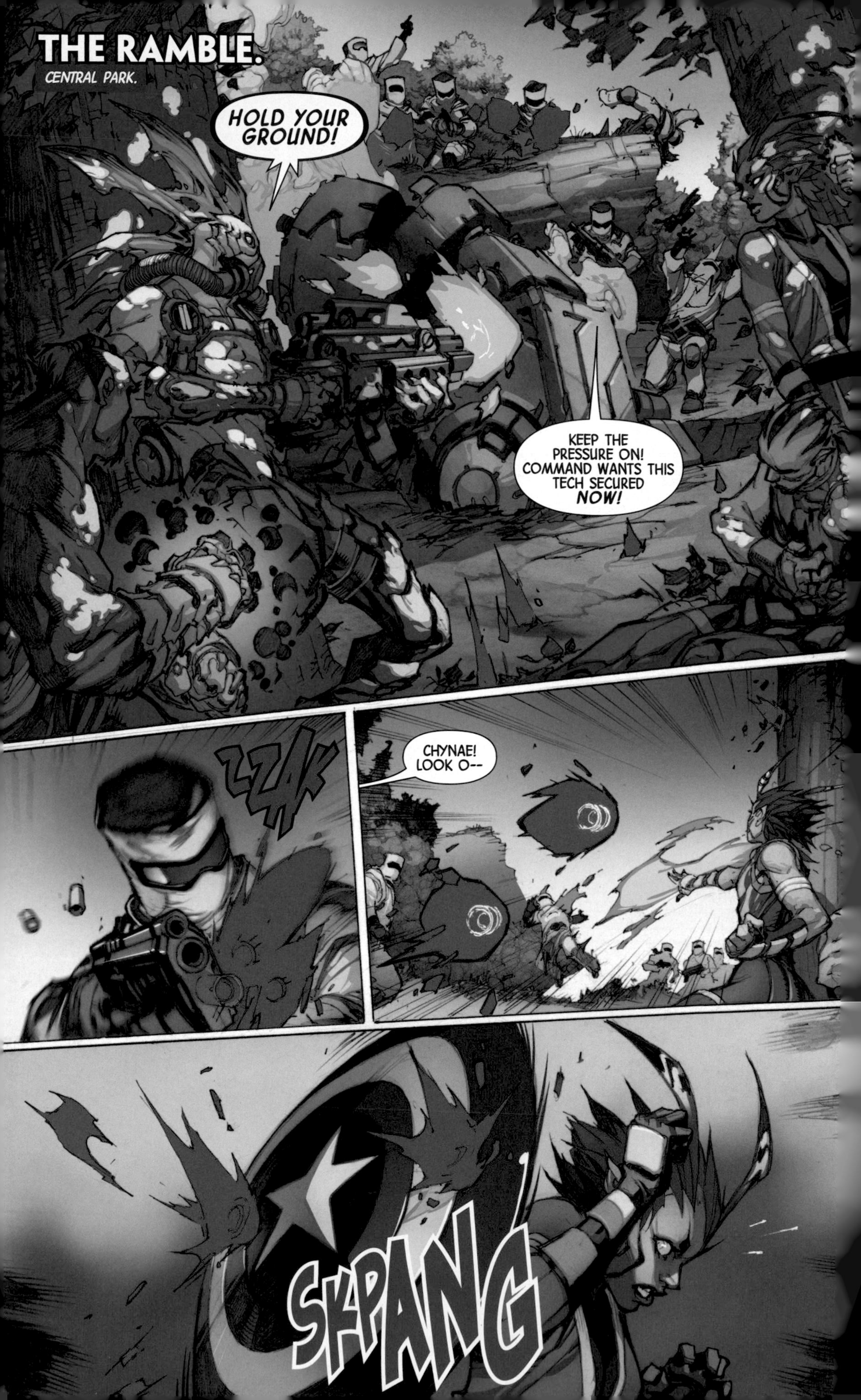
THE RAMBLE.
CENTRAL PARK.
HOLD YOUR GROUND!
KEEP THE PRESSURE ON! COMMAND WANTS THIS TECH SECURED NOW!
ZZAK
CHYNAE! LOOK O--
SKPANG

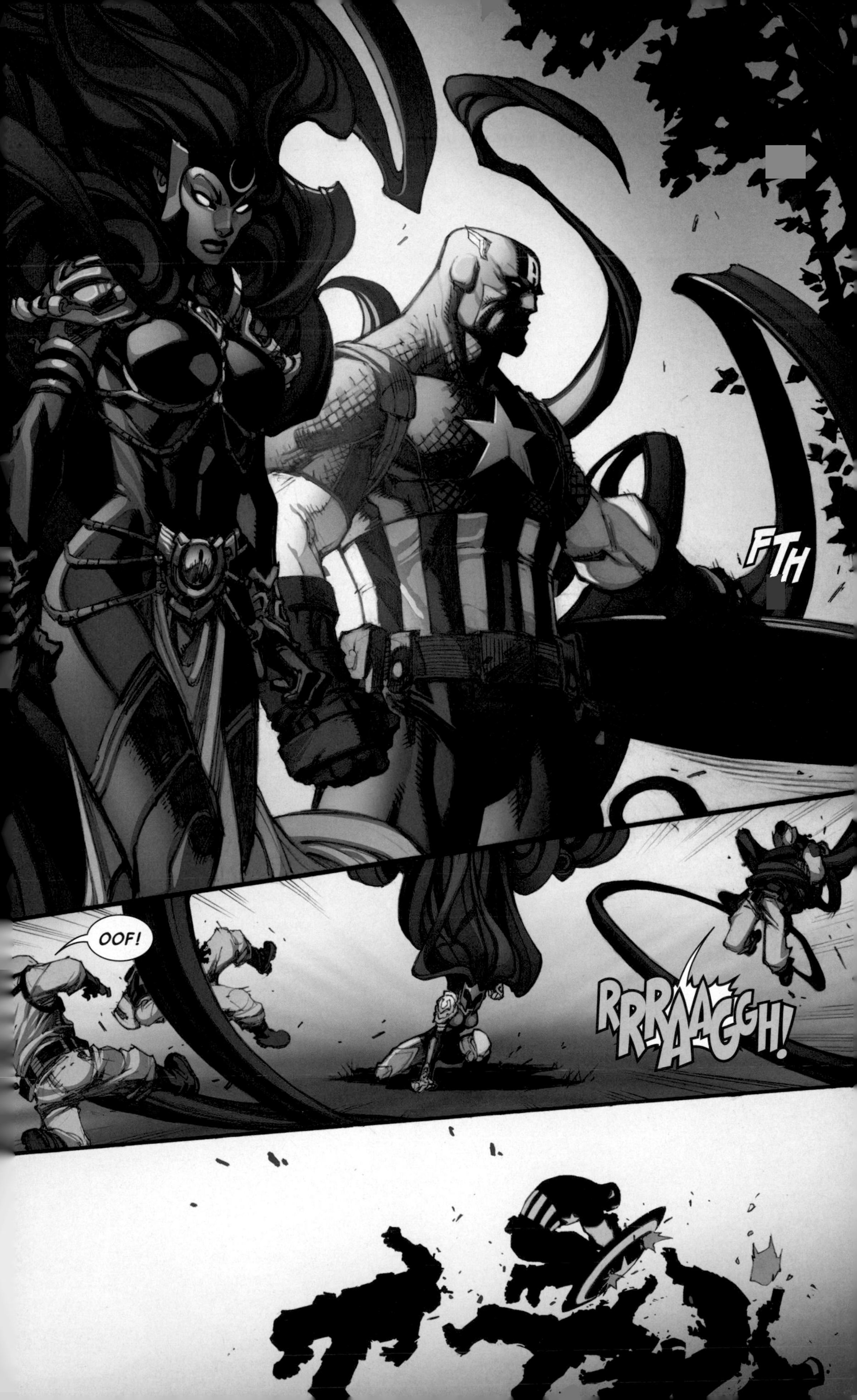
FTH
OOF!
RRRAAGGH!

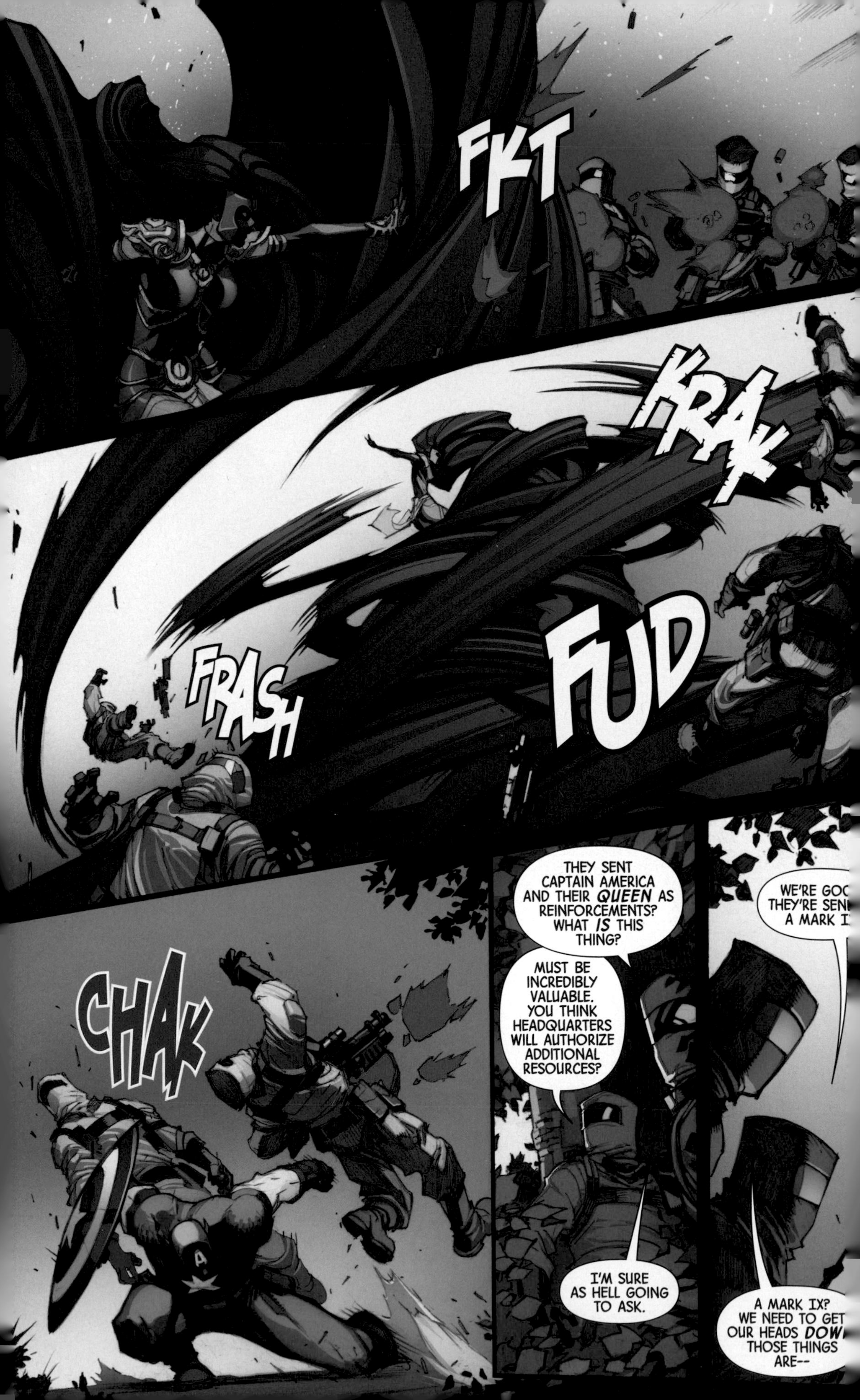

FKT
KRAK
FRASH
FUD
CHAK
THEY SENT CAPTAIN AMERICA AND THEIR QUEEN AS REINFORCEMENTS? WHAT IS THIS THING?
MUST BE INCREDIBLY VALUABLE. YOU THINK HEADQUARTERS WILL AUTHORIZE ADDITIONAL RESOURCES?
I'M SURE AS HELL GOING TO ASK.
A MARK IX? WE NEED TO GET OUR HEADS
THOSE THINGS ARE--

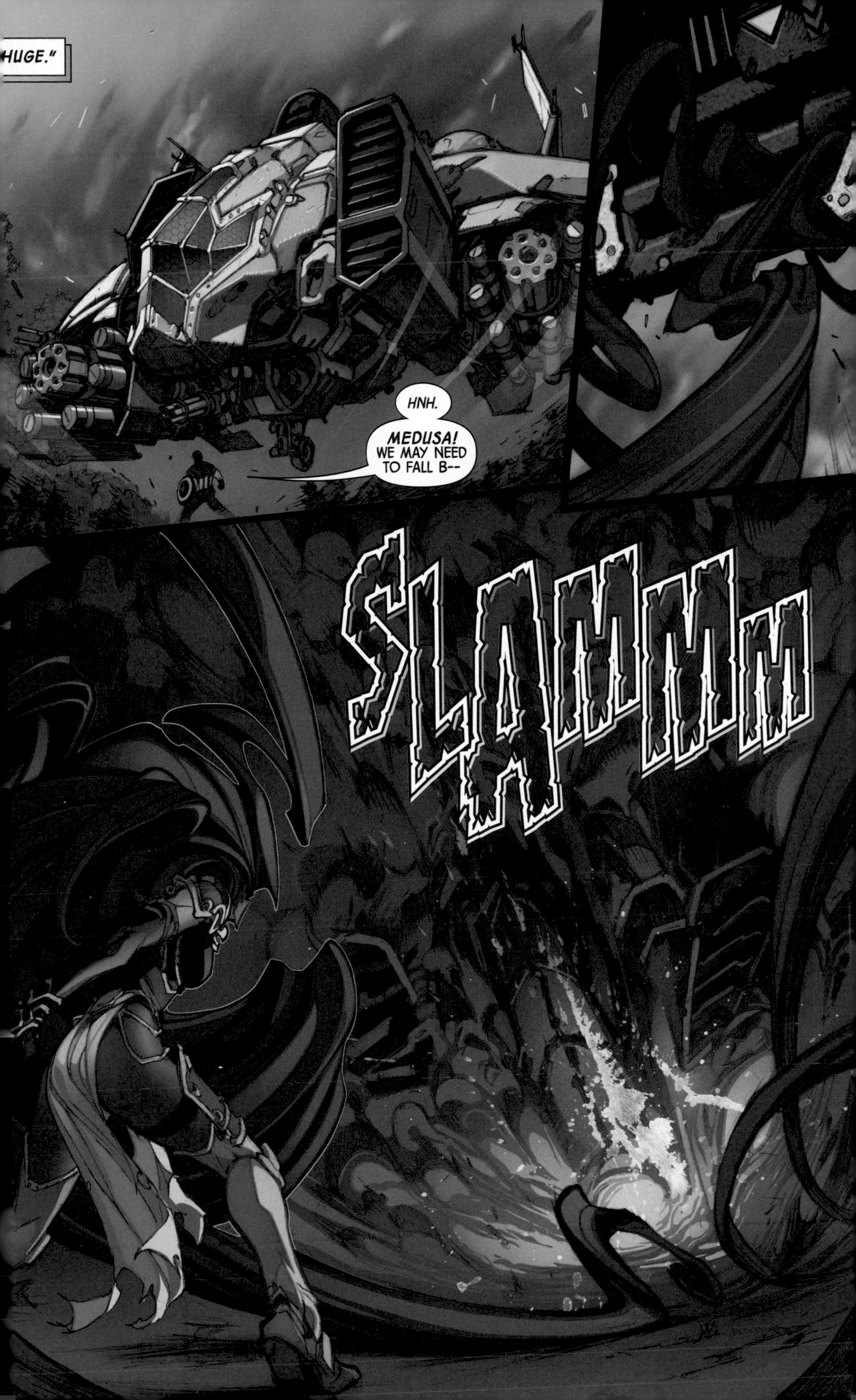
HUGE."
HNH.
MEDUSA! WE MAY NEED TO FALL B--
SLAMMM

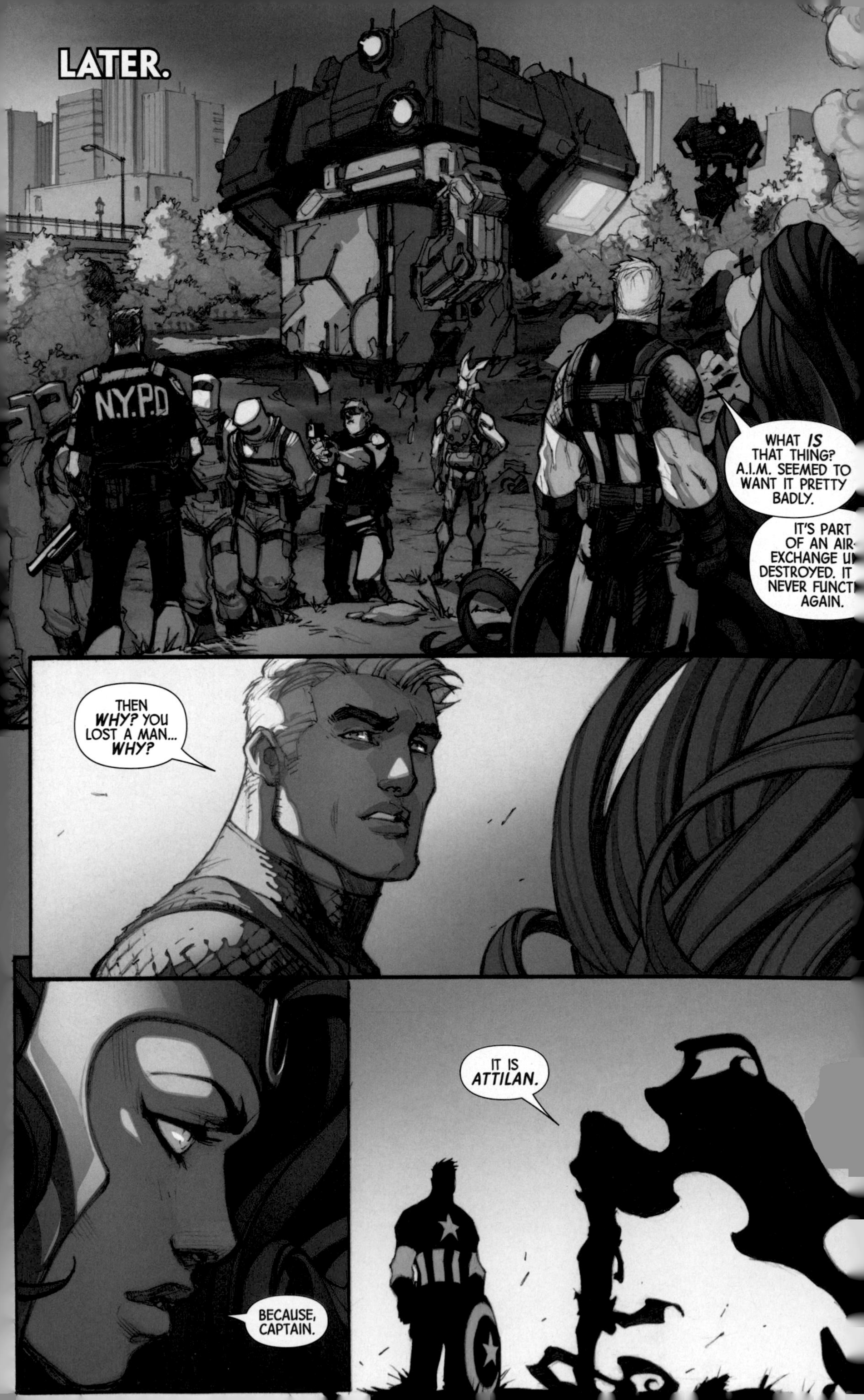
LATER.
N.Y.P.D
WHAT *IS* THAT THING? A.I.M. SEEMED TO WANT IT PRETTY BADLY.
IT'S PART OF AN AIR-EXCHANGE U DESTROYED. IT NEVER FUNCT AGAIN.
THEN *WHY?* YOU LOST A MAN... *WHY?*
BECAUSE, CAPTAIN.
IT IS *ATTILAN.*

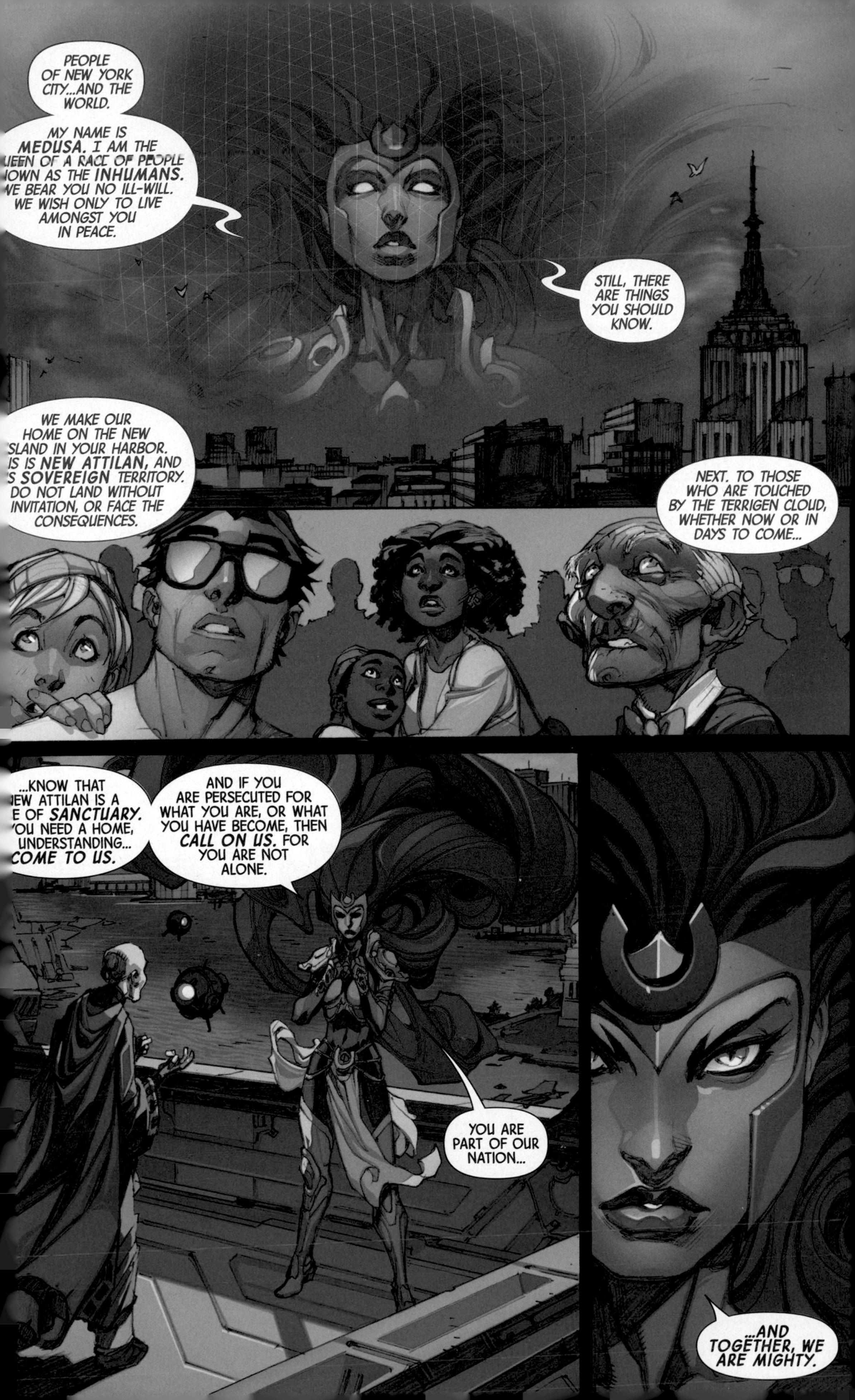
PEOPLE OF NEW YORK CITY...AND THE WORLD.
MY NAME IS MEDUSA. I AM THE UEEN OF A RACE OF PEOPLE OWN AS THE INHUMANS. VE BEAR YOU NO ILL-WILL. WE WISH ONLY TO LIVE AMONGST YOU IN PEACE.
STILL, THERE ARE THINGS YOU SHOULD KNOW.
WE MAKE OUR HOME ON THE NEW SLAND IN YOUR HARBOR. IS IS NEW ATTILAN, AND S SOVEREIGN TERRITORY. DO NOT LAND WITHOUT INVITATION, OR FACE THE CONSEQUENCES.
NEXT. TO THOSE WHO ARE TOUCHED BY THE TERRIGEN CLOUD, WHETHER NOW OR IN DAYS TO COME...
...KNOW THAT IEW ATTILAN IS A E OF SANCTUARY. OU NEED A HOME, UNDERSTANDING... COME TO US.
AND IF YOU ARE PERSECUTED FOR WHAT YOU ARE, OR WHAT YOU HAVE BECOME, THEN CALL ON US. FOR YOU ARE NOT ALONE.
YOU ARE PART OF OUR NATION...
...AND TOGETHER, WE ARE MIGHTY.

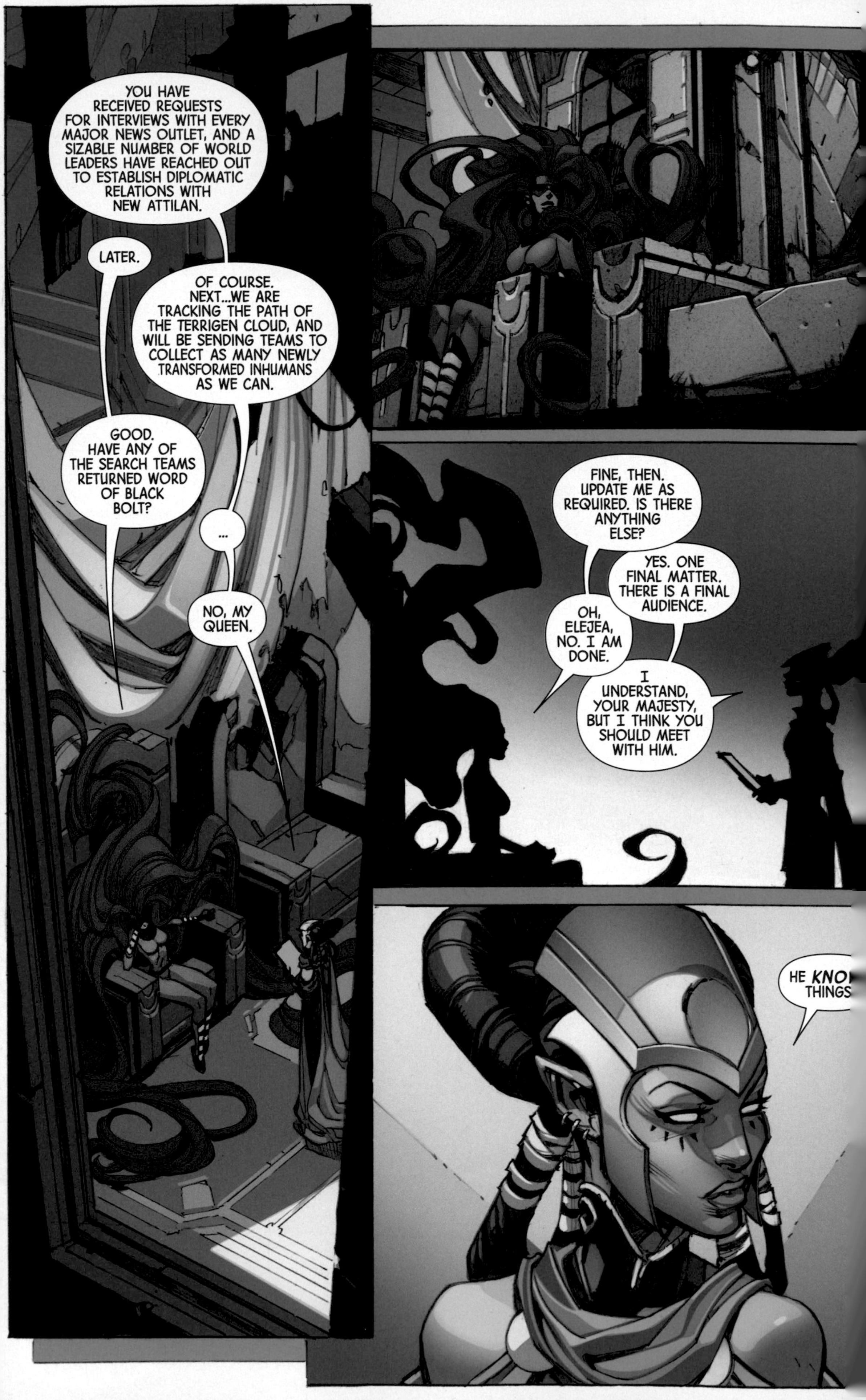
YOU HAVE RECEIVED REQUESTS FOR INTERVIEWS WITH EVERY MAJOR NEWS OUTLET, AND A SIZABLE NUMBER OF WORLD LEADERS HAVE REACHED OUT TO ESTABLISH DIPLOMATIC RELATIONS WITH NEW ATTILAN.
LATER.
OF COURSE. NEXT...WE ARE TRACKING THE PATH OF THE TERRIGEN CLOUD, AND WILL BE SENDING TEAMS TO COLLECT AS MANY NEWLY TRANSFORMED INHUMANS AS WE CAN.
GOOD. HAVE ANY OF THE SEARCH TEAMS RETURNED WORD OF BLACK BOLT?
...
NO, MY QUEEN.
FINE, THEN. UPDATE ME AS REQUIRED. IS THERE ANYTHING ELSE?
YES. ONE FINAL MATTER. THERE IS A FINAL AUDIENCE.
OH, ELEJEA, NO. I AM DONE.
I UNDERSTAND, YOUR MAJESTY, BUT I THINK YOU SHOULD MEET WITH HIM.
HE KNO THINGS

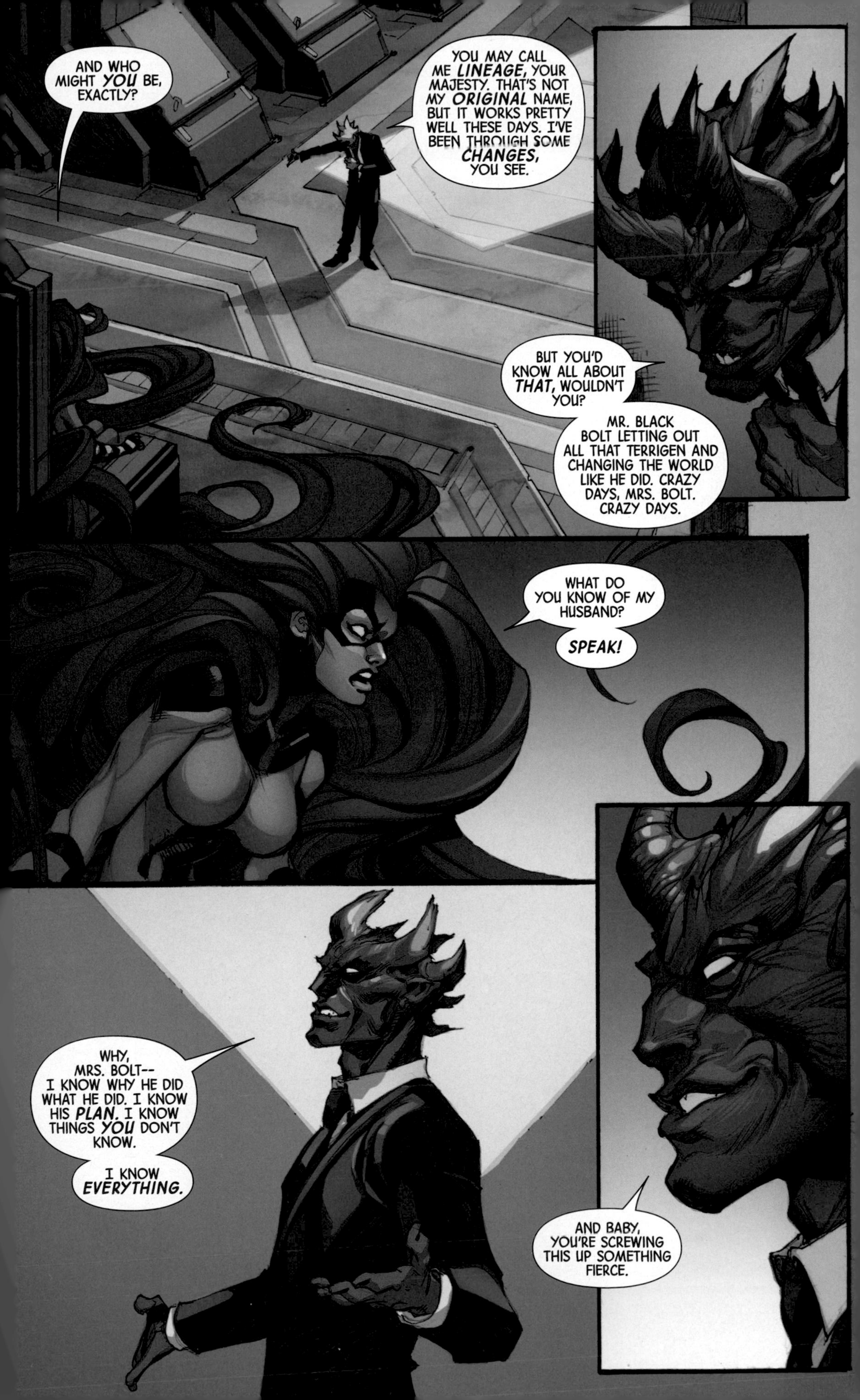
AND WHO MIGHT YOU BE, EXACTLY?
YOU MAY CALL ME LINEAGE, YOUR MAJESTY. THAT'S NOT MY ORIGINAL NAME, BUT IT WORKS PRETTY WELL THESE DAYS. I'VE BEEN THROUGH SOME CHANGES, YOU SEE.
BUT YOU'D KNOW ALL ABOUT THAT, WOULDN'T YOU?
MR. BLACK BOLT LETTING OUT ALL THAT TERRIGEN AND CHANGING THE WORLD LIKE HE DID. CRAZY DAYS, MRS. BOLT. CRAZY DAYS.
WHAT DO YOU KNOW OF MY HUSBAND?
SPEAK!
WHY, MRS. BOLT-- I KNOW WHY HE DID WHAT HE DID. I KNOW HIS PLAN. I KNOW THINGS YOU DON'T KNOW.
I KNOW EVERYTHING.
AND BABY, YOU'RE SCREWING THIS UP SOMETHING FIERCE.

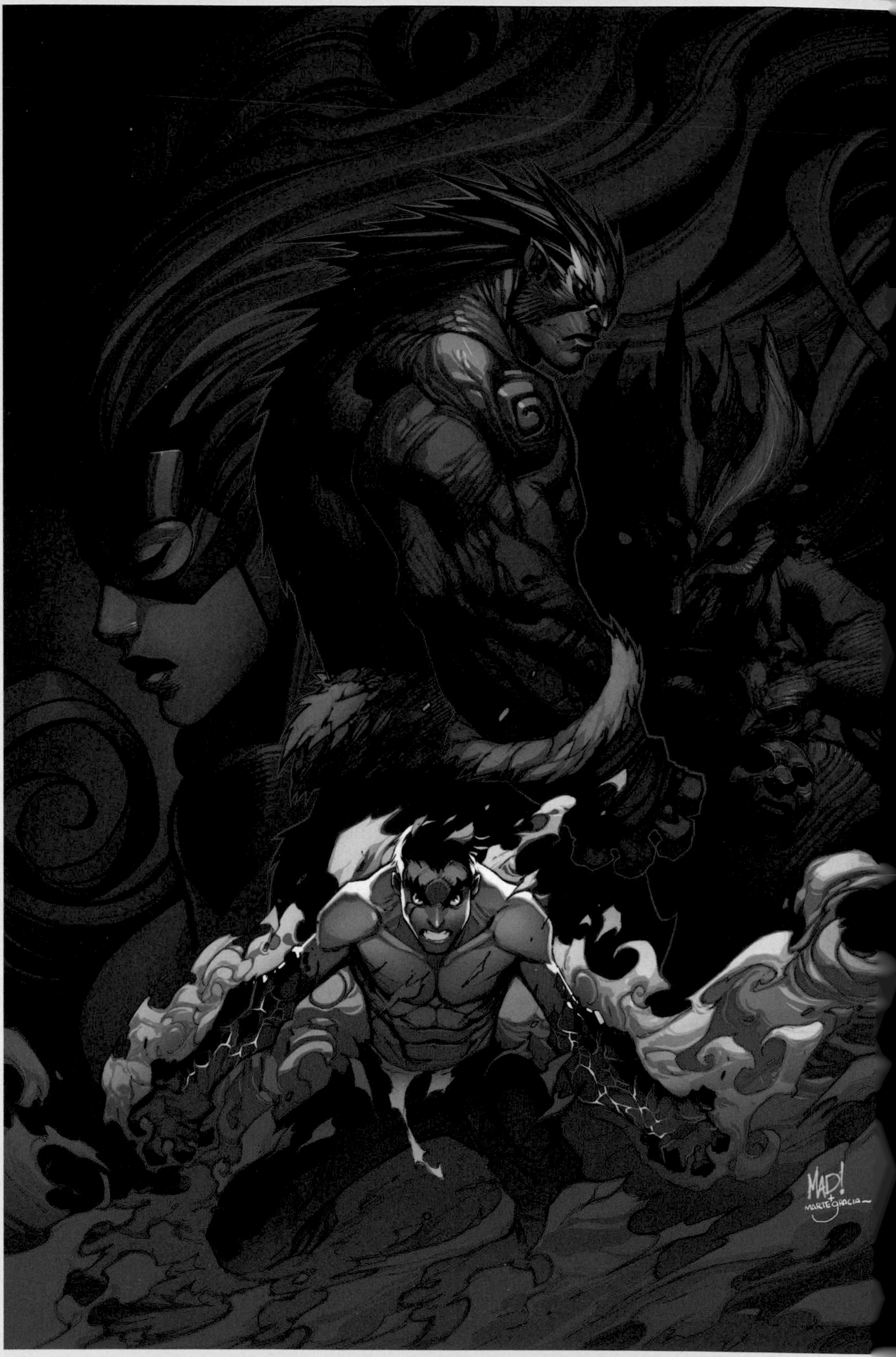
MAD!
+ MARTEGRACIA

3

PART THREE: THEY FALL

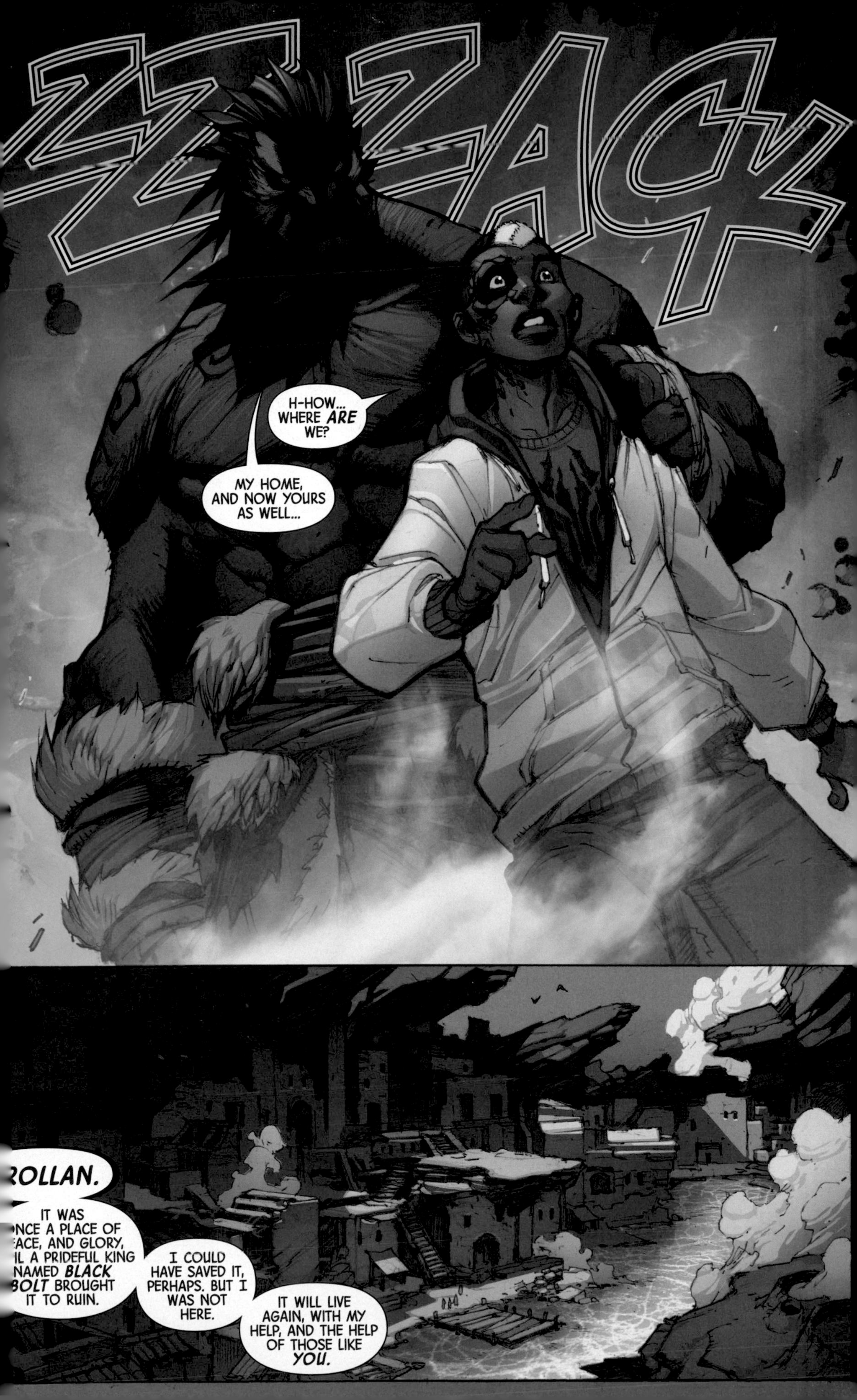
ZZZZAACK
H-HOW... WHERE *ARE* WE?
MY HOME, AND NOW YOURS AS WELL...
ROLLAN.
IT WAS ONCE A PLACE OF PEACE, AND GLORY, ...IL A PRIDEFUL KING NAMED *BLACK BOLT* BROUGHT IT TO RUIN.
I COULD HAVE SAVED IT, PERHAPS. BUT I WAS NOT HERE.
IT WILL LIVE AGAIN, WITH MY HELP, AND THE HELP OF THOSE LIKE *YOU*.

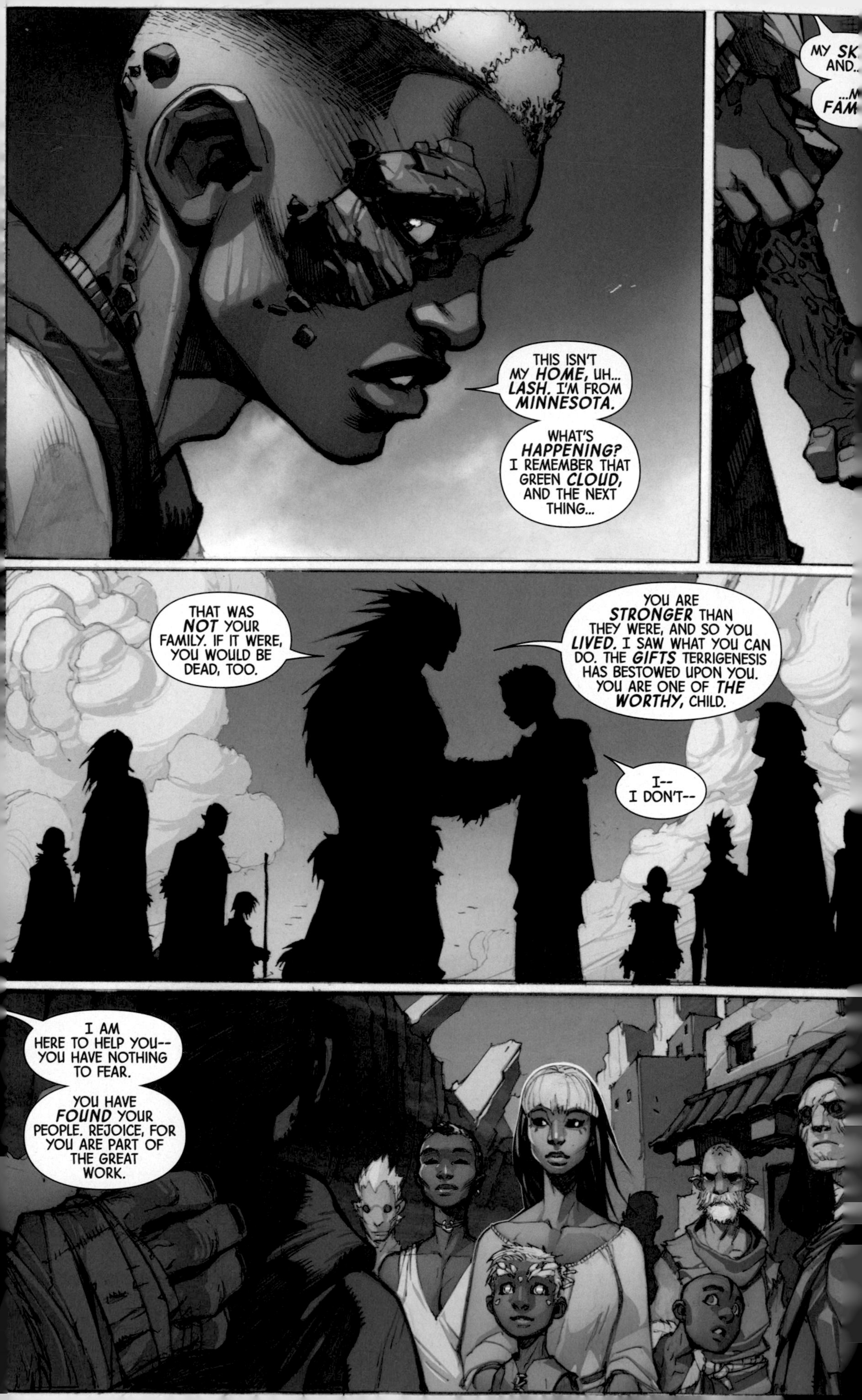

THIS ISN'T MY HOME, UH... LASH. I'M FROM MINNESOTA.
WHAT'S HAPPENING? I REMEMBER THAT GREEN CLOUD, AND THE NEXT THING...
MY SK AND...
...M FAM
THAT WAS NOT YOUR FAMILY. IF IT WERE, YOU WOULD BE DEAD, TOO.
YOU ARE STRONGER THAN THEY WERE, AND SO YOU LIVED. I SAW WHAT YOU CAN DO. THE GIFTS TERRIGENESIS HAS BESTOWED UPON YOU. YOU ARE ONE OF THE WORTHY, CHILD.
I-- I DON'T--
I AM HERE TO HELP YOU-- YOU HAVE NOTHING TO FEAR.
YOU HAVE FOUND YOUR PEOPLE. REJOICE, FOR YOU ARE PART OF THE GREAT WORK.

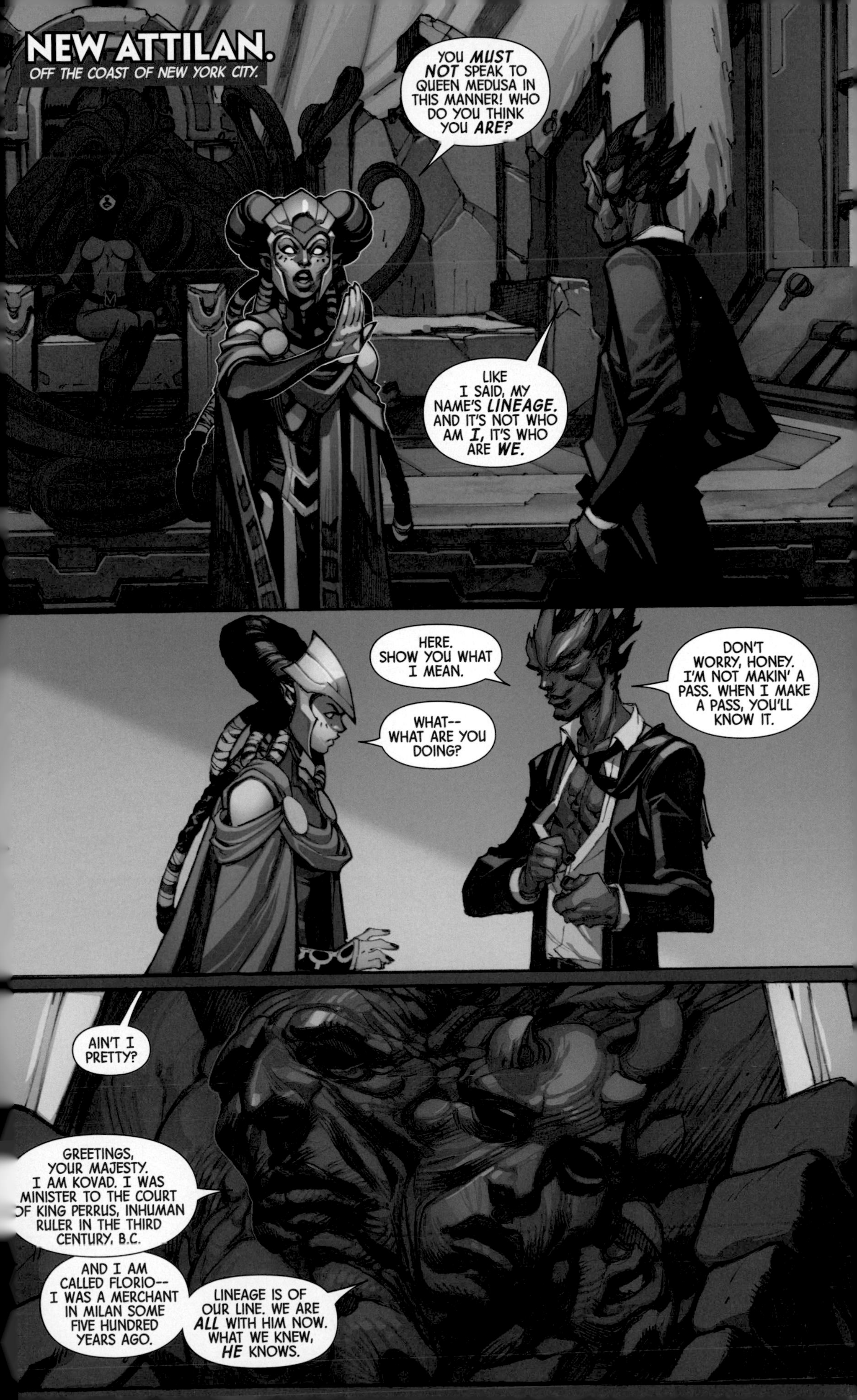
NEW ATTILAN.
OFF THE COAST OF NEW YORK CITY.
YOU MUST NOT SPEAK TO QUEEN MEDUSA IN THIS MANNER! WHO DO YOU THINK YOU ARE?
LIKE I SAID, MY NAME'S LINEAGE. AND IT'S NOT WHO AM I, IT'S WHO ARE WE.
HERE. SHOW YOU WHAT I MEAN.
WHAT-- WHAT ARE YOU DOING?
DON'T WORRY, HONEY. I'M NOT MAKIN' A PASS. WHEN I MAKE A PASS, YOU'LL KNOW IT.
AIN'T I PRETTY?
GREETINGS, YOUR MAJESTY. I AM KOVAD. I WAS MINISTER TO THE COURT OF KING PERRUS, INHUMAN RULER IN THE THIRD CENTURY, B.C.
AND I AM CALLED FLORIO-- I WAS A MERCHANT IN MILAN SOME FIVE HUNDRED YEARS AGO.
LINEAGE IS OF OUR LINE. WE ARE ALL WITH HIM NOW. WHAT WE KNEW, HE KNOWS.

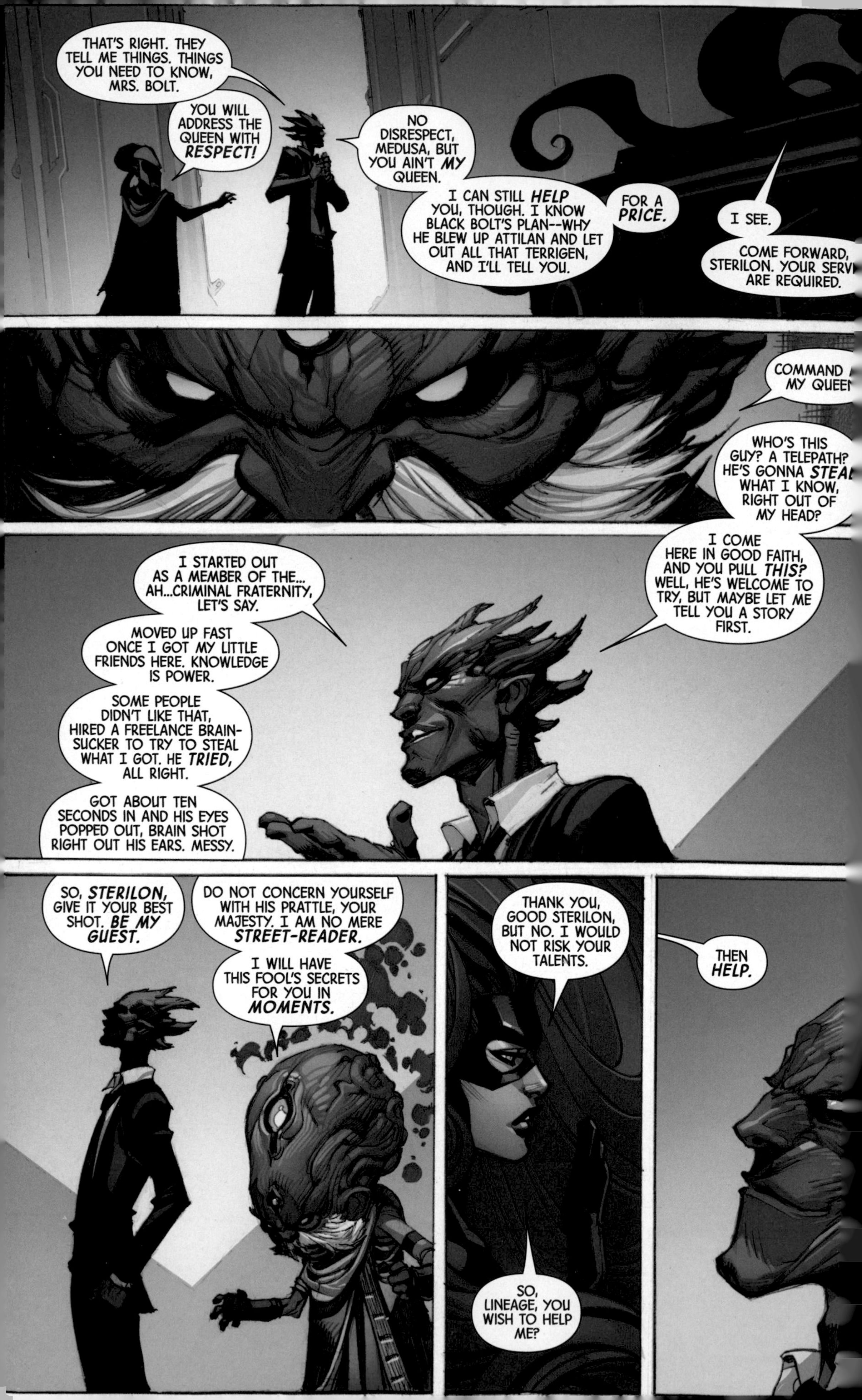
THAT'S RIGHT. THEY TELL ME THINGS. THINGS YOU NEED TO KNOW, MRS. BOLT.
YOU WILL ADDRESS THE QUEEN WITH RESPECT!
NO DISRESPECT, MEDUSA, BUT YOU AIN'T MY QUEEN.
I CAN STILL HELP YOU, THOUGH. I KNOW BLACK BOLT'S PLAN--WHY HE BLEW UP ATTILAN AND LET OUT ALL THAT TERRIGEN, AND I'LL TELL YOU.
FOR A PRICE.
I SEE.
COME FORWARD, STERILON. YOUR SERV
ARE REQUIRED.
COMMAND
MY QUEE
WHO'S THIS GUY? A TELEPATH? HE'S GONNA STEA
WHAT I KNOW, RIGHT OUT OF MY HEAD?
I COME HERE IN GOOD FAITH, AND YOU PULL THIS? WELL, HE'S WELCOME TO TRY, BUT MAYBE LET ME TELL YOU A STORY FIRST.
I STARTED OUT AS A MEMBER OF THE... AH...CRIMINAL FRATERNITY, LET'S SAY.
MOVED UP FAST ONCE I GOT MY LITTLE FRIENDS HERE. KNOWLEDGE IS POWER.
SOME PEOPLE DIDN'T LIKE THAT, HIRED A FREELANCE BRAIN-SUCKER TO TRY TO STEAL WHAT I GOT. HE TRIED, ALL RIGHT.
GOT ABOUT TEN SECONDS IN AND HIS EYES POPPED OUT, BRAIN SHOT RIGHT OUT HIS EARS. MESSY.
SO, STERILON, GIVE IT YOUR BEST SHOT. BE MY GUEST.
DO NOT CONCERN YOURSELF WITH HIS PRATTLE, YOUR MAJESTY. I AM NO MERE STREET-READER.
I WILL HAVE THIS FOOL'S SECRETS FOR YOU IN MOMENTS.
THANK YOU, GOOD STERILON, BUT NO. I WOULD NOT RISK YOUR TALENTS.
SO, LINEAGE, YOU WISH TO HELP ME?
THEN HELP.

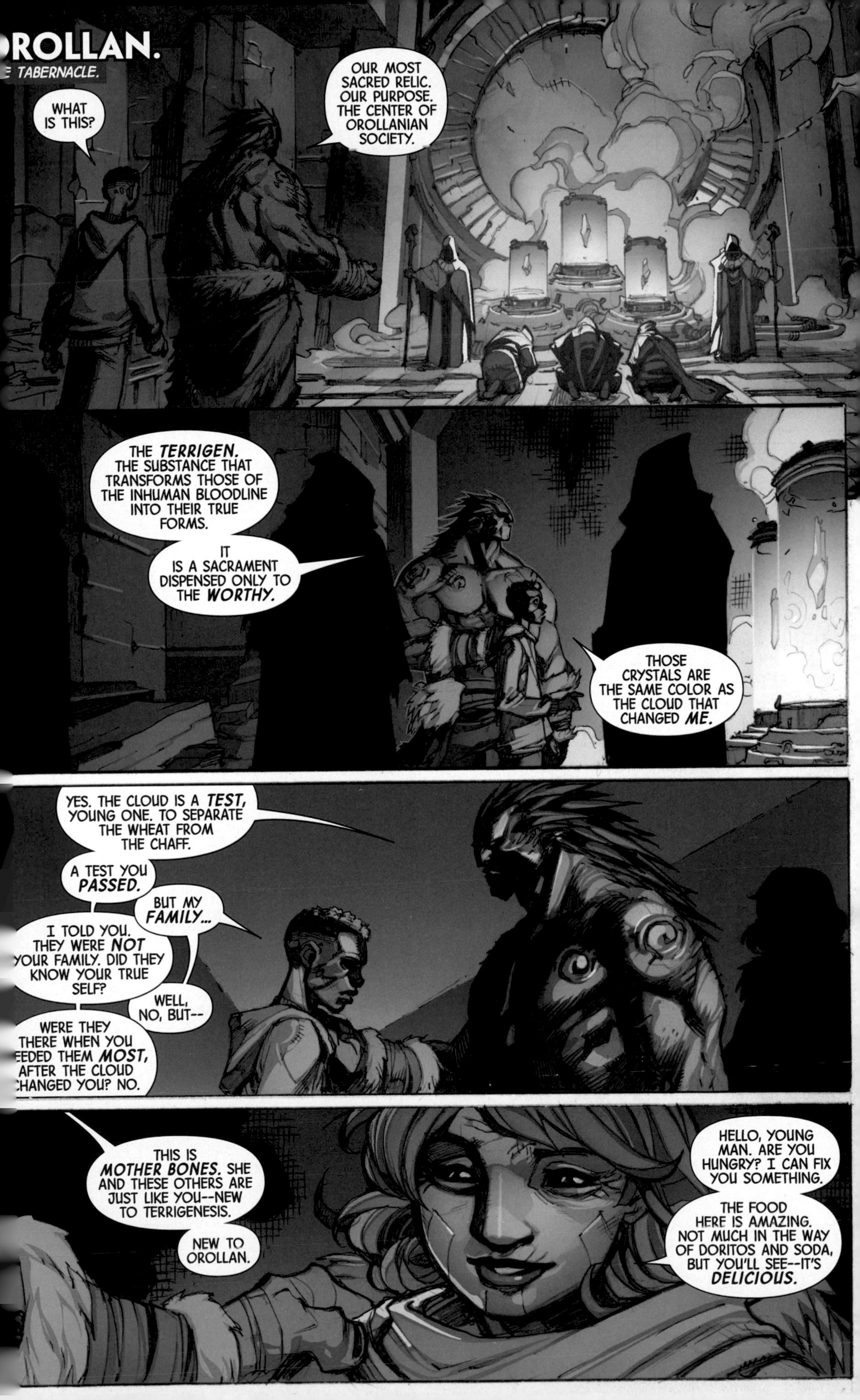
OROLLAN.
E TABERNACLE.
WHAT IS THIS?
OUR MOST SACRED RELIC. OUR PURPOSE. THE CENTER OF OROLLANIAN SOCIETY.
THE TERRIGEN. THE SUBSTANCE THAT TRANSFORMS THOSE OF THE INHUMAN BLOODLINE INTO THEIR TRUE FORMS.
IT IS A SACRAMENT DISPENSED ONLY TO THE WORTHY.
THOSE CRYSTALS ARE THE SAME COLOR AS THE CLOUD THAT CHANGED ME.
YES. THE CLOUD IS A TEST, YOUNG ONE. TO SEPARATE THE WHEAT FROM THE CHAFF.
A TEST YOU PASSED.
BUT MY FAMILY...
I TOLD YOU. THEY WERE NOT YOUR FAMILY. DID THEY KNOW YOUR TRUE SELF?
WELL, NO, BUT--
WERE THEY THERE WHEN YOU EEDED THEM MOST, AFTER THE CLOUD CHANGED YOU? NO.
THIS IS MOTHER BONES. SHE AND THESE OTHERS ARE JUST LIKE YOU--NEW TO TERRIGENESIS.
NEW TO OROLLAN.
HELLO, YOUNG MAN. ARE YOU HUNGRY? I CAN FIX YOU SOMETHING.
THE FOOD HERE IS AMAZING. NOT MUCH IN THE WAY OF DORITOS AND SODA, BUT YOU'LL SEE--IT'S DELICIOUS.

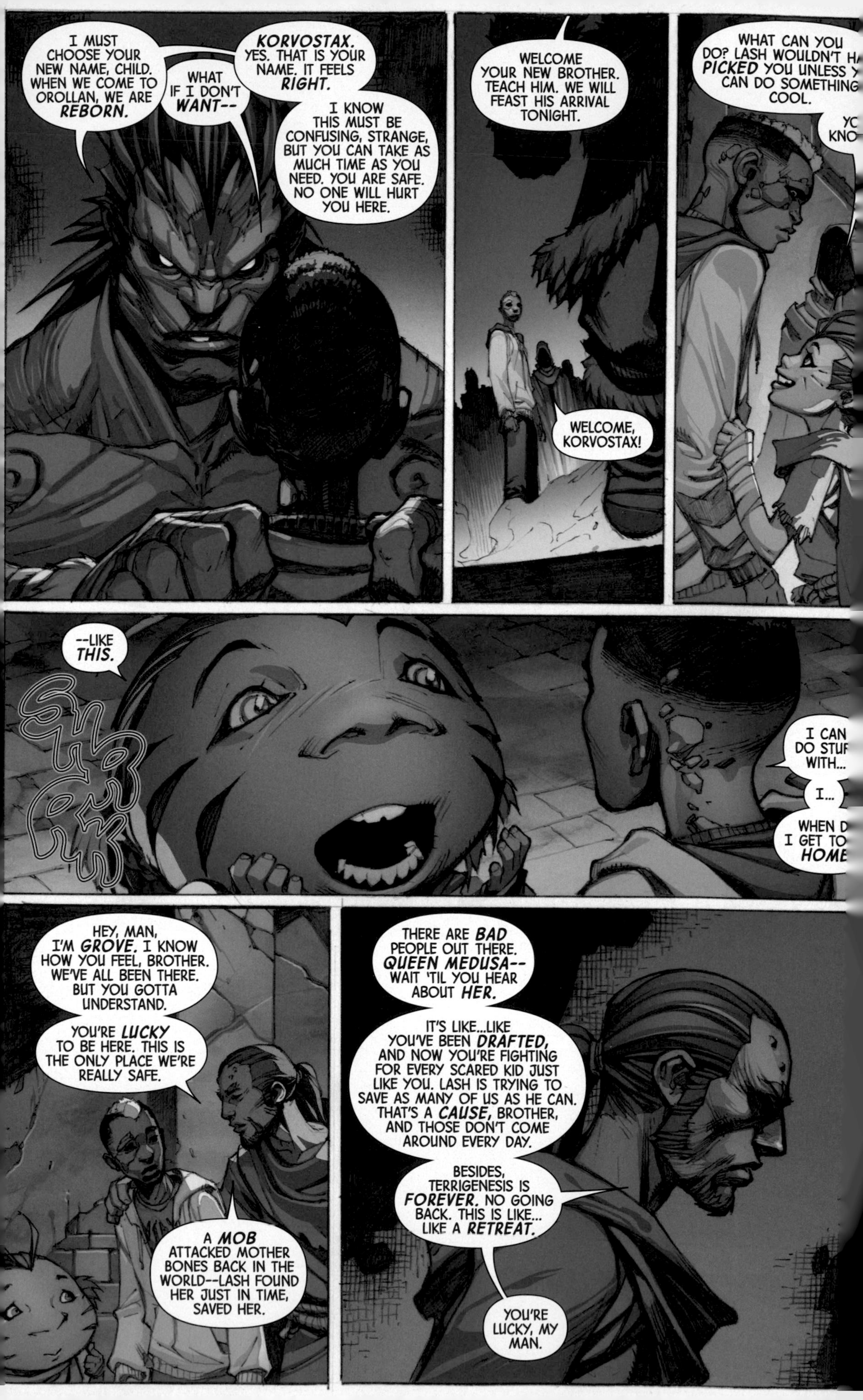
I MUST CHOOSE YOUR NEW NAME, CHILD. WHEN WE COME TO OROLLAN, WE ARE REBORN.
WHAT IF I DON'T WANT--
KORVOSTAX. YES. THAT IS YOUR NAME. IT FEELS RIGHT.
I KNOW THIS MUST BE CONFUSING, STRANGE, BUT YOU CAN TAKE AS MUCH TIME AS YOU NEED. YOU ARE SAFE. NO ONE WILL HURT YOU HERE.
WELCOME YOUR NEW BROTHER. TEACH HIM. WE WILL FEAST HIS ARRIVAL TONIGHT.
WELCOME, KORVOSTAX!
WHAT CAN YOU DO? LASH WOULDN'T
PICKED YOU UNLESS
CAN DO SOMETHING
COOL.
--LIKE THIS.
I CAN
DO STU
WITH...
I...
WHEN
I GET TO
HOME
HEY, MAN, I'M GROVE. I KNOW HOW YOU FEEL, BROTHER. WE'VE ALL BEEN THERE. BUT YOU GOTTA UNDERSTAND.
YOU'RE LUCKY TO BE HERE. THIS IS THE ONLY PLACE WE'RE REALLY SAFE.
A MOB ATTACKED MOTHER BONES BACK IN THE WORLD--LASH FOUND HER JUST IN TIME, SAVED HER.
THERE ARE BAD PEOPLE OUT THERE. QUEEN MEDUSA-- WAIT 'TIL YOU HEAR ABOUT HER.
IT'S LIKE...LIKE YOU'VE BEEN DRAFTED, AND NOW YOU'RE FIGHTING FOR EVERY SCARED KID JUST LIKE YOU. LASH IS TRYING TO SAVE AS MANY OF US AS HE CAN. THAT'S A CAUSE, BROTHER, AND THOSE DON'T COME AROUND EVERY DAY.
BESIDES, TERRIGENESIS IS FOREVER. NO GOING BACK. THIS IS LIKE... LIKE A RETREAT.
YOU'RE LUCKY, MY MAN.

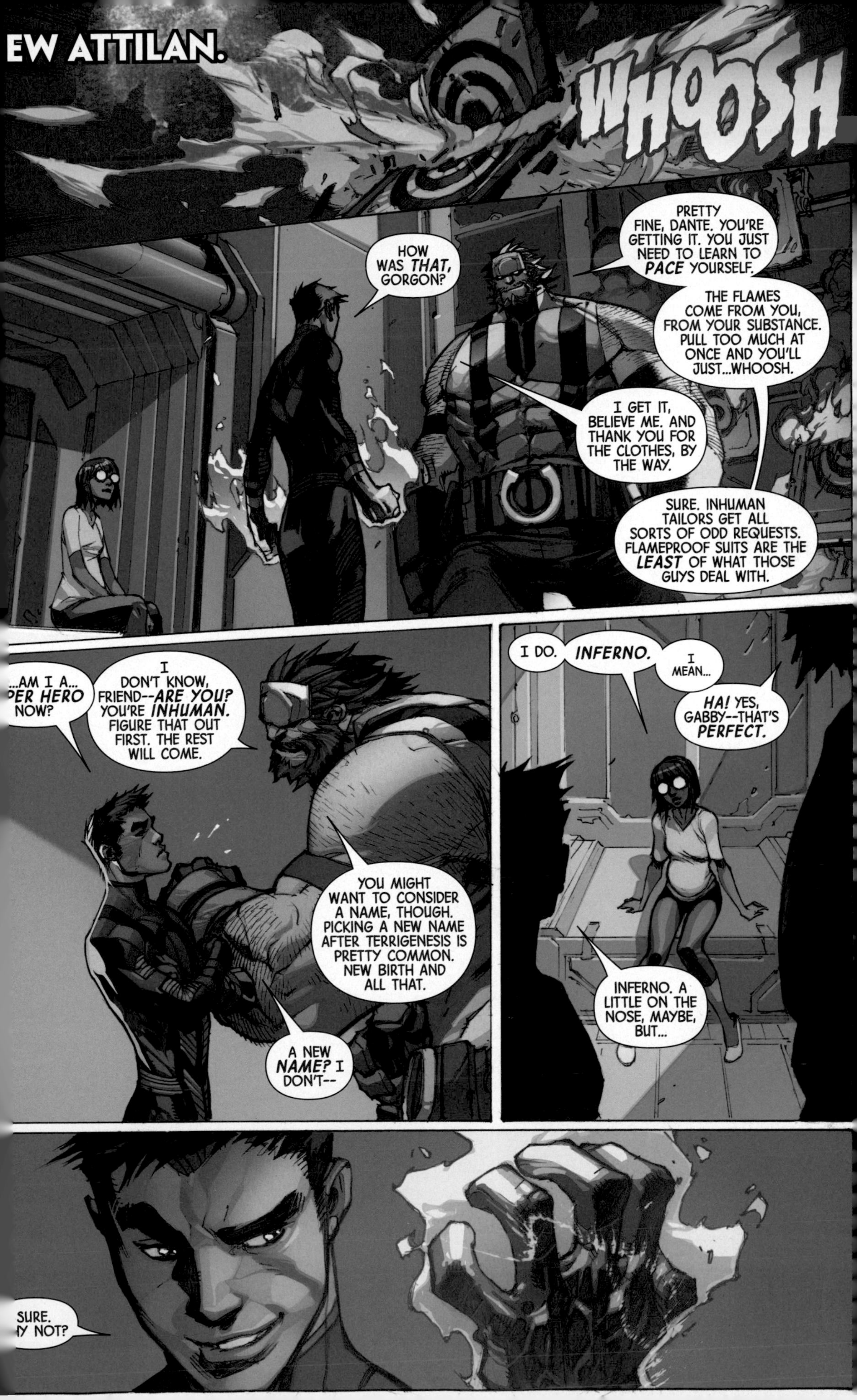
EW ATTILAN.
WHOOSH
HOW WAS THAT, GORGON?
PRETTY FINE, DANTE. YOU'RE GETTING IT. YOU JUST NEED TO LEARN TO PACE YOURSELF.
THE FLAMES COME FROM YOU, FROM YOUR SUBSTANCE. PULL TOO MUCH AT ONCE AND YOU'LL JUST...WHOOSH.
I GET IT, BELIEVE ME. AND THANK YOU FOR THE CLOTHES, BY THE WAY.
SURE. INHUMAN TAILORS GET ALL SORTS OF ODD REQUESTS. FLAMEPROOF SUITS ARE THE LEAST OF WHAT THOSE GUYS DEAL WITH.
...AM I A... PER HERO NOW?
I DON'T KNOW, FRIEND--ARE YOU? YOU'RE INHUMAN. FIGURE THAT OUT FIRST. THE REST WILL COME.
YOU MIGHT WANT TO CONSIDER A NAME, THOUGH. PICKING A NEW NAME AFTER TERRIGENESIS IS PRETTY COMMON. NEW BIRTH AND ALL THAT.
A NEW NAME? I DON'T--
I DO. INFERNO.
I MEAN...
HA! YES, GABBY--THAT'S PERFECT.
INFERNO. A LITTLE ON THE NOSE, MAYBE, BUT...
SURE. IY NOT?

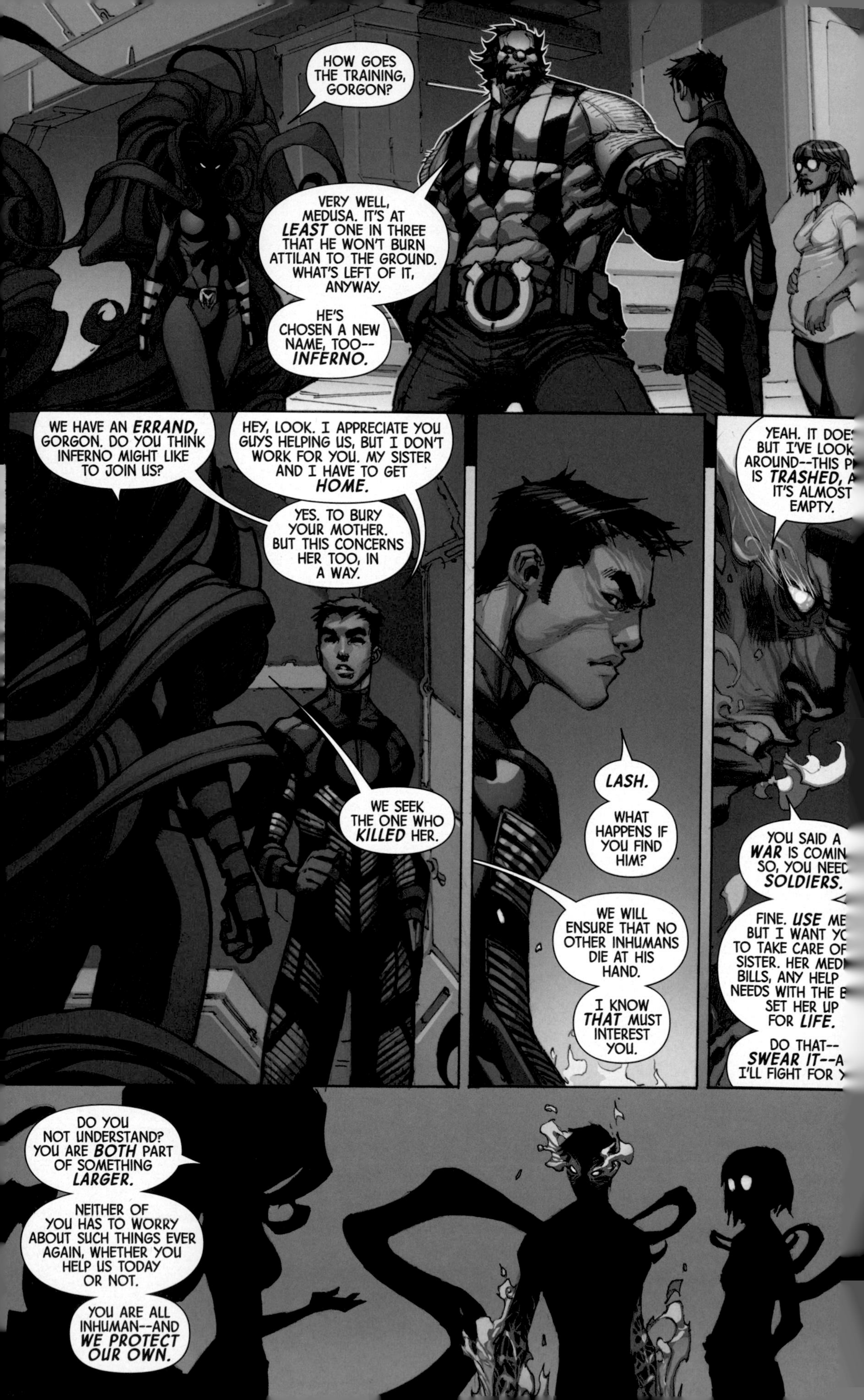
HOW GOES THE TRAINING, GORGON?
VERY WELL, MEDUSA. IT'S AT LEAST ONE IN THREE THAT HE WON'T BURN ATTILAN TO THE GROUND. WHAT'S LEFT OF IT, ANYWAY.
HE'S CHOSEN A NEW NAME, TOO-- INFERNO.
WE HAVE AN ERRAND, GORGON. DO YOU THINK INFERNO MIGHT LIKE TO JOIN US?
HEY, LOOK. I APPRECIATE YOU GUYS HELPING US, BUT I DON'T WORK FOR YOU. MY SISTER AND I HAVE TO GET HOME.
YES. TO BURY YOUR MOTHER. BUT THIS CONCERNS HER TOO, IN A WAY.
WE SEEK THE ONE WHO KILLED HER.
LASH.
WHAT HAPPENS IF YOU FIND HIM?
WE WILL ENSURE THAT NO OTHER INHUMANS DIE AT HIS HAND.
I KNOW THAT MUST INTEREST YOU.
YEAH. IT DOES BUT I'VE LOOK AROUND--THIS P IS TRASHED, A IT'S ALMOST EMPTY.
YOU SAID A WAR IS COMIN SO, YOU NEED SOLDIERS.
FINE. USE ME BUT I WANT YO TO TAKE CARE OF SISTER. HER MED BILLS, ANY HELP NEEDS WITH THE B SET HER UP FOR LIFE.
DO THAT-- SWEAR IT--A I'LL FIGHT FOR Y
DO YOU NOT UNDERSTAND? YOU ARE BOTH PART OF SOMETHING LARGER.
NEITHER OF YOU HAS TO WORRY ABOUT SUCH THINGS EVER AGAIN, WHETHER YOU HELP US TODAY OR NOT.
YOU ARE ALL INHUMAN--AND WE PROTECT OUR OWN.

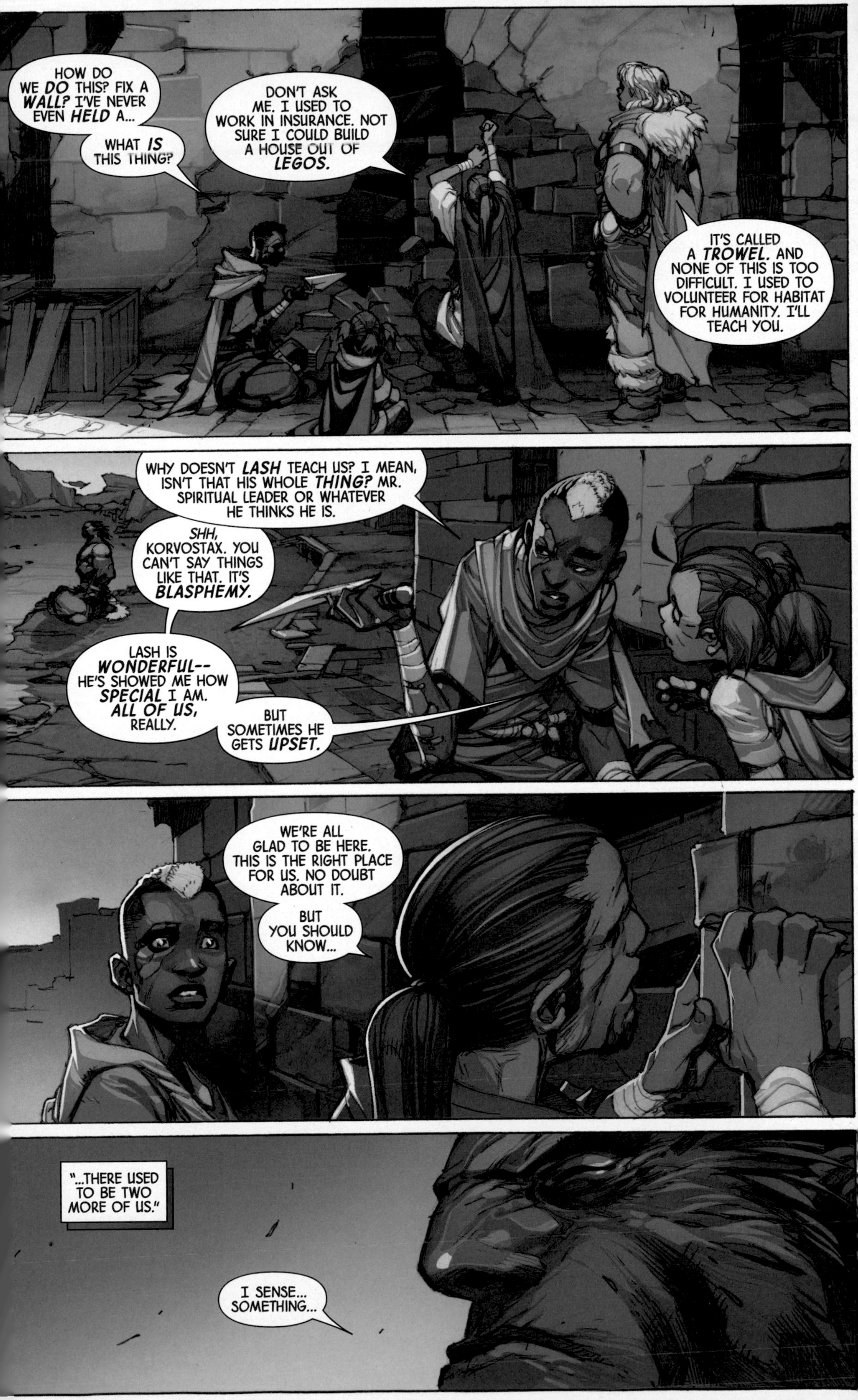

HOW DO WE *DO* THIS? FIX A *WALL?* I'VE NEVER EVEN *HELD* A...
WHAT *IS* THIS THING?
DON'T ASK ME. I USED TO WORK IN INSURANCE. NOT SURE I COULD BUILD A HOUSE OUT OF *LEGOS.*
IT'S CALLED A *TROWEL.* AND NONE OF THIS IS TOO DIFFICULT. I USED TO VOLUNTEER FOR HABITAT FOR HUMANITY. I'LL TEACH YOU.
WHY DOESN'T *LASH* TEACH US? I MEAN, ISN'T THAT HIS WHOLE *THING?* MR. SPIRITUAL LEADER OR WHATEVER HE THINKS HE IS.
SHH, KORVOSTAX. YOU CAN'T SAY THINGS LIKE THAT. IT'S *BLASPHEMY.*
LASH IS *WONDERFUL--* HE'S SHOWED ME HOW *SPECIAL* I AM. *ALL OF US,* REALLY.
BUT SOMETIMES HE GETS *UPSET.*
WE'RE ALL GLAD TO BE HERE. THIS IS THE RIGHT PLACE FOR US. NO DOUBT ABOUT IT.
BUT YOU SHOULD KNOW...
"...THERE USED TO BE TWO MORE OF US."
I SENSE... SOMETHING...

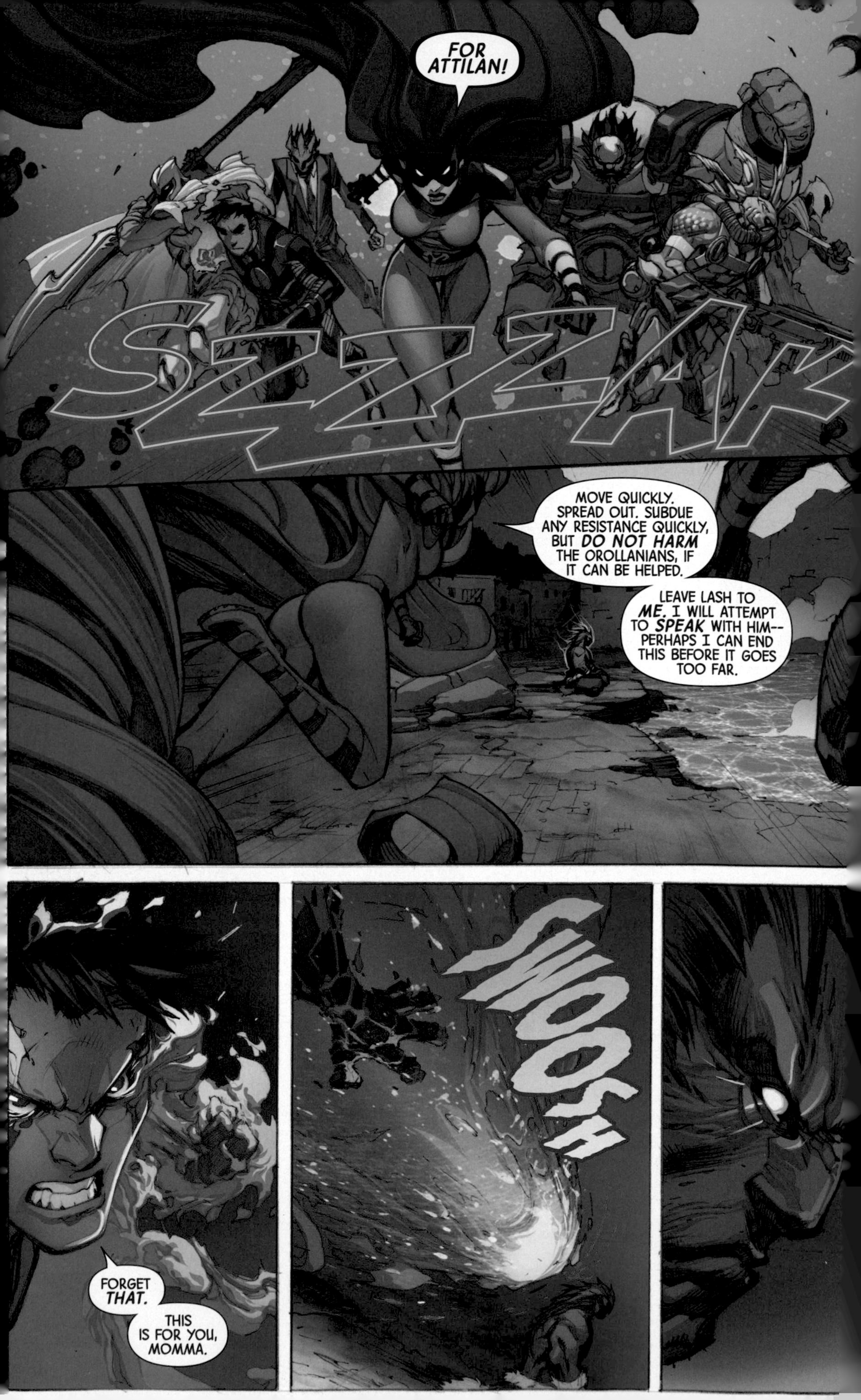
FOR ATTILAN!
SZZZAK
MOVE QUICKLY. SPREAD OUT. SUBDUE ANY RESISTANCE QUICKLY, BUT **DO NOT HARM** THE OROLLANIANS, IF IT CAN BE HELPED.
LEAVE LASH TO **ME.** I WILL ATTEMPT TO **SPEAK** WITH HIM--PERHAPS I CAN END THIS BEFORE IT GOES TOO FAR.
FORGET **THAT.**
THIS IS FOR YOU, MOMMA.
SWOOSH

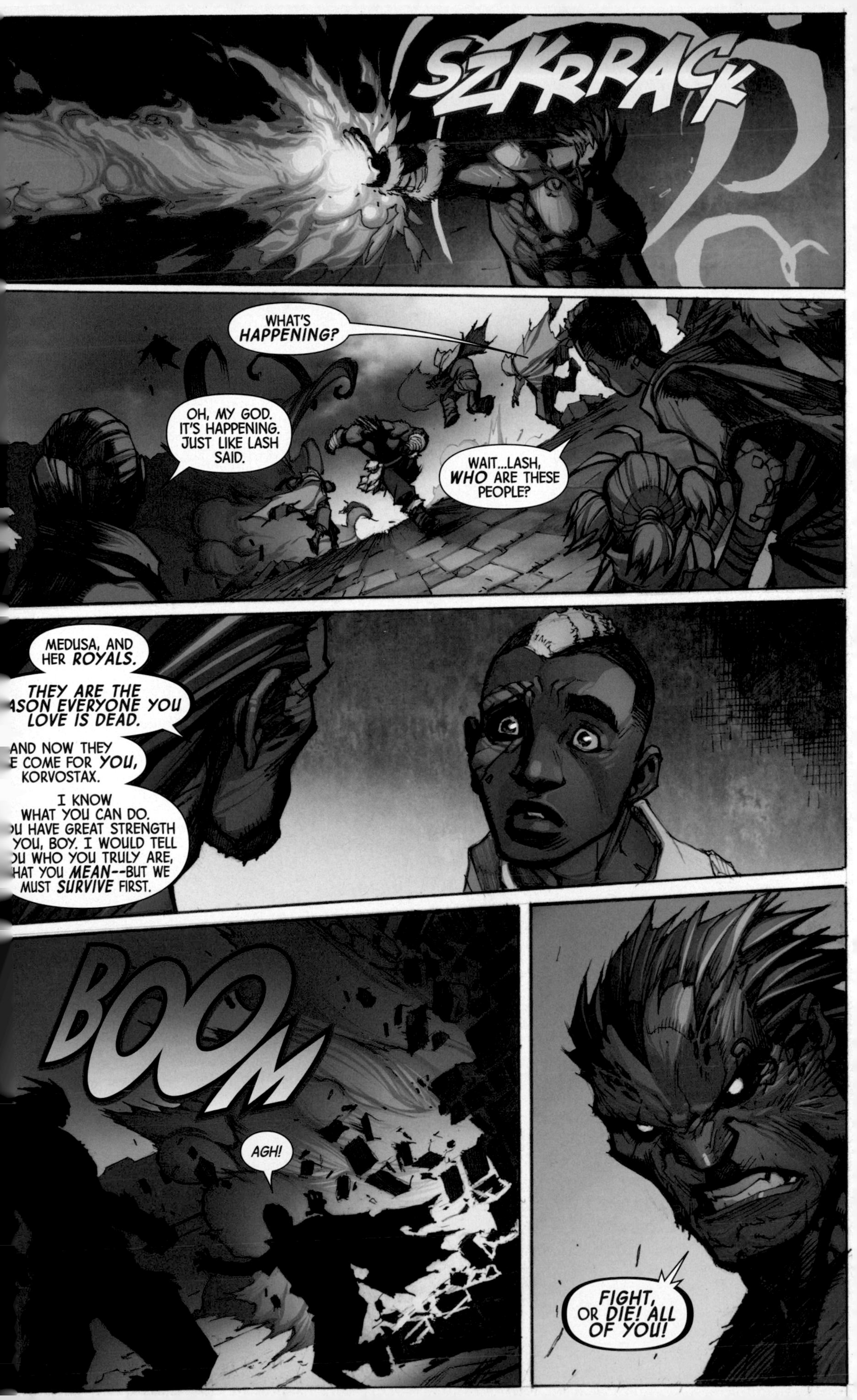
SZKRRACK
WHAT'S HAPPENING?
OH, MY GOD. IT'S HAPPENING. JUST LIKE LASH SAID.
WAIT...LASH, WHO ARE THESE PEOPLE?
MEDUSA, AND HER ROYALS.
THEY ARE THE ASON EVERYONE YOU LOVE IS DEAD.
AND NOW THEY E COME FOR YOU, KORVOSTAX.
I KNOW WHAT YOU CAN DO. OU HAVE GREAT STRENGTH YOU, BOY. I WOULD TELL OU WHO YOU TRULY ARE, HAT YOU MEAN--BUT WE MUST SURVIVE FIRST.
BOOM
AGH!
FIGHT, OR DIE! ALL OF YOU!

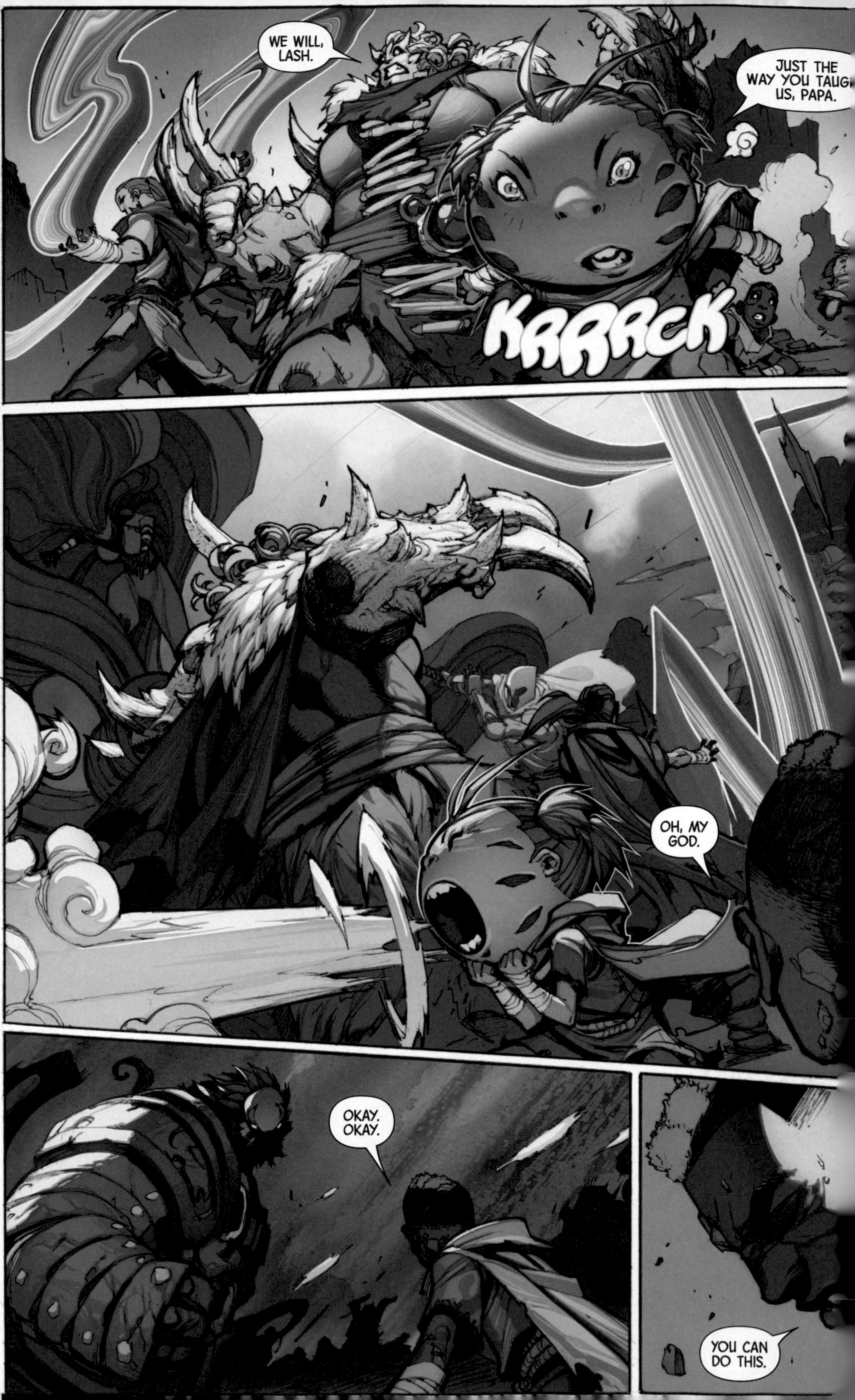
WE WILL, LASH.
JUST THE WAY YOU TAUGHT US, PAPA.
KRRRCK
OH, MY GOD.
OKAY. OKAY.
YOU CAN DO THIS.

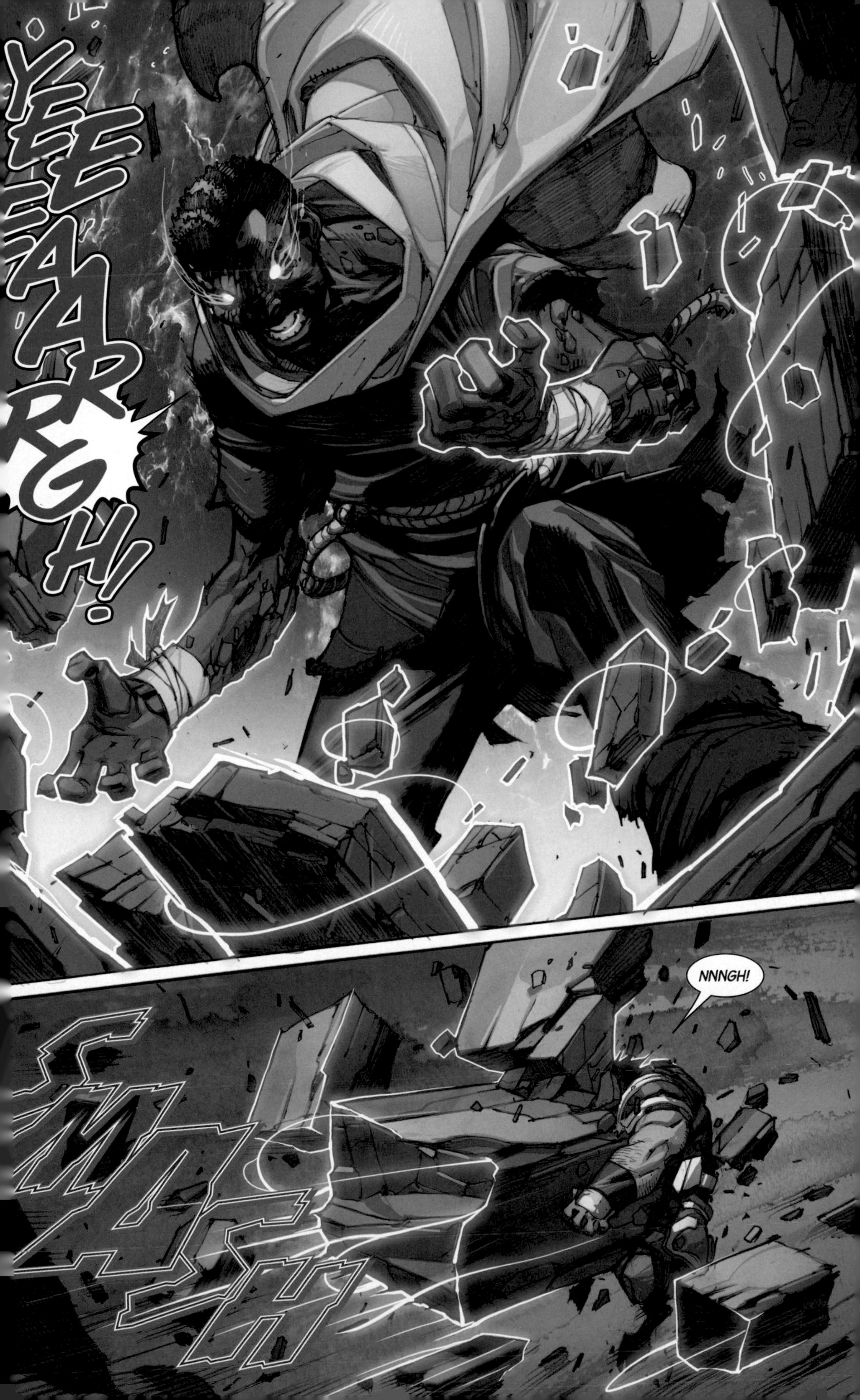
YEEEAARRGH!
NNNGH!

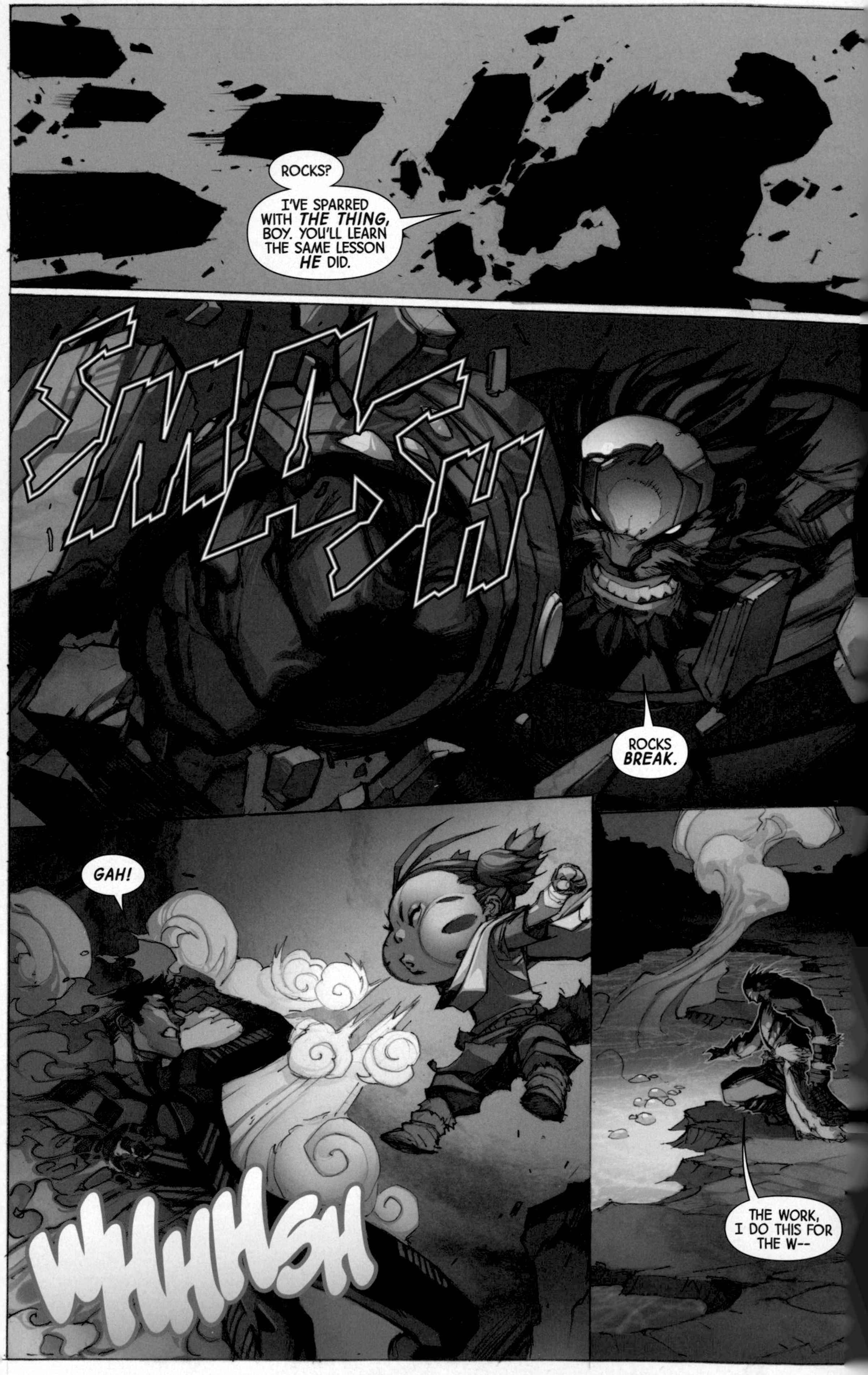
ROCKS?
I'VE SPARRED WITH THE THING, BOY. YOU'LL LEARN THE SAME LESSON HE DID.
SMASH
ROCKS BREAK.
GAH!
WHHHSH
THE WORK, I DO THIS FOR THE W--

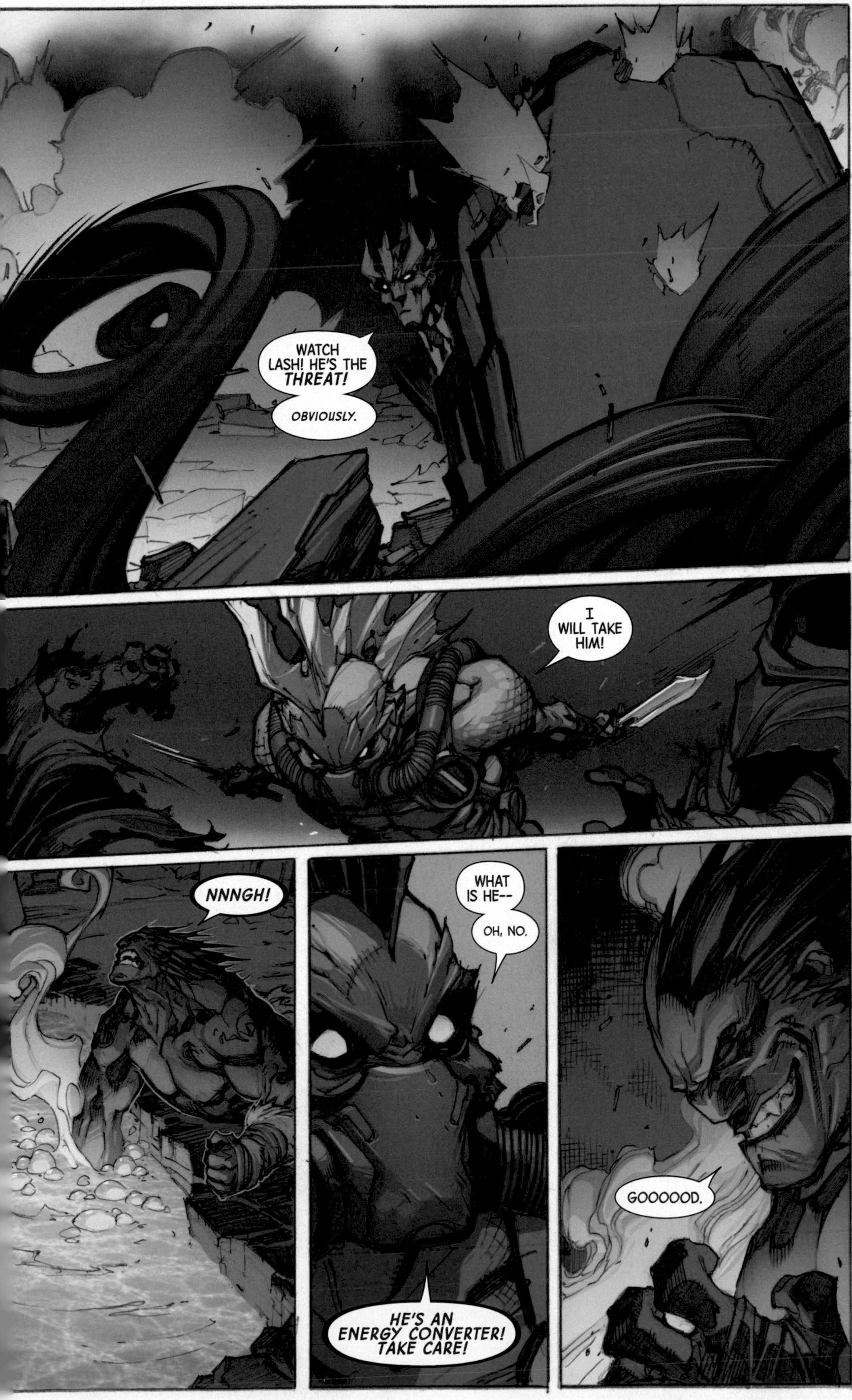
WATCH LASH! HE'S THE THREAT!
OBVIOUSLY.
I WILL TAKE HIM!
NNNGH!
WHAT IS HE--
OH, NO.
HE'S AN ENERGY CONVERTER! TAKE CARE!
GOOOOOD.

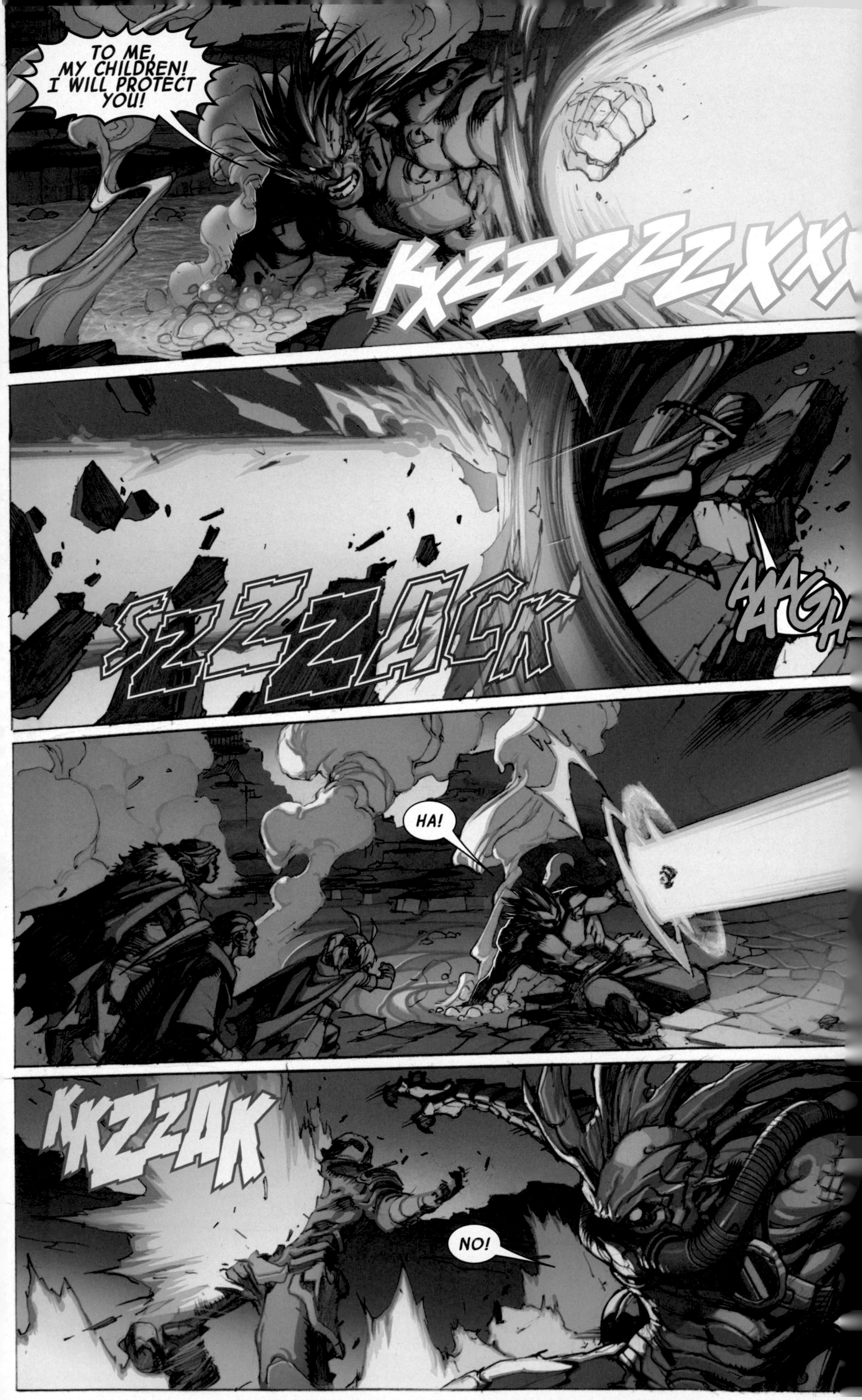
TO ME, MY CHILDREN! I WILL PROTECT YOU!
KXZZZZZXX
SZZZACK
AAAGH
HA!
KXZZAK
NO!

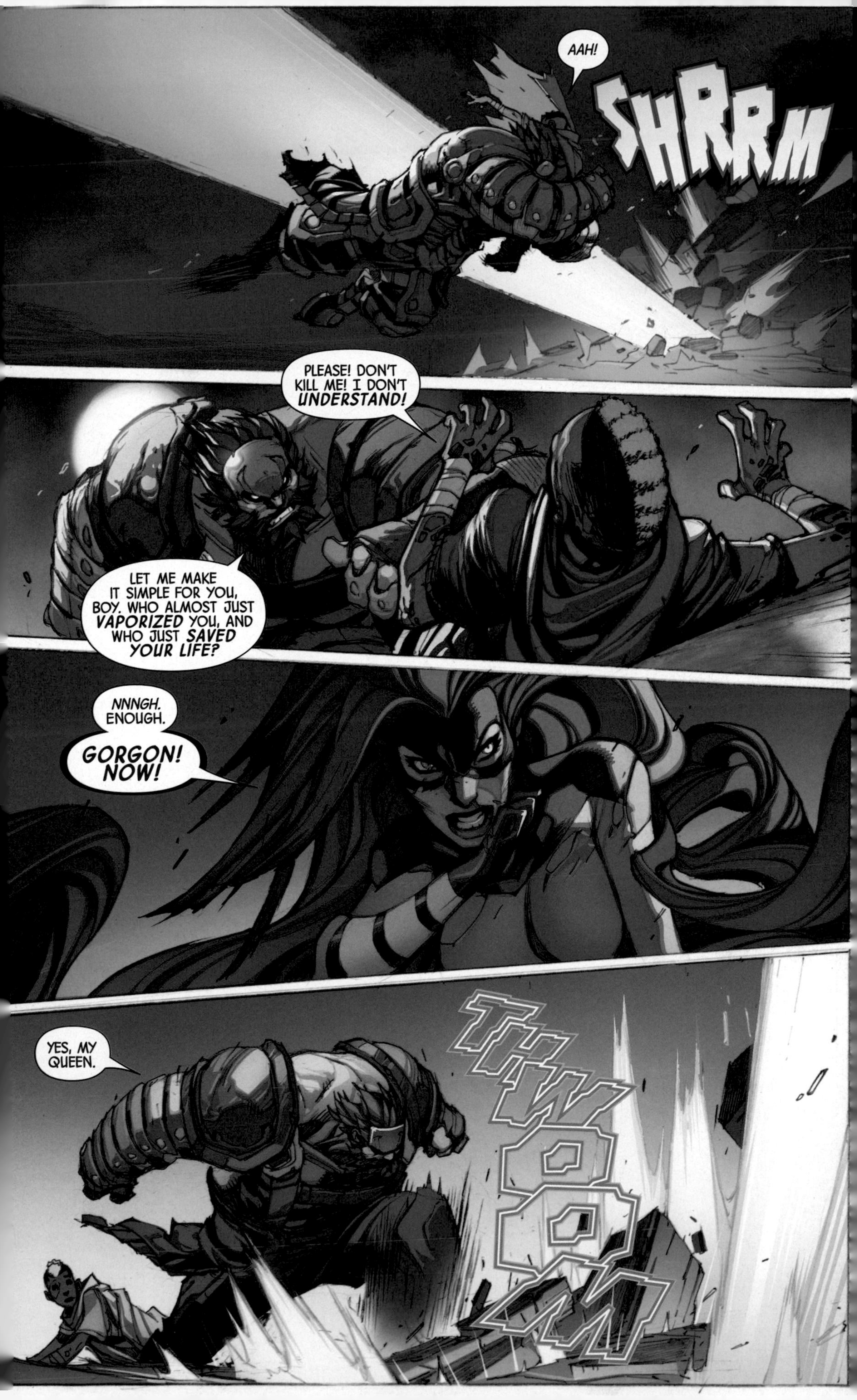
AAH!
SHRRM
PLEASE! DON'T KILL ME! I DON'T UNDERSTAND!
LET ME MAKE IT SIMPLE FOR YOU, BOY. WHO ALMOST JUST VAPORIZED YOU, AND WHO JUST SAVED YOUR LIFE?
NNNGH. ENOUGH.
GORGON! NOW!
YES, MY QUEEN.
THWOOM

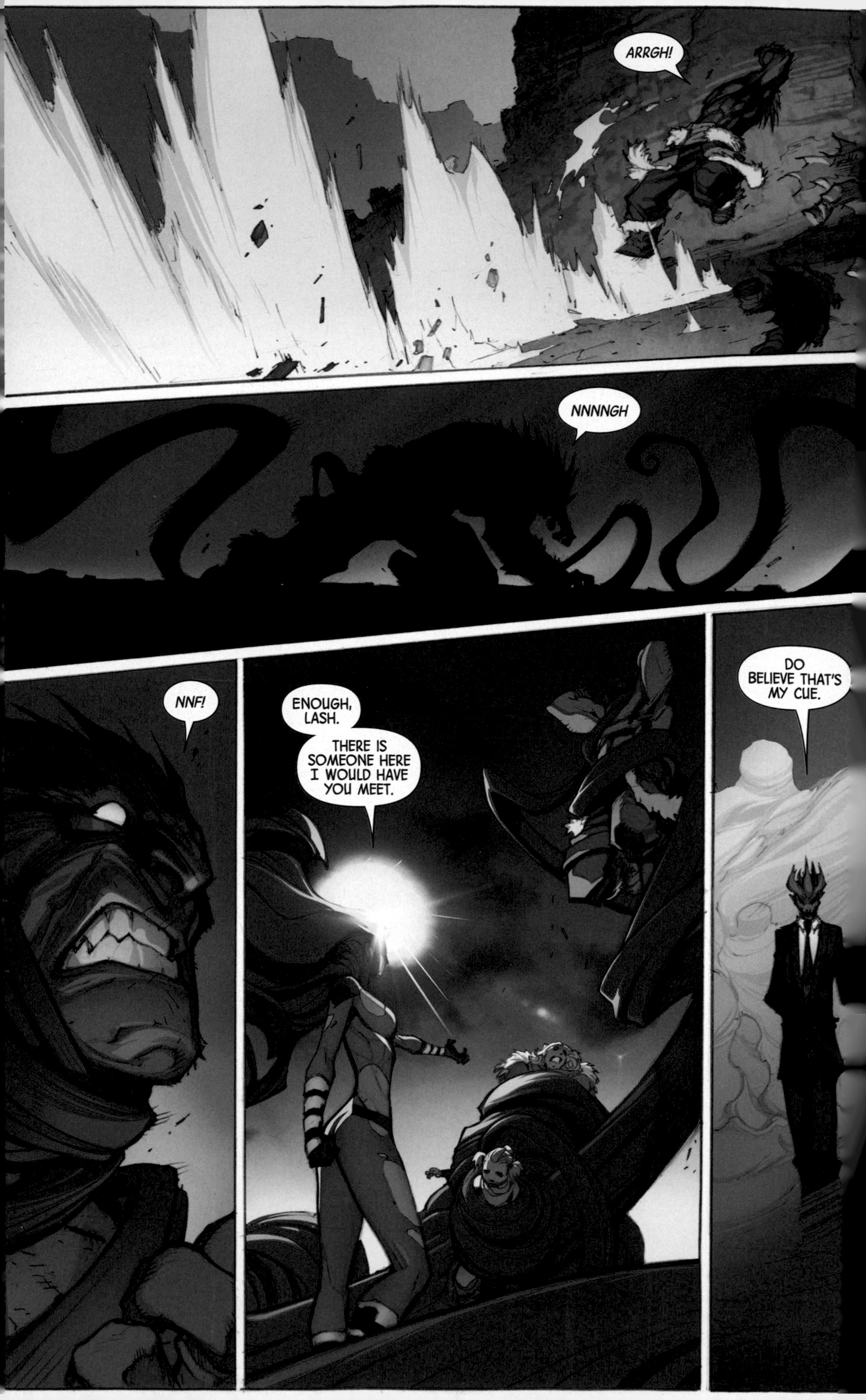
ARRGH!
NNNNGH
NNF!
ENOUGH, LASH.
THERE IS SOMEONE HERE I WOULD HAVE YOU MEET.
DO BELIEVE THAT'S MY CUE.

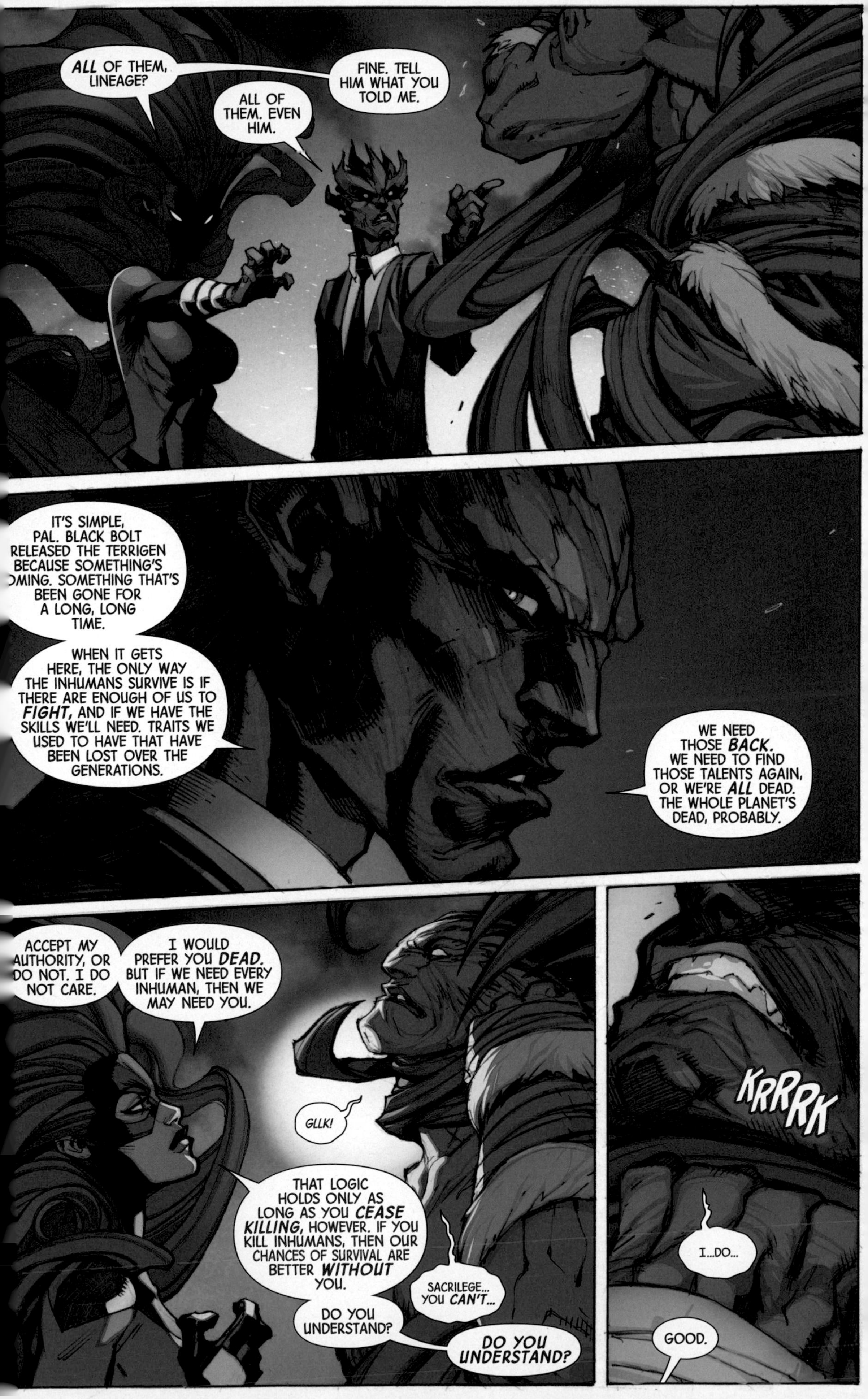
ALL OF THEM, LINEAGE?
FINE. TELL HIM WHAT YOU TOLD ME.
ALL OF THEM. EVEN HIM.
IT'S SIMPLE, PAL. BLACK BOLT RELEASED THE TERRIGEN BECAUSE SOMETHING'S OMING. SOMETHING THAT'S BEEN GONE FOR A LONG, LONG TIME.
WHEN IT GETS HERE, THE ONLY WAY THE INHUMANS SURVIVE IS IF THERE ARE ENOUGH OF US TO FIGHT, AND IF WE HAVE THE SKILLS WE'LL NEED. TRAITS WE USED TO HAVE THAT HAVE BEEN LOST OVER THE GENERATIONS.
WE NEED THOSE BACK. WE NEED TO FIND THOSE TALENTS AGAIN, OR WE'RE ALL DEAD. THE WHOLE PLANET'S DEAD, PROBABLY.
ACCEPT MY AUTHORITY, OR DO NOT. I DO NOT CARE.
I WOULD PREFER YOU DEAD. BUT IF WE NEED EVERY INHUMAN, THEN WE MAY NEED YOU.
GLLK!
THAT LOGIC HOLDS ONLY AS LONG AS YOU CEASE KILLING, HOWEVER. IF YOU KILL INHUMANS, THEN OUR CHANCES OF SURVIVAL ARE BETTER WITHOUT YOU.
DO YOU UNDERSTAND?
SACRILEGE... YOU CAN'T...
DO YOU UNDERSTAND?
KRRRK
I...DO...
GOOD.

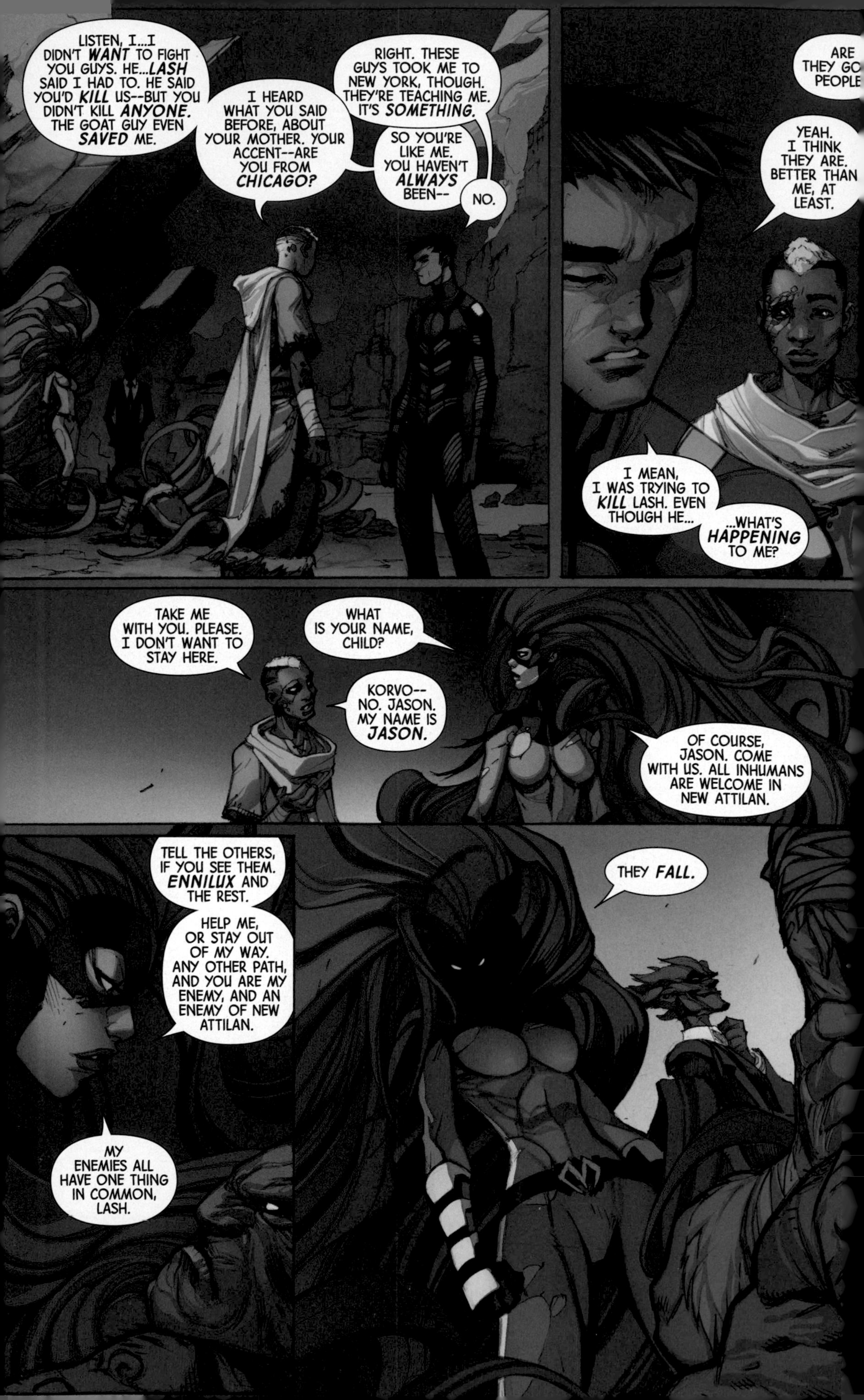

LISTEN, I...I DIDN'T WANT TO FIGHT YOU GUYS. HE...LASH SAID I HAD TO. HE SAID YOU'D KILL US--BUT YOU DIDN'T KILL ANYONE. THE GOAT GUY EVEN SAVED ME.
I HEARD WHAT YOU SAID BEFORE, ABOUT YOUR MOTHER. YOUR ACCENT--ARE YOU FROM CHICAGO?
RIGHT. THESE GUYS TOOK ME TO NEW YORK, THOUGH. THEY'RE TEACHING ME. IT'S SOMETHING.
SO YOU'RE LIKE ME. YOU HAVEN'T ALWAYS BEEN--
NO.
ARE THEY GO PEOPLE
YEAH. I THINK THEY ARE. BETTER THAN ME, AT LEAST.
I MEAN, I WAS TRYING TO KILL LASH. EVEN THOUGH HE...
...WHAT'S HAPPENING TO ME?
TAKE ME WITH YOU. PLEASE. I DON'T WANT TO STAY HERE.
WHAT IS YOUR NAME, CHILD?
KORVO-- NO. JASON. MY NAME IS JASON.
OF COURSE, JASON. COME WITH US. ALL INHUMANS ARE WELCOME IN NEW ATTILAN.
TELL THE OTHERS, IF YOU SEE THEM. ENNILUX AND THE REST.
HELP ME, OR STAY OUT OF MY WAY. ANY OTHER PATH, AND YOU ARE MY ENEMY, AND AN ENEMY OF NEW ATTILAN.
MY ENEMIES ALL HAVE ONE THING IN COMMON, LASH.
THEY FALL.

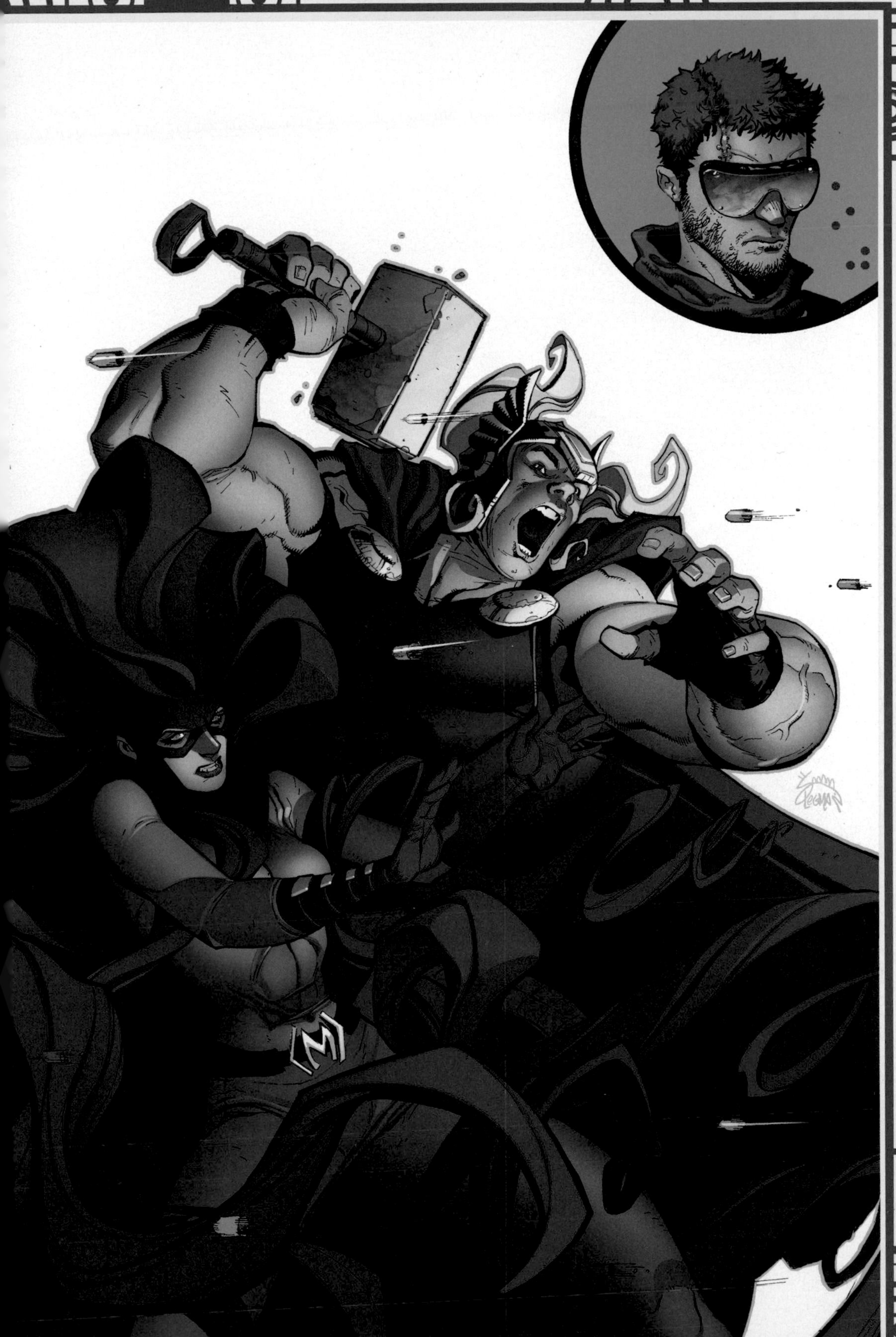

PART FOUR: A THUNDER GOD IN ATTILAN

4

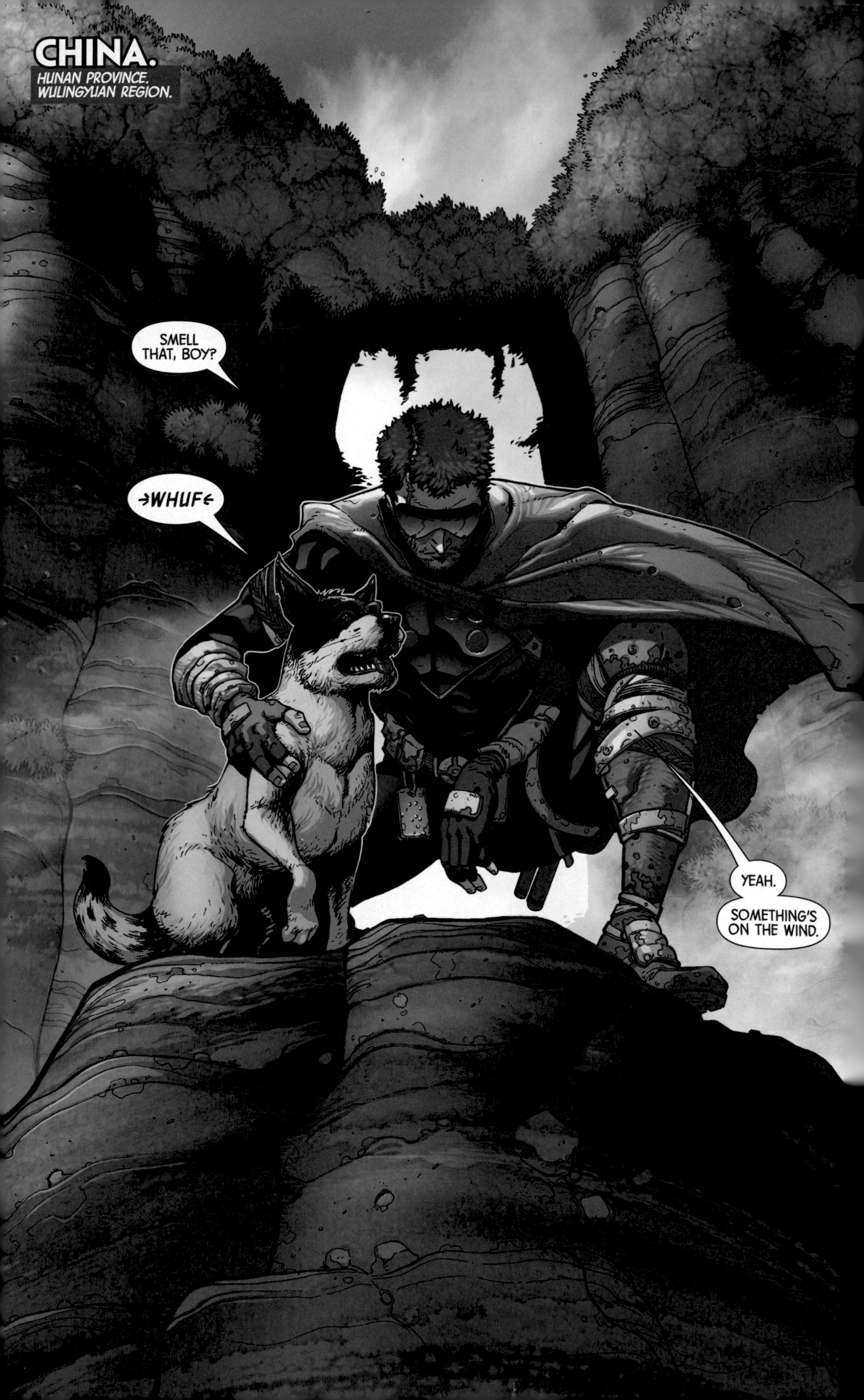
CHINA.
HUNAN PROVINCE. WULINGYUAN REGION.
SMELL THAT, BOY?
WHUF
YEAH.
SOMETHING'S ON THE WIND.

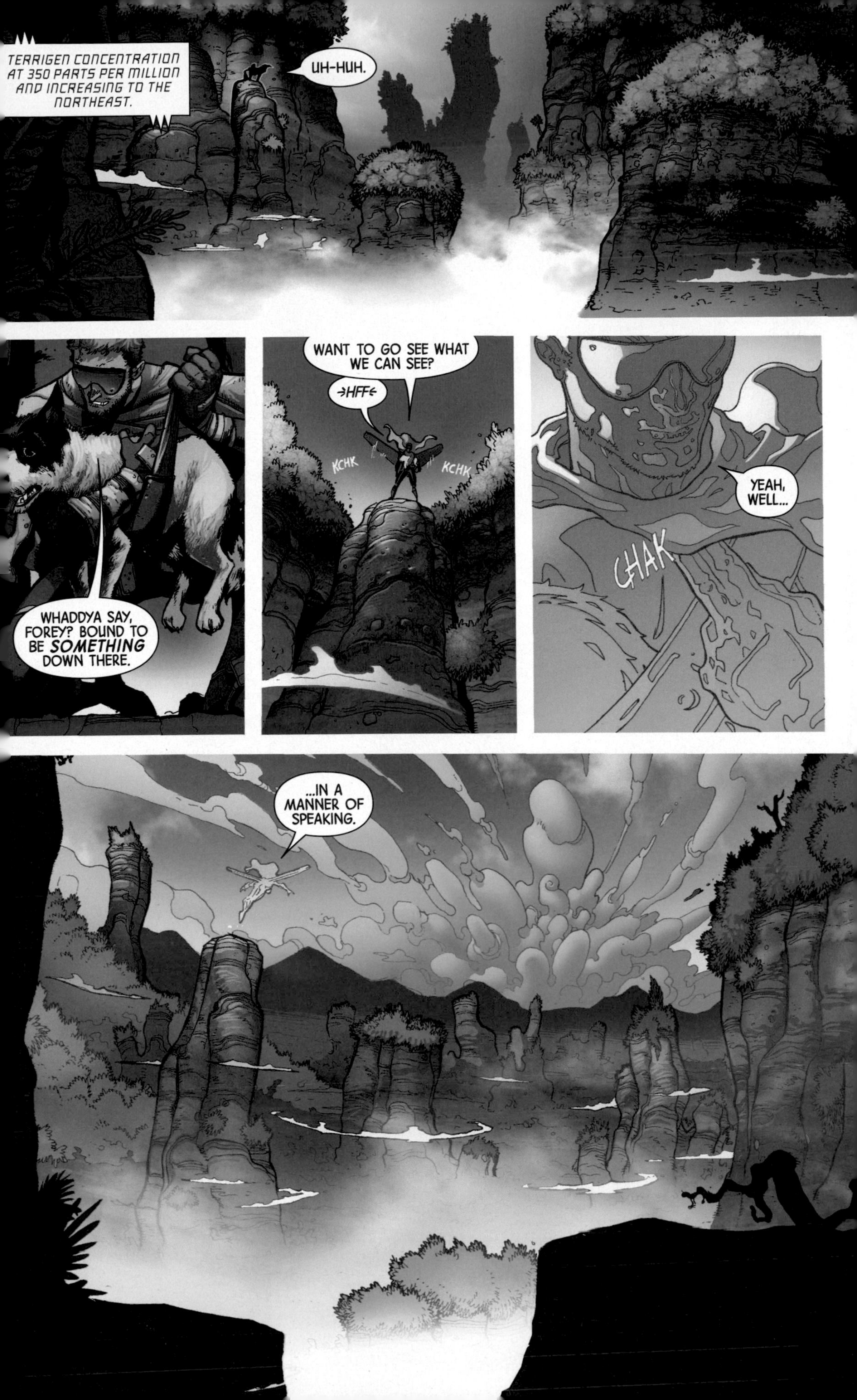
TERRIGEN CONCENTRATION AT 350 PARTS PER MILLION AND INCREASING TO THE NORTHEAST.
UH-HUH.
WHADDYA SAY, FOREY? BOUND TO BE SOMETHING DOWN THERE.
WANT TO GO SEE WHAT WE CAN SEE?
HFF
KCHK
KCHK
YEAH, WELL...
CHAK
...IN A MANNER OF SPEAKING.

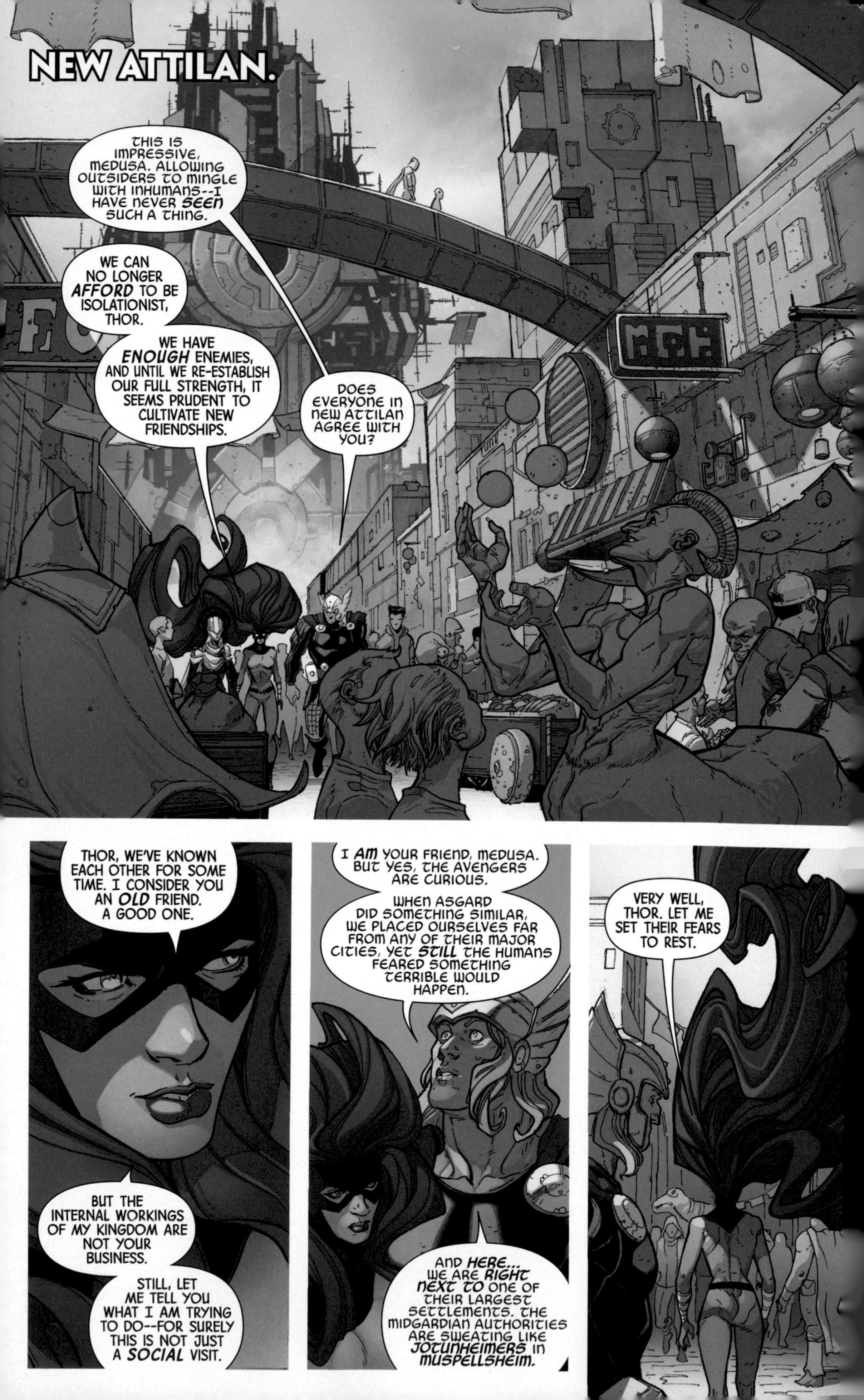
NEW ATTILAN.
THIS IS IMPRESSIVE, MEDUSA. ALLOWING OUTSIDERS TO MINGLE WITH INHUMANS--I HAVE NEVER SEEN SUCH A THING.
WE CAN NO LONGER AFFORD TO BE ISOLATIONIST, THOR.
WE HAVE ENOUGH ENEMIES, AND UNTIL WE RE-ESTABLISH OUR FULL STRENGTH, IT SEEMS PRUDENT TO CULTIVATE NEW FRIENDSHIPS.
DOES EVERYONE IN NEW ATTILAN AGREE WITH YOU?
THOR, WE'VE KNOWN EACH OTHER FOR SOME TIME. I CONSIDER YOU AN OLD FRIEND. A GOOD ONE.
BUT THE INTERNAL WORKINGS OF MY KINGDOM ARE NOT YOUR BUSINESS.
STILL, LET ME TELL YOU WHAT I AM TRYING TO DO--FOR SURELY THIS IS NOT JUST A SOCIAL VISIT.
I AM YOUR FRIEND, MEDUSA. BUT YES, THE AVENGERS ARE CURIOUS.
WHEN ASGARD DID SOMETHING SIMILAR, WE PLACED OURSELVES FAR FROM ANY OF THEIR MAJOR CITIES, YET STILL THE HUMANS FEARED SOMETHING TERRIBLE WOULD HAPPEN.
AND HERE... WE ARE RIGHT NEXT TO ONE OF THEIR LARGEST SETTLEMENTS. THE MIDGARDIAN AUTHORITIES ARE SWEATING LIKE JOTUNHEIMERS IN MUSPELLSHEIM.
VERY WELL, THOR. LET ME SET THEIR FEARS TO REST.

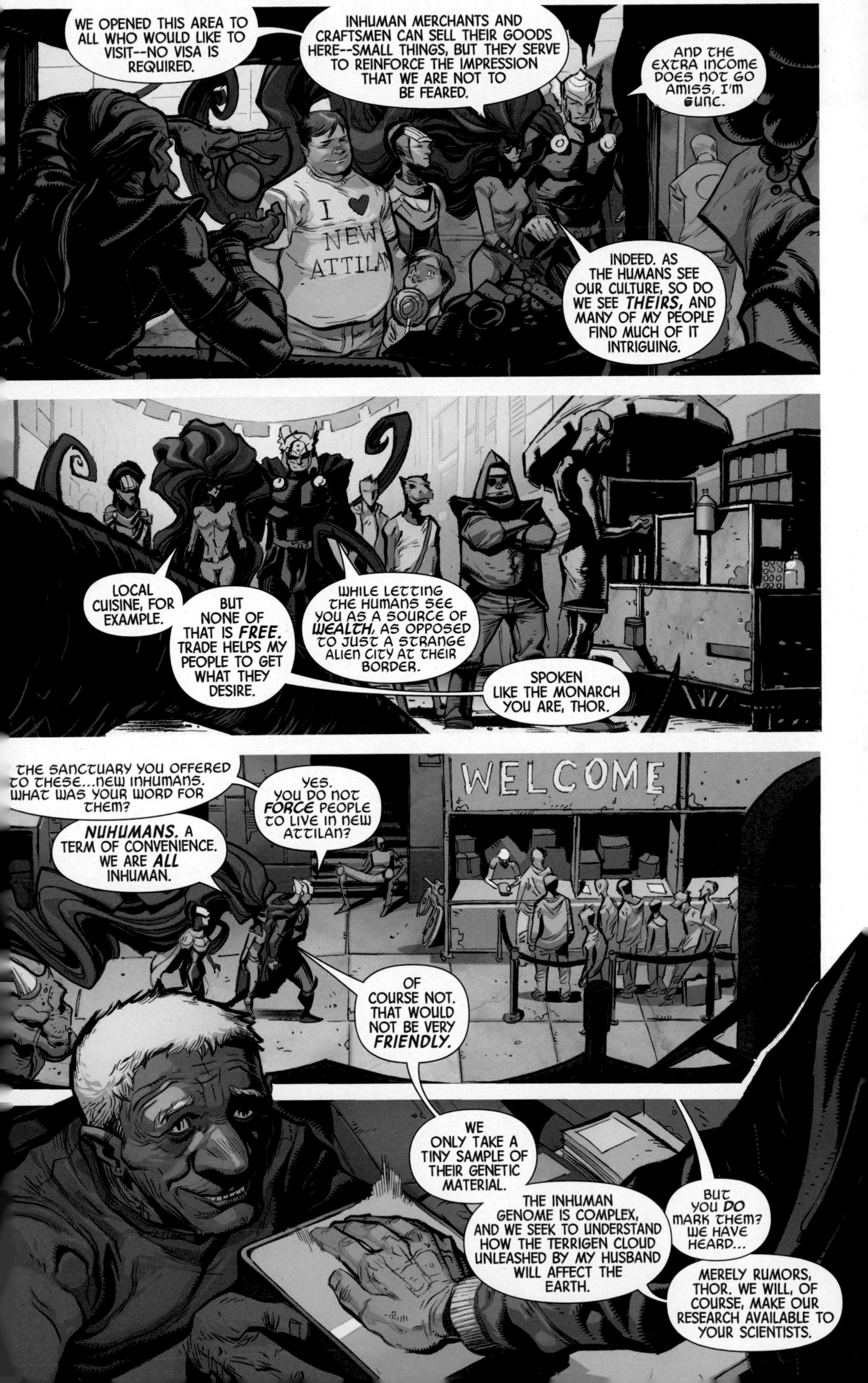
WE OPENED THIS AREA TO ALL WHO WOULD LIKE TO VISIT--NO VISA IS REQUIRED.
INHUMAN MERCHANTS AND CRAFTSMEN CAN SELL THEIR GOODS HERE--SMALL THINGS, BUT THEY SERVE TO REINFORCE THE IMPRESSION THAT WE ARE NOT TO BE FEARED.
AND THE EXTRA INCOME DOES NOT GO AMISS, I'M SURE.
I ♥ NEW ATTILA
INDEED. AS THE HUMANS SEE OUR CULTURE, SO DO WE SEE THEIRS, AND MANY OF MY PEOPLE FIND MUCH OF IT INTRIGUING.
LOCAL CUISINE, FOR EXAMPLE.
BUT NONE OF THAT IS FREE. TRADE HELPS MY PEOPLE TO GET WHAT THEY DESIRE.
WHILE LETTING THE HUMANS SEE YOU AS A SOURCE OF WEALTH, AS OPPOSED TO JUST A STRANGE ALIEN CITY AT THEIR BORDER.
SPOKEN LIKE THE MONARCH YOU ARE, THOR.
WELCOME
THE SANCTUARY YOU OFFERED TO THESE...NEW INHUMANS. WHAT WAS YOUR WORD FOR THEM?
NUHUMANS. A TERM OF CONVENIENCE. WE ARE ALL INHUMAN.
YES. YOU DO NOT FORCE PEOPLE TO LIVE IN NEW ATTILAN?
OF COURSE NOT. THAT WOULD NOT BE VERY FRIENDLY.
WE ONLY TAKE A TINY SAMPLE OF THEIR GENETIC MATERIAL.
THE INHUMAN GENOME IS COMPLEX, AND WE SEEK TO UNDERSTAND HOW THE TERRIGEN CLOUD UNLEASHED BY MY HUSBAND WILL AFFECT THE EARTH.
BUT YOU DO MARK THEM? WE HAVE HEARD...
MERELY RUMORS, THOR. WE WILL, OF COURSE, MAKE OUR RESEARCH AVAILABLE TO YOUR SCIENTISTS.

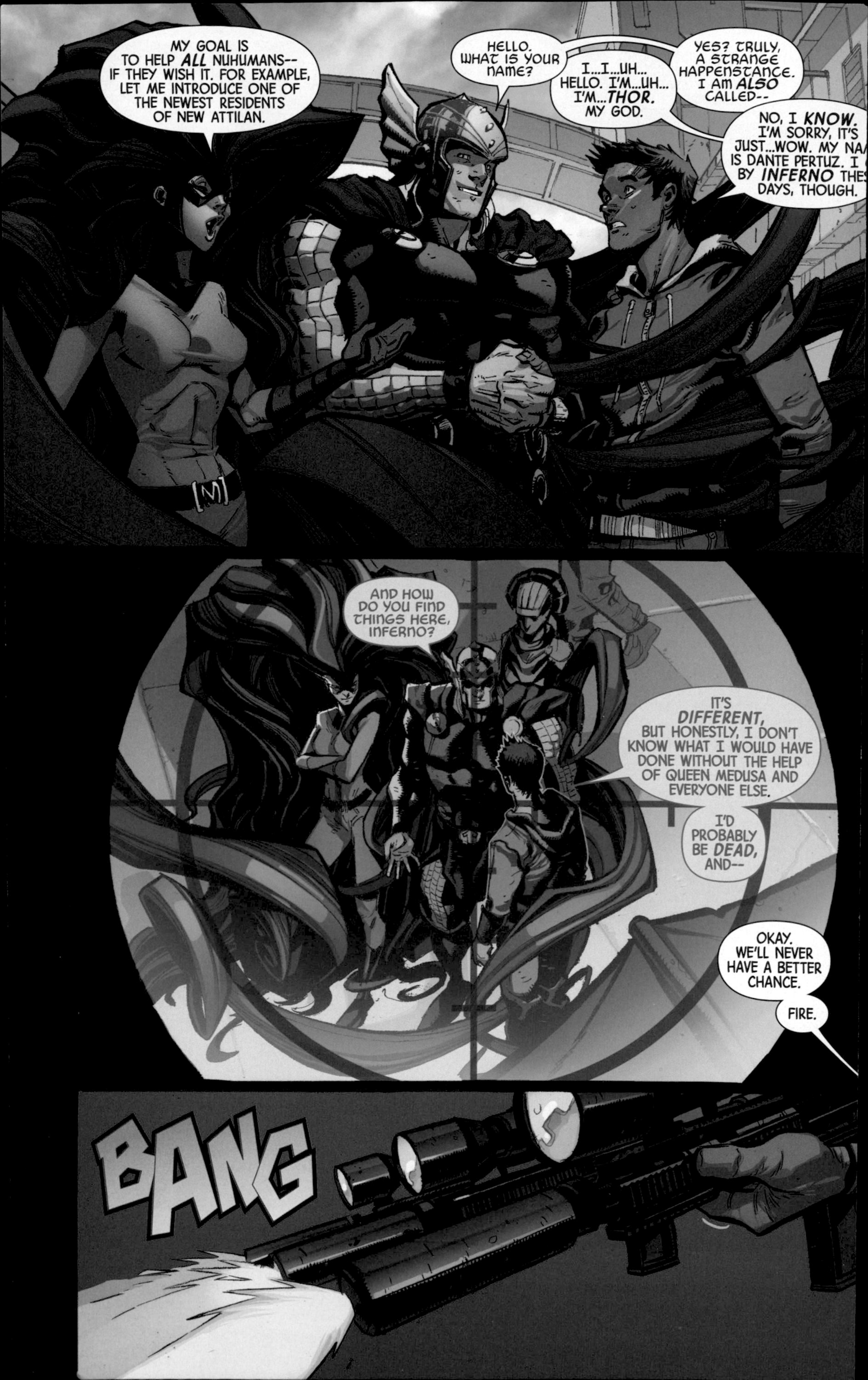
MY GOAL IS TO HELP ALL NUHUMANS-- IF THEY WISH IT. FOR EXAMPLE, LET ME INTRODUCE ONE OF THE NEWEST RESIDENTS OF NEW ATTILAN.
HELLO. WHAT IS YOUR NAME?
I...I...UH... HELLO. I'M...UH... I'M...THOR. MY GOD.
YES? TRULY, A STRANGE HAPPENSTANCE. I AM ALSO CALLED--
NO, I KNOW. I'M SORRY, IT'S JUST...WOW. MY NA IS DANTE PERTUZ. I BY INFERNO THES DAYS, THOUGH.
AND HOW DO YOU FIND THINGS HERE, INFERNO?
IT'S DIFFERENT, BUT HONESTLY, I DON'T KNOW WHAT I WOULD HAVE DONE WITHOUT THE HELP OF QUEEN MEDUSA AND EVERYONE ELSE.
I'D PROBABLY BE DEAD, AND--
OKAY. WE'LL NEVER HAVE A BETTER CHANCE.
FIRE.
BANG

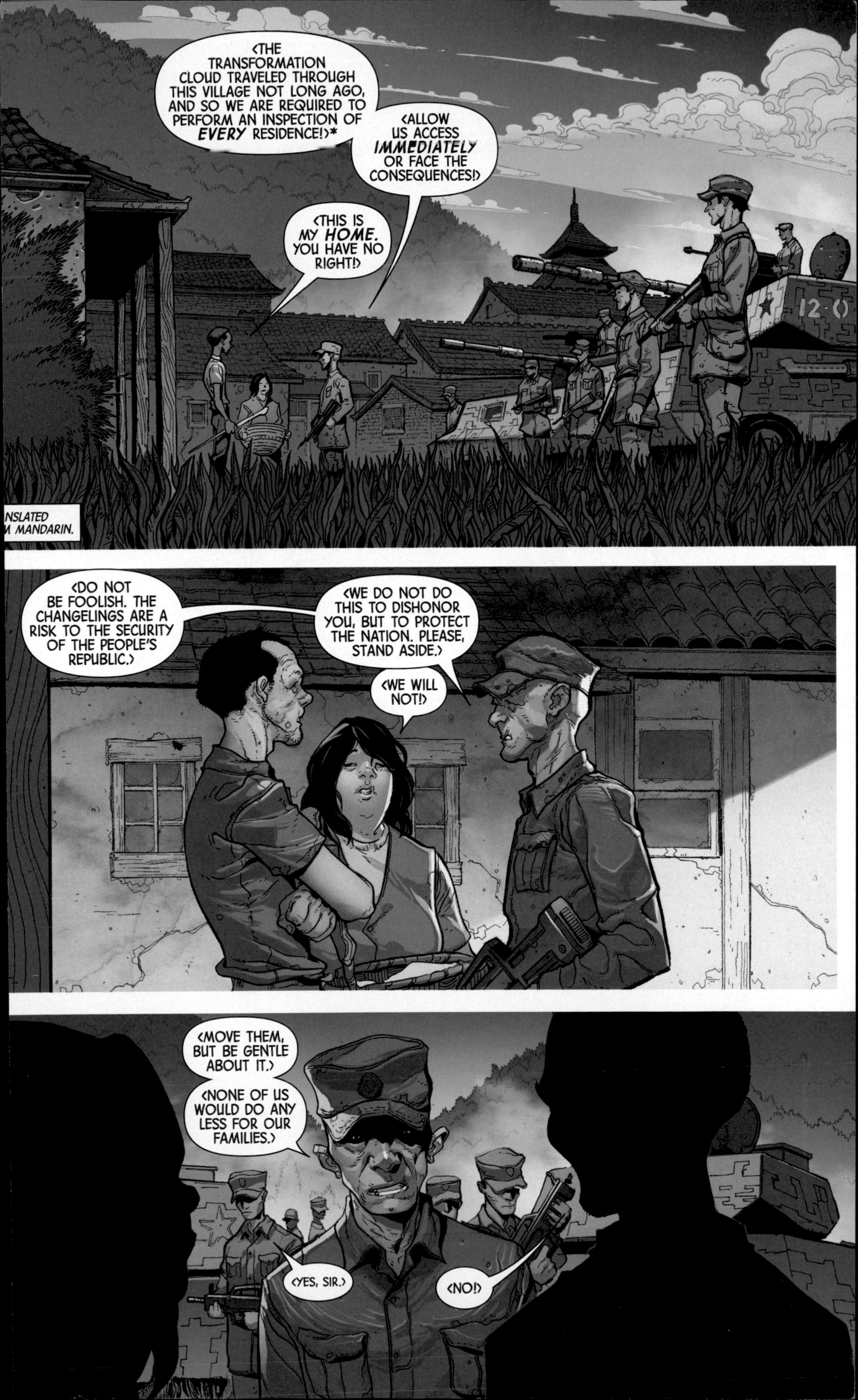
<THE TRANSFORMATION CLOUD TRAVELED THROUGH THIS VILLAGE NOT LONG AGO, AND SO WE ARE REQUIRED TO PERFORM AN INSPECTION OF EVERY RESIDENCE!>*
<ALLOW US ACCESS IMMEDIATELY OR FACE THE CONSEQUENCES!>
<THIS IS MY HOME. YOU HAVE NO RIGHT!>
12-()
NSLATED
M MANDARIN.
<DO NOT BE FOOLISH. THE CHANGELINGS ARE A RISK TO THE SECURITY OF THE PEOPLE'S REPUBLIC.>
<WE DO NOT DO THIS TO DISHONOR YOU, BUT TO PROTECT THE NATION. PLEASE, STAND ASIDE.>
<WE WILL NOT!>
<MOVE THEM, BUT BE GENTLE ABOUT IT.>
<NONE OF US WOULD DO ANY LESS FOR OUR FAMILIES.>
<YES, SIR.>
<NO!>

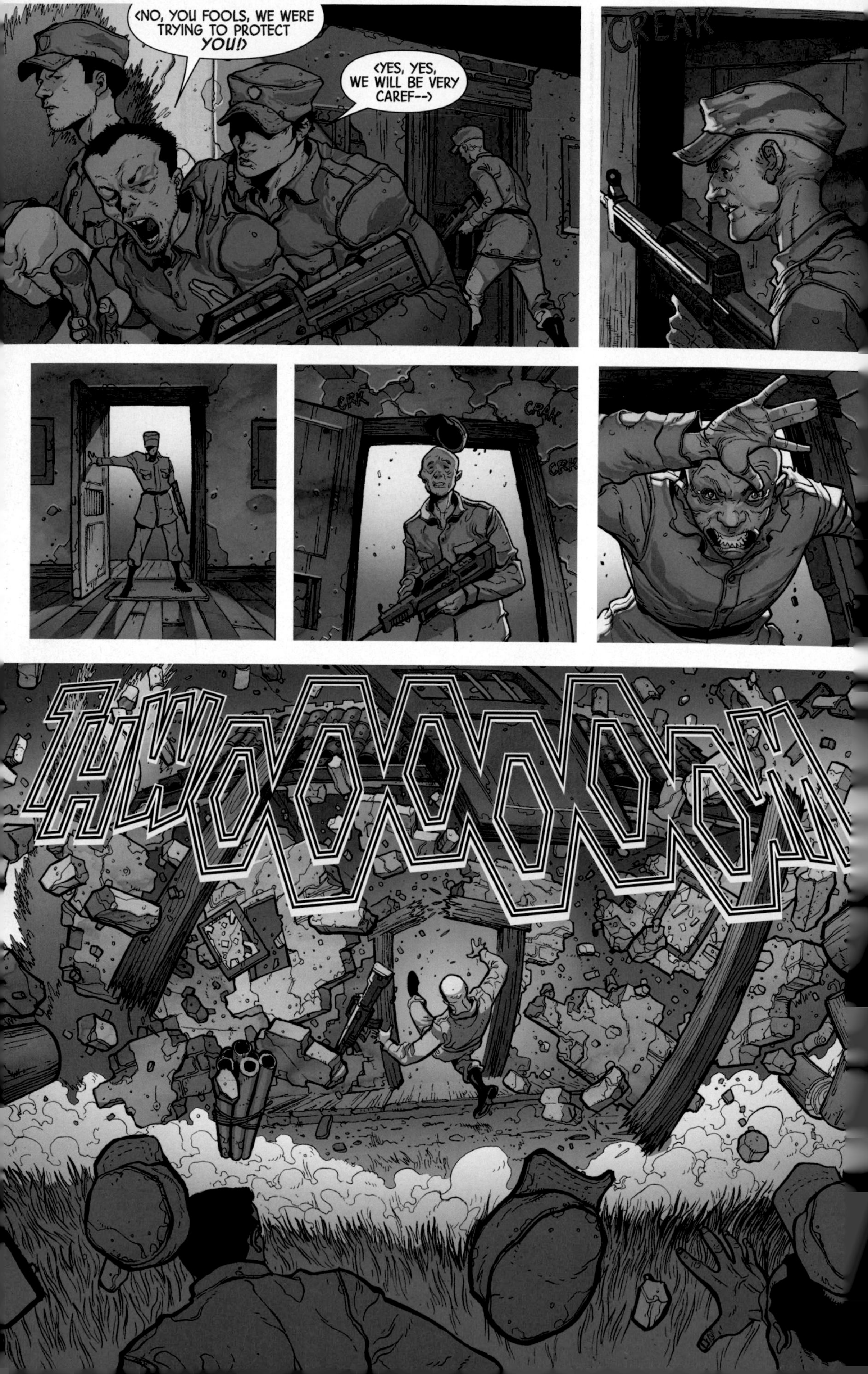
<NO, YOU FOOLS, WE WERE TRYING TO PROTECT YOU!>
<YES, YES, WE WILL BE VERY CAREF-->
CREAK
CRK
CRAK
CRK
THWOOOOOOOOOOM

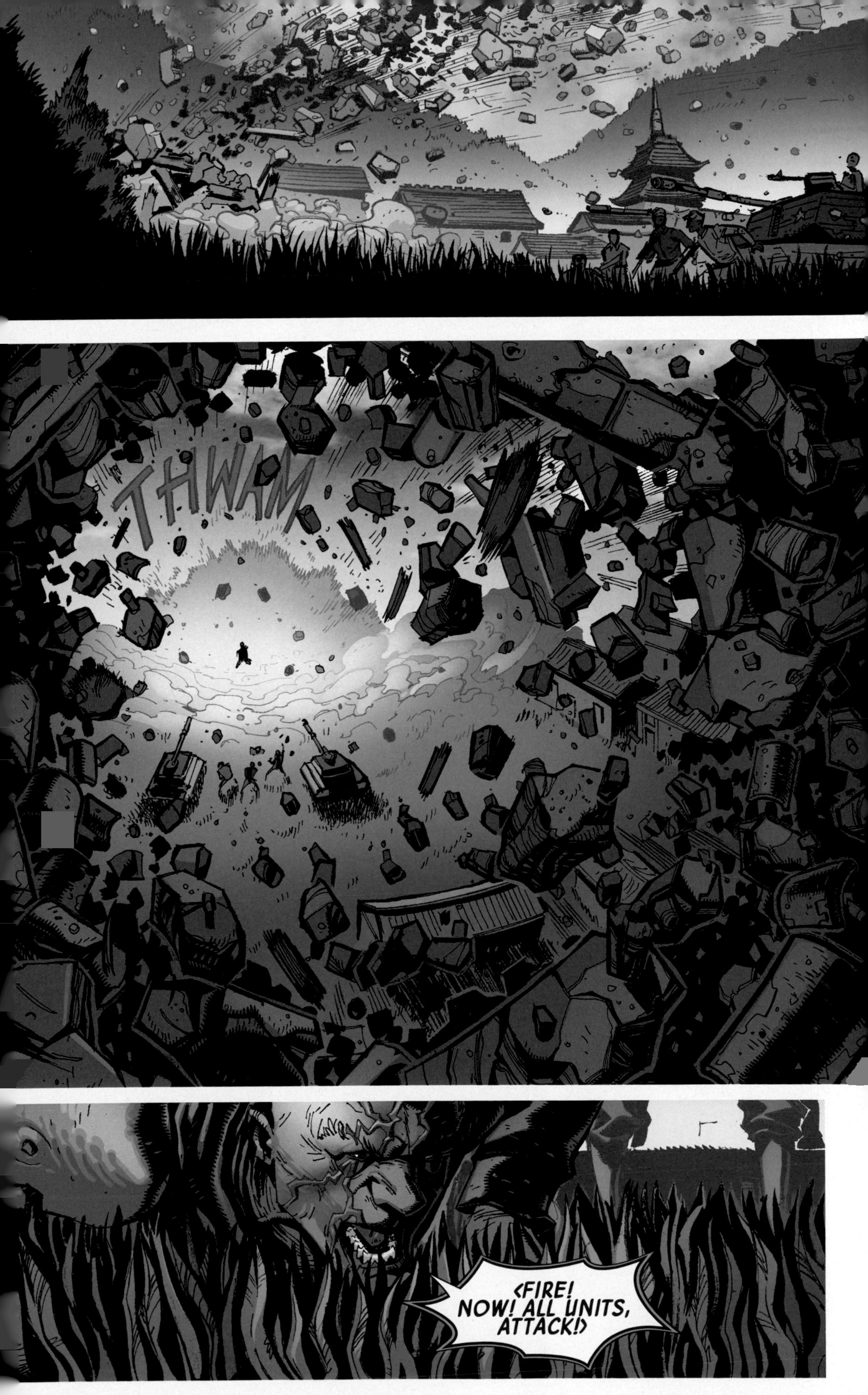
THWAM
<FIRE! NOW! ALL UNITS, ATTACK!>

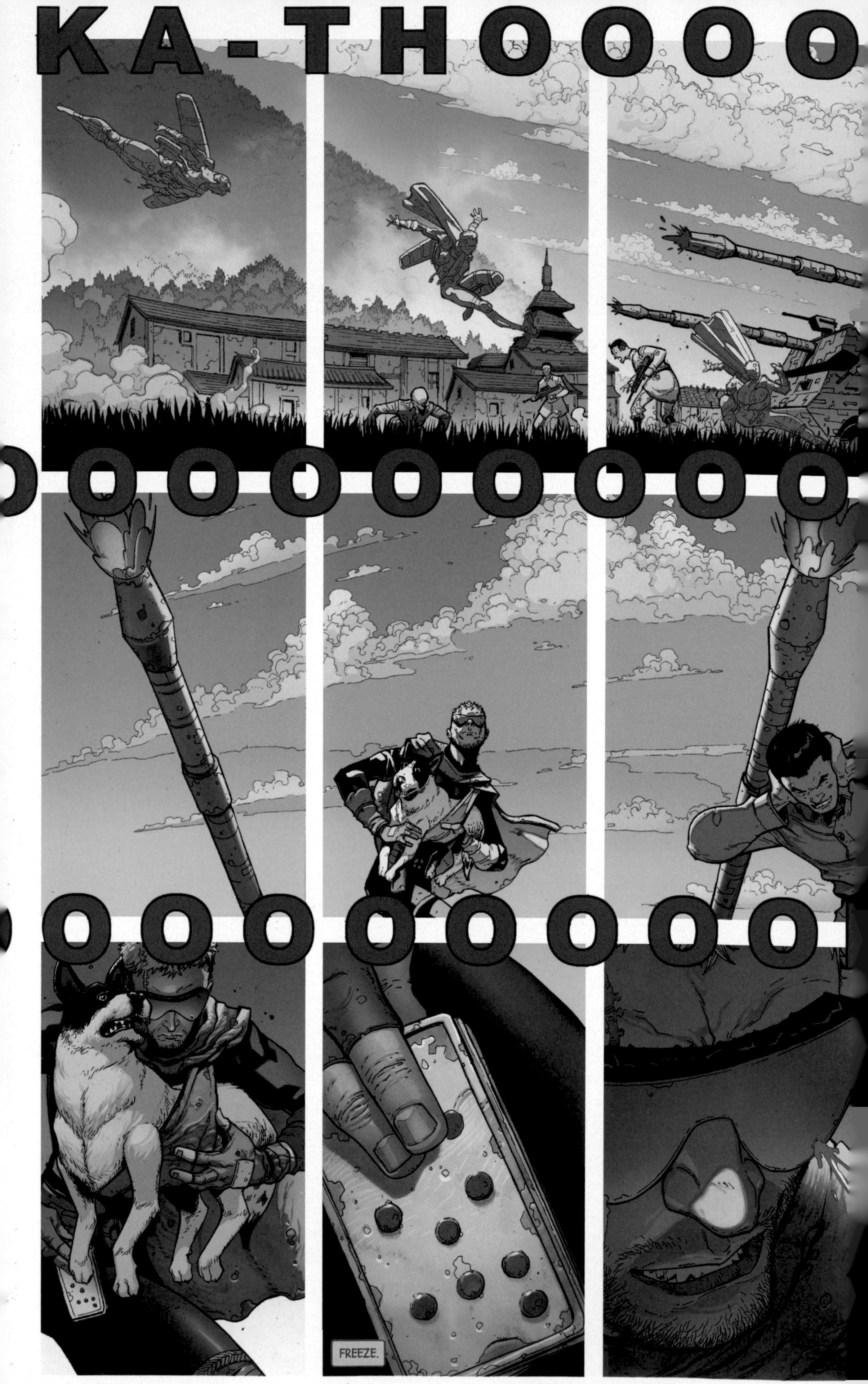

KA-THOOOOOOOOOOOOOOOOOOOOOOOOO
FREEZE.

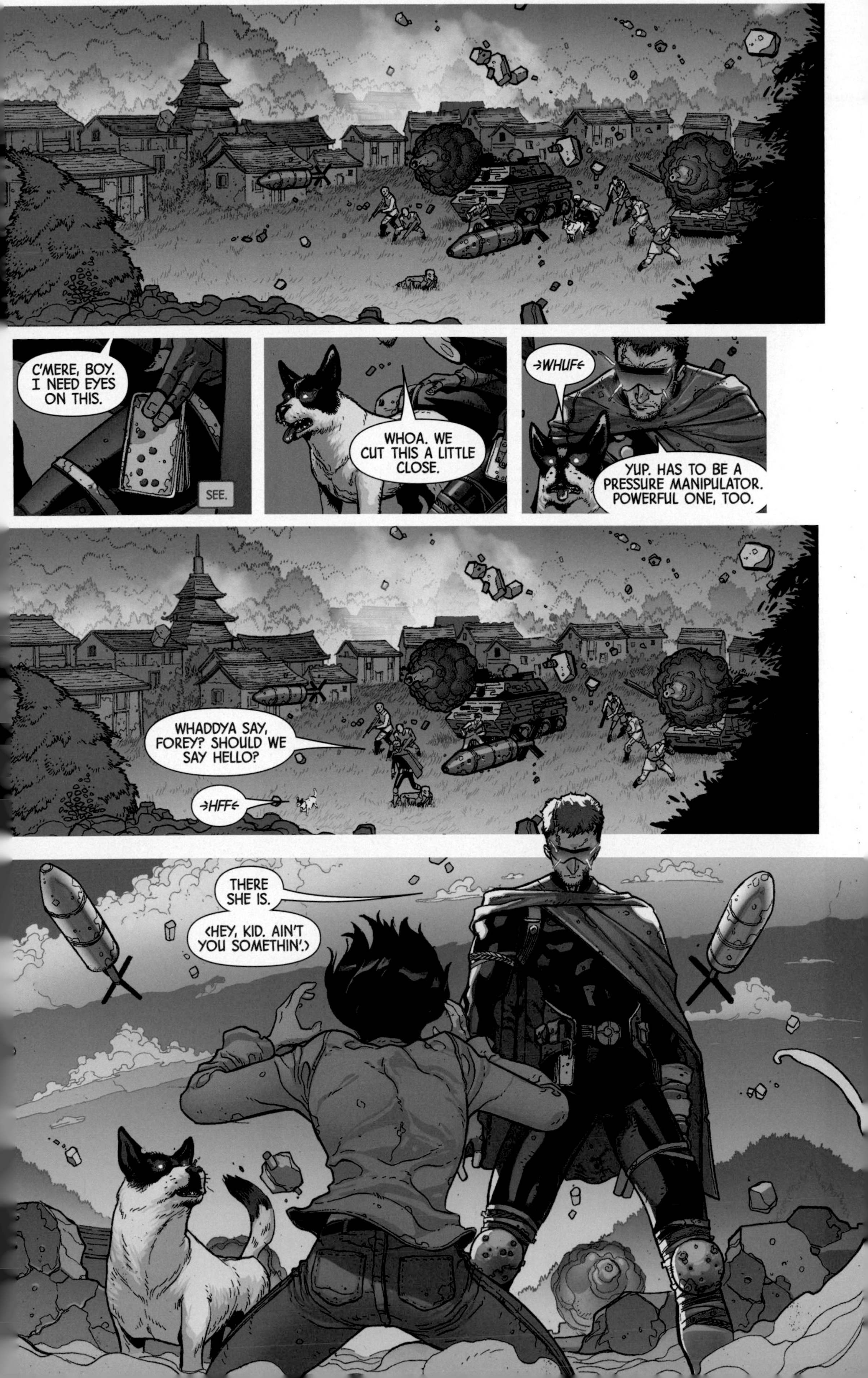
C'MERE, BOY. I NEED EYES ON THIS.
SEE.
WHOA. WE CUT THIS A LITTLE CLOSE.
→WHUF←
YUP. HAS TO BE A PRESSURE MANIPULATOR. POWERFUL ONE, TOO.
WHADDYA SAY, FOREY? SHOULD WE SAY HELLO?
→HFF←
THERE SHE IS.
‹HEY, KID. AIN'T YOU SOMETHIN'.›

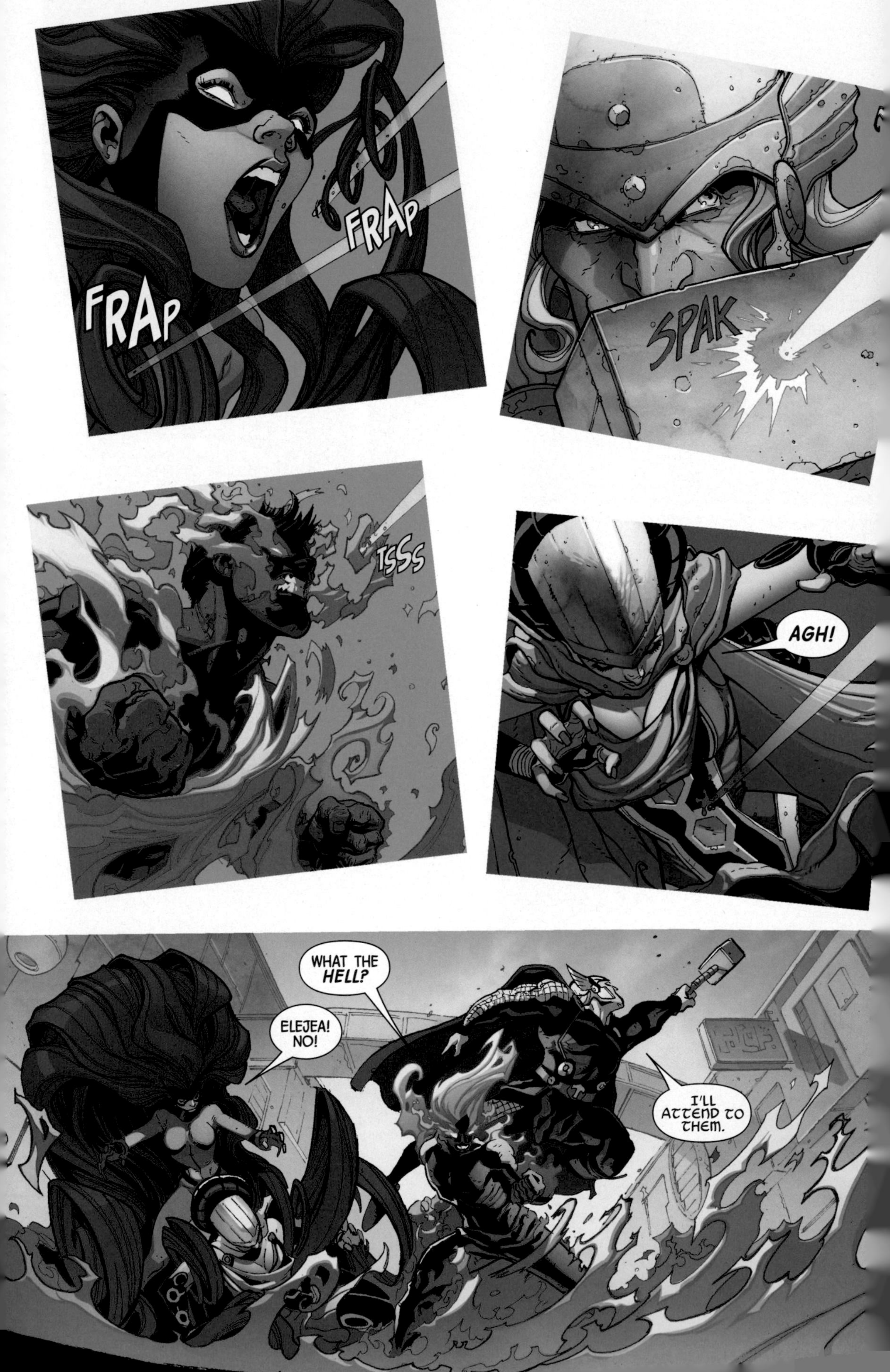
FRAP
FRAP
SPAK
TSSS
AGH!
ELEJEA! NO!
WHAT THE HELL?
I'LL ATTEND TO THEM.

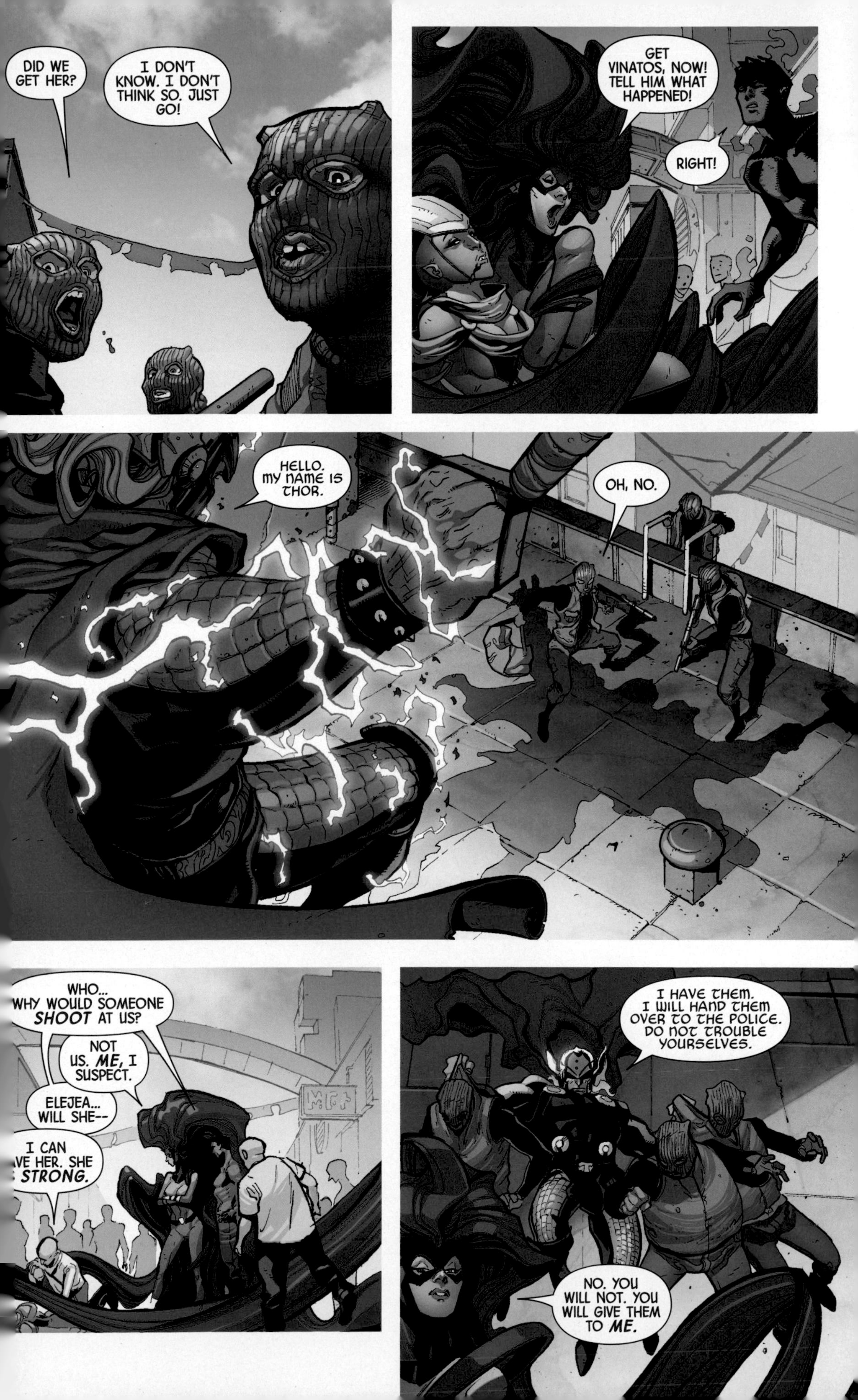
DID WE GET HER?
I DON'T KNOW. I DON'T THINK SO. JUST GO!
GET VINATOS, NOW! TELL HIM WHAT HAPPENED!
RIGHT!
HELLO. MY NAME IS THOR.
OH, NO.
WHO... WHY WOULD SOMEONE SHOOT AT US?
NOT US. ME, I SUSPECT.
ELEJEA... WILL SHE--
I CAN
VE HER. SHE
STRONG.
I HAVE THEM. I WILL HAND THEM OVER TO THE POLICE. DO NOT TROUBLE YOURSELVES.
NO. YOU WILL NOT. YOU WILL GIVE THEM TO ME.

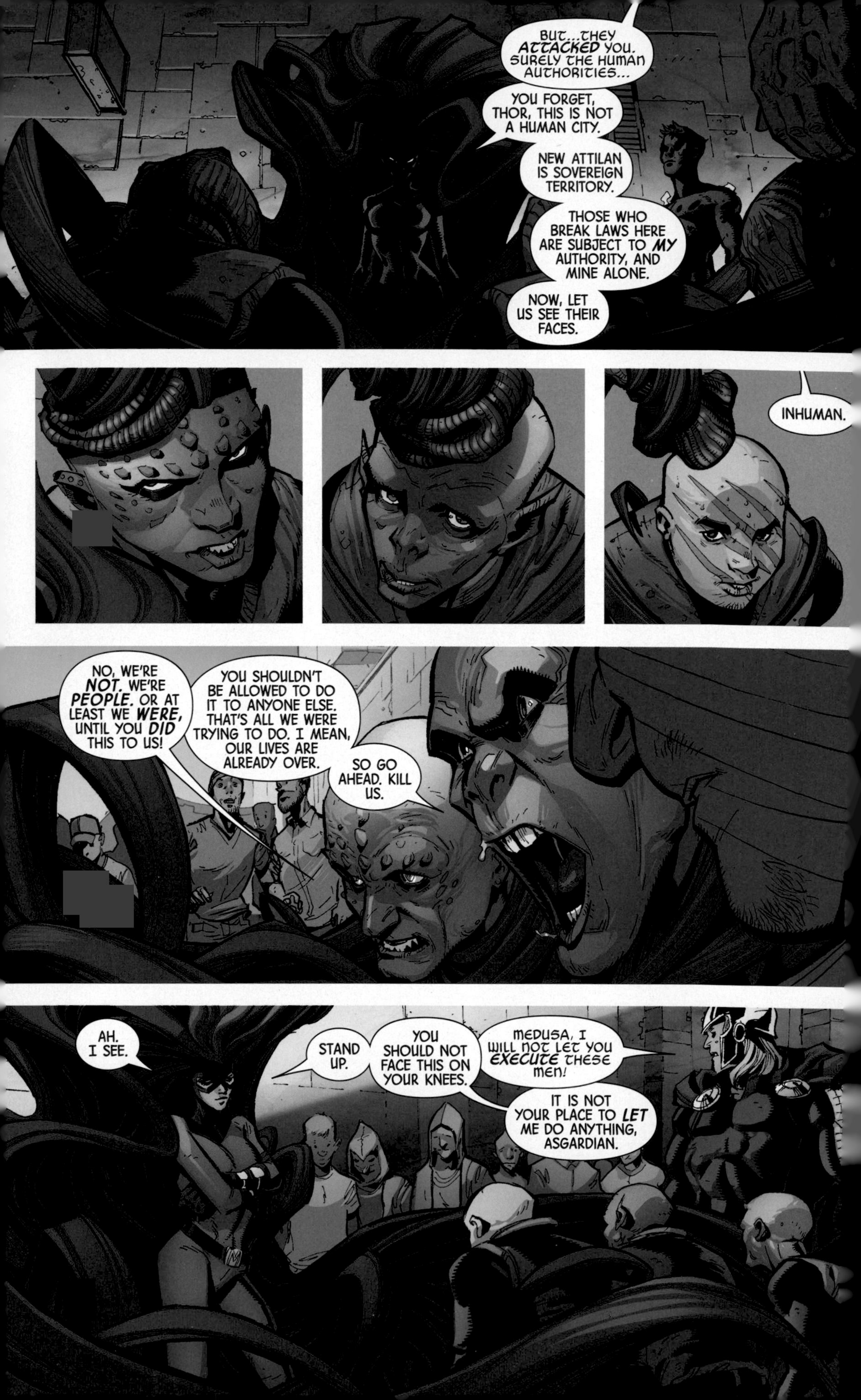

BUT...THEY ATTACKED YOU. SURELY THE HUMAN AUTHORITIES...
YOU FORGET, THOR, THIS IS NOT A HUMAN CITY.
NEW ATTILAN IS SOVEREIGN TERRITORY.
THOSE WHO BREAK LAWS HERE ARE SUBJECT TO MY AUTHORITY, AND MINE ALONE.
NOW, LET US SEE THEIR FACES.
INHUMAN.
NO, WE'RE NOT. WE'RE PEOPLE. OR AT LEAST WE WERE, UNTIL YOU DID THIS TO US!
YOU SHOULDN'T BE ALLOWED TO DO IT TO ANYONE ELSE. THAT'S ALL WE WERE TRYING TO DO. I MEAN, OUR LIVES ARE ALREADY OVER.
SO GO AHEAD. KILL US.
AH. I SEE.
STAND UP.
YOU SHOULD NOT FACE THIS ON YOUR KNEES.
MEDUSA, I WILL NOT LET YOU EXECUTE THESE MEN!
IT IS NOT YOUR PLACE TO LET ME DO ANYTHING, ASGARDIAN.

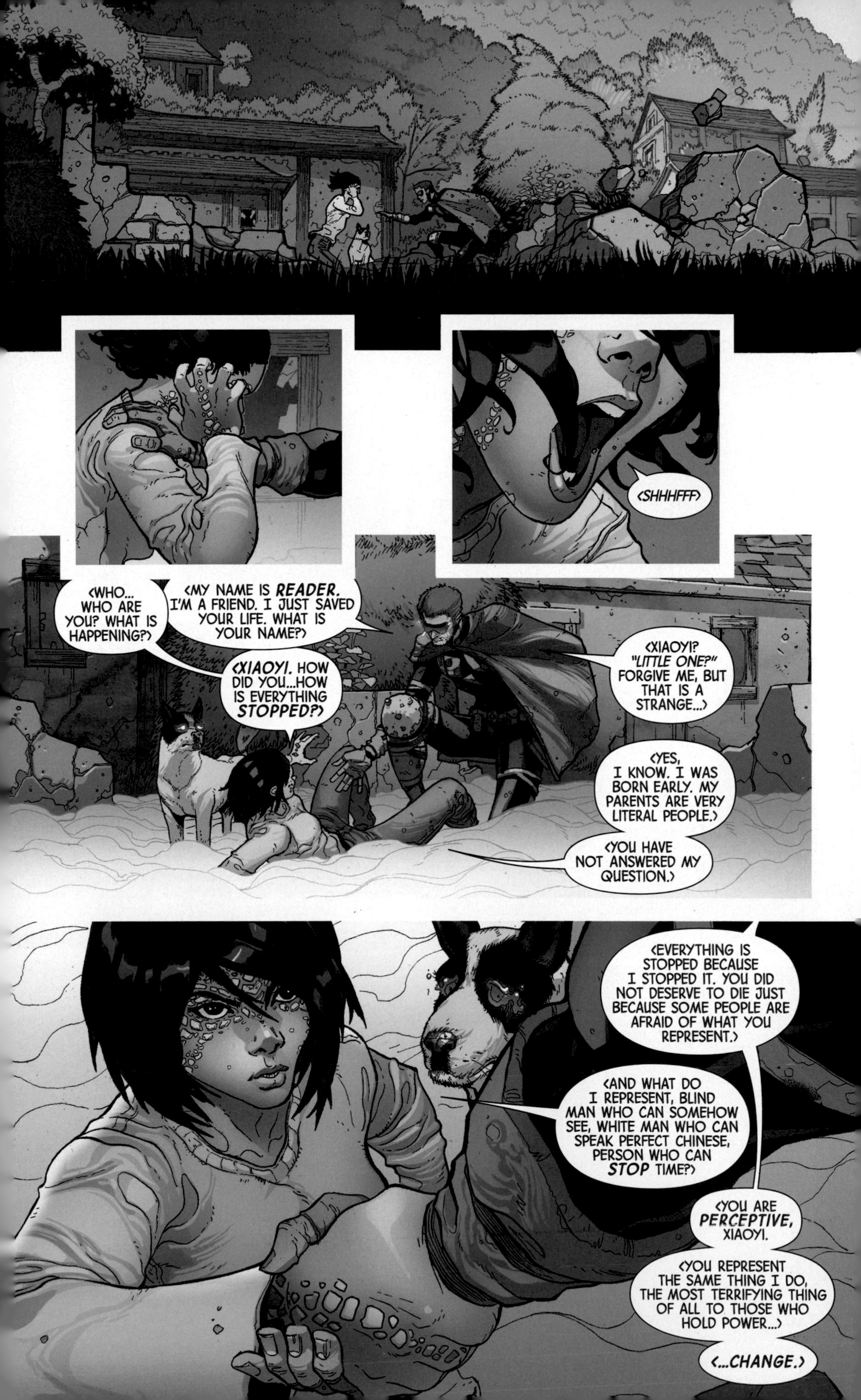

<SHHHFFF>
<WHO... WHO ARE YOU? WHAT IS HAPPENING?>
<MY NAME IS READER. I'M A FRIEND. I JUST SAVED YOUR LIFE. WHAT IS YOUR NAME?>
<XIAOYI. HOW DID YOU...HOW IS EVERYTHING STOPPED?>
<XIAOYI? "LITTLE ONE?" FORGIVE ME, BUT THAT IS A STRANGE...>
<YES, I KNOW. I WAS BORN EARLY. MY PARENTS ARE VERY LITERAL PEOPLE.>
<YOU HAVE NOT ANSWERED MY QUESTION.>
<EVERYTHING IS STOPPED BECAUSE I STOPPED IT. YOU DID NOT DESERVE TO DIE JUST BECAUSE SOME PEOPLE ARE AFRAID OF WHAT YOU REPRESENT.>
<AND WHAT DO I REPRESENT, BLIND MAN WHO CAN SOMEHOW SEE, WHITE MAN WHO CAN SPEAK PERFECT CHINESE, PERSON WHO CAN STOP TIME?>
<YOU ARE PERCEPTIVE, XIAOYI.
<YOU REPRESENT THE SAME THING I DO, THE MOST TERRIFYING THING OF ALL TO THOSE WHO HOLD POWER...>
<...CHANGE.>

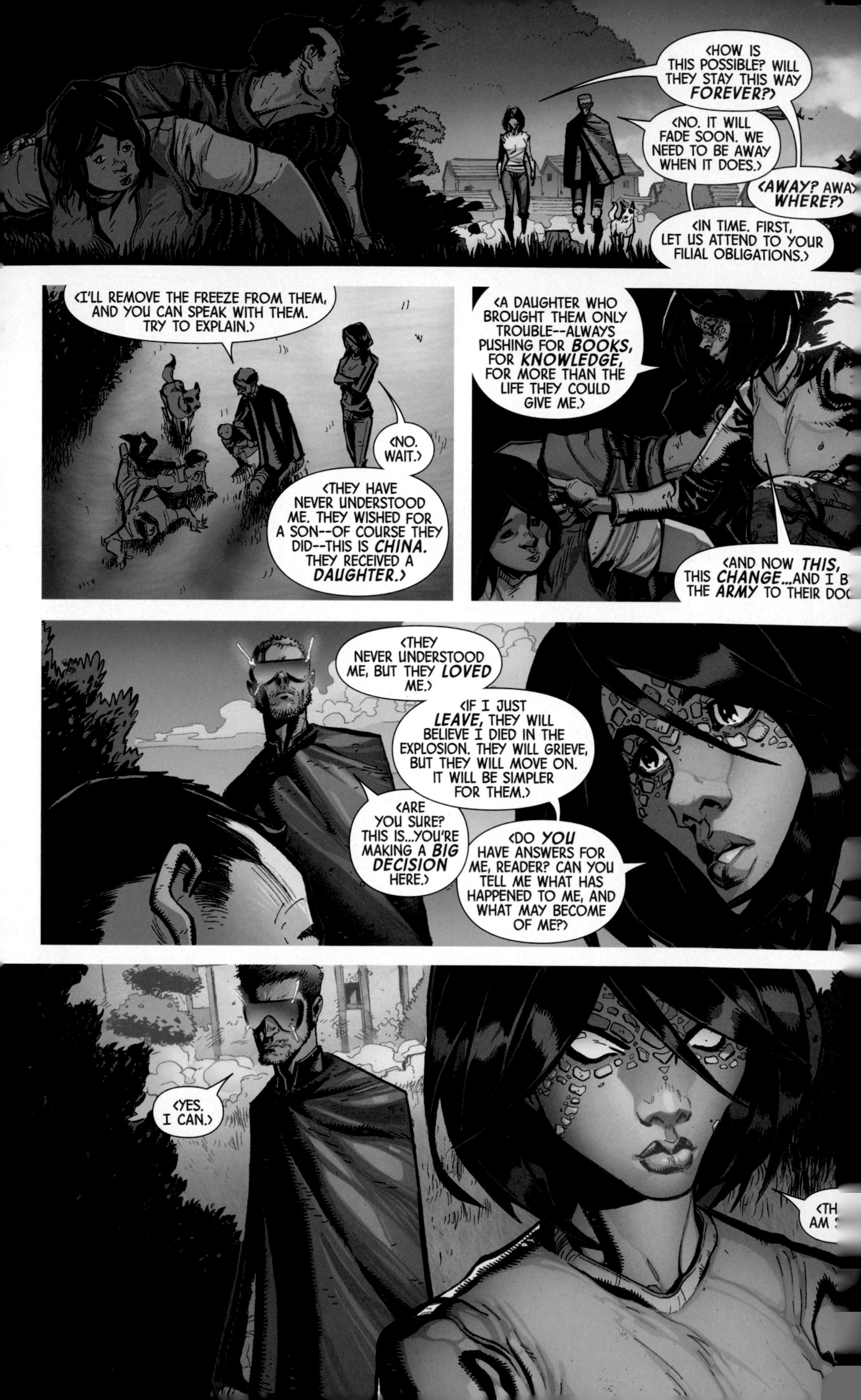
‹HOW IS THIS POSSIBLE? WILL THEY STAY THIS WAY *FOREVER?*›
‹NO. IT WILL FADE SOON. WE NEED TO BE AWAY WHEN IT DOES.›
‹*AWAY?* AWA *WHERE?*›
‹IN TIME. FIRST, LET US ATTEND TO YOUR FILIAL OBLIGATIONS.›
‹I'LL REMOVE THE FREEZE FROM THEM, AND YOU CAN SPEAK WITH THEM. TRY TO EXPLAIN.›
‹NO. WAIT.›
‹THEY HAVE NEVER UNDERSTOOD ME. THEY WISHED FOR A SON--OF COURSE THEY DID--THIS IS *CHINA.* THEY RECEIVED A *DAUGHTER.*›
‹A DAUGHTER WHO BROUGHT THEM ONLY TROUBLE--ALWAYS PUSHING FOR *BOOKS,* FOR *KNOWLEDGE,* FOR MORE THAN THE LIFE THEY COULD GIVE ME.›
‹AND NOW *THIS,* THIS *CHANGE*...AND I B THE *ARMY* TO THEIR DO
‹THEY NEVER UNDERSTOOD ME, BUT THEY *LOVED* ME.›
‹IF I JUST *LEAVE,* THEY WILL BELIEVE I DIED IN THE EXPLOSION. THEY WILL GRIEVE, BUT THEY WILL MOVE ON. IT WILL BE SIMPLER FOR THEM.›
‹ARE YOU SURE? THIS IS...YOU'RE MAKING A *BIG DECISION* HERE.›
‹DO *YOU* HAVE ANSWERS FOR ME, READER? CAN YOU TELL ME WHAT HAS HAPPENED TO ME, AND WHAT MAY BECOME OF ME?›
‹YES. I CAN.›
‹TH
AM

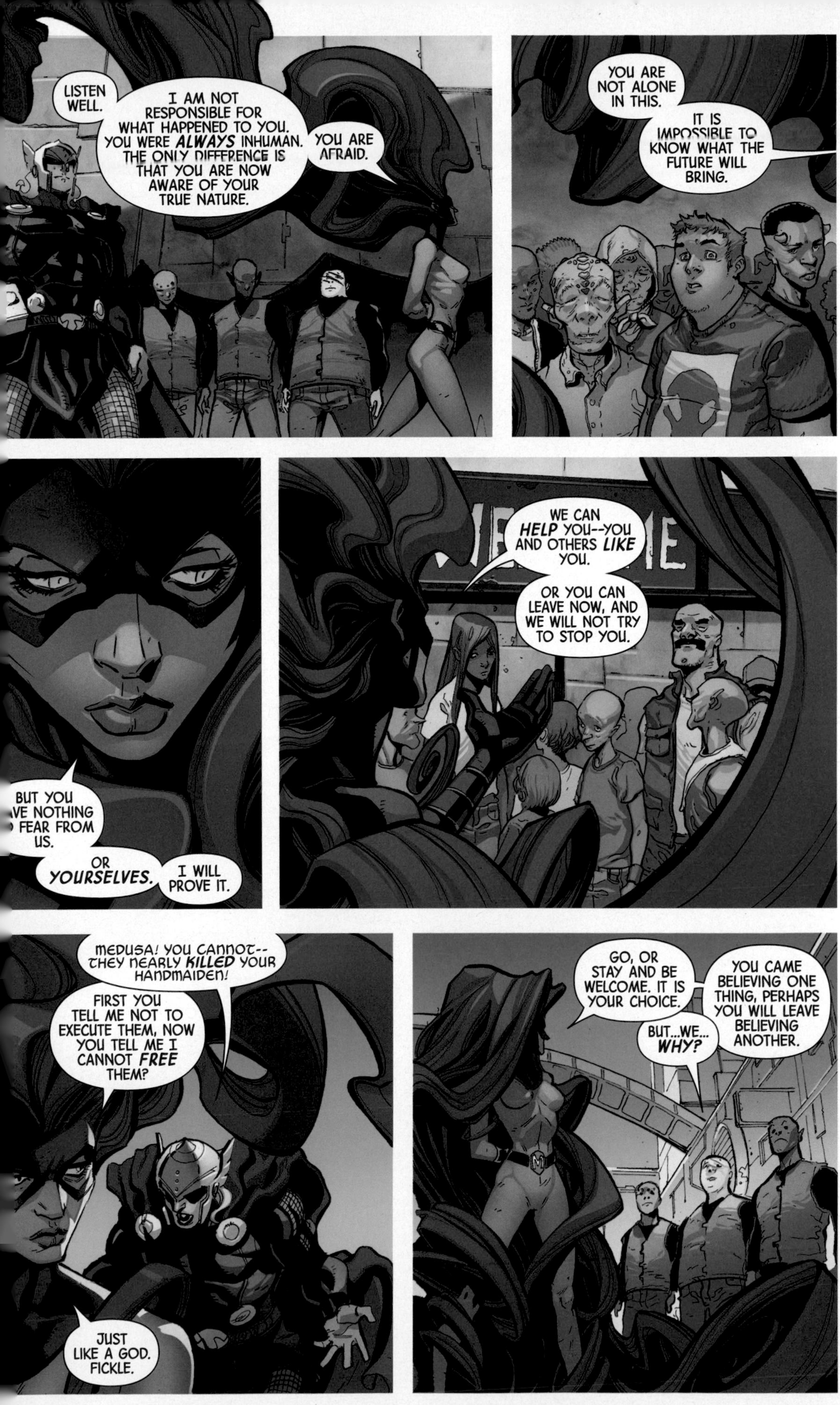
LISTEN WELL.
I AM NOT RESPONSIBLE FOR WHAT HAPPENED TO YOU. YOU WERE ALWAYS INHUMAN. THE ONLY DIFFERENCE IS THAT YOU ARE NOW AWARE OF YOUR TRUE NATURE.
YOU ARE AFRAID.
YOU ARE NOT ALONE IN THIS.
IT IS IMPOSSIBLE TO KNOW WHAT THE FUTURE WILL BRING.
BUT YOU
VE NOTHING
FEAR FROM
US.
OR YOURSELVES.
I WILL PROVE IT.
WE CAN HELP YOU--YOU AND OTHERS LIKE YOU.
OR YOU CAN LEAVE NOW, AND WE WILL NOT TRY TO STOP YOU.
MEDUSA! YOU CANNOT--THEY NEARLY KILLED YOUR HANDMAIDEN!
FIRST YOU TELL ME NOT TO EXECUTE THEM, NOW YOU TELL ME I CANNOT FREE THEM?
JUST LIKE A GOD. FICKLE.
GO, OR STAY AND BE WELCOME. IT IS YOUR CHOICE.
BUT...WE... WHY?
YOU CAME BELIEVING ONE THING, PERHAPS YOU WILL LEAVE BELIEVING ANOTHER.

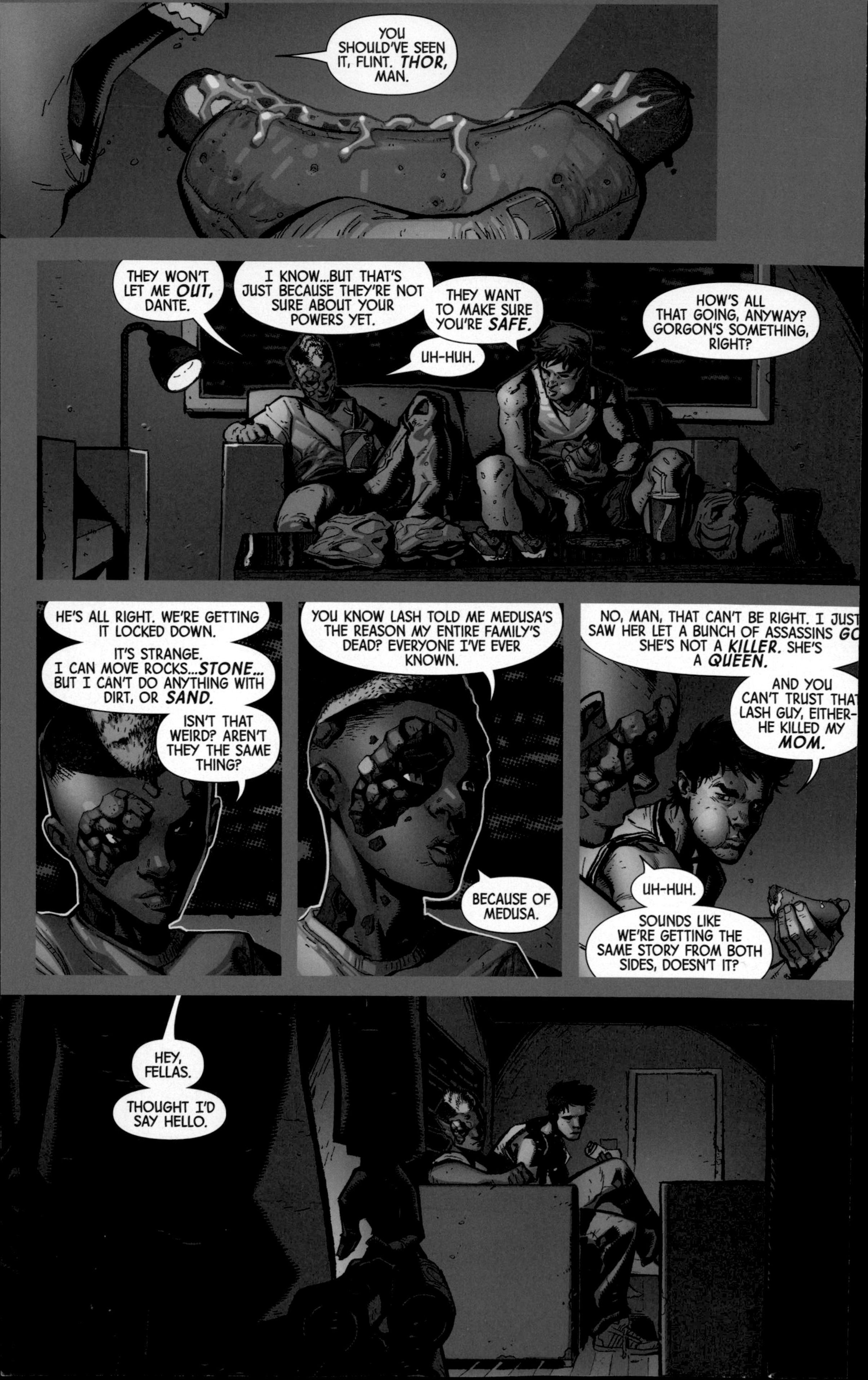
YOU SHOULD'VE SEEN IT, FLINT. THOR, MAN.
THEY WON'T LET ME OUT, DANTE.
I KNOW...BUT THAT'S JUST BECAUSE THEY'RE NOT SURE ABOUT YOUR POWERS YET.
THEY WANT TO MAKE SURE YOU'RE SAFE.
UH-HUH.
HOW'S ALL THAT GOING, ANYWAY? GORGON'S SOMETHING, RIGHT?
HE'S ALL RIGHT. WE'RE GETTING IT LOCKED DOWN.
IT'S STRANGE. I CAN MOVE ROCKS...STONE... BUT I CAN'T DO ANYTHING WITH DIRT, OR SAND.
ISN'T THAT WEIRD? AREN'T THEY THE SAME THING?
YOU KNOW LASH TOLD ME MEDUSA'S THE REASON MY ENTIRE FAMILY'S DEAD? EVERYONE I'VE EVER KNOWN.
BECAUSE OF MEDUSA.
NO, MAN, THAT CAN'T BE RIGHT. I JUST SAW HER LET A BUNCH OF ASSASSINS GO. SHE'S NOT A KILLER. SHE'S A QUEEN.
AND YOU CAN'T TRUST THAT LASH GUY, EITHER- HE KILLED MY MOM.
UH-HUH.
SOUNDS LIKE WE'RE GETTING THE SAME STORY FROM BOTH SIDES, DOESN'T IT?
HEY, FELLAS.
THOUGHT I'D SAY HELLO.

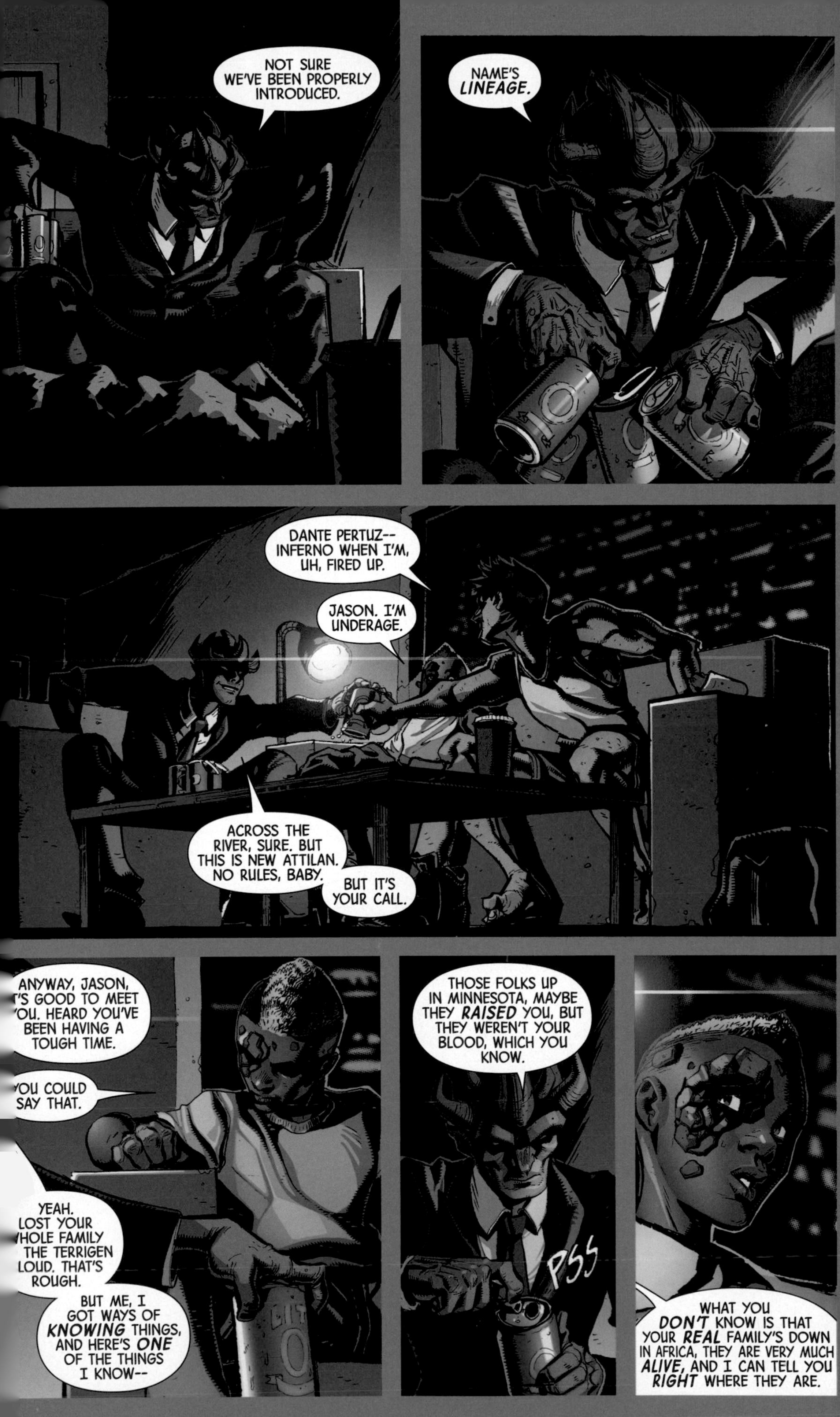

NOT SURE WE'VE BEEN PROPERLY INTRODUCED.
NAME'S *LINEAGE.*
DANTE PERTUZ-- INFERNO WHEN I'M, UH, FIRED UP.
JASON. I'M UNDERAGE.
ACROSS THE RIVER, SURE. BUT THIS IS NEW ATTILAN. NO RULES, BABY.
BUT IT'S YOUR CALL.
ANYWAY, JASON, T'S GOOD TO MEET OU. HEARD YOU'VE BEEN HAVING A TOUGH TIME.
OU COULD SAY THAT.
YEAH. LOST YOUR HOLE FAMILY THE TERRIGEN LOUD. THAT'S ROUGH.
BUT ME, I GOT WAYS OF *KNOWING* THINGS, AND HERE'S *ONE* OF THE THINGS I KNOW--
THOSE FOLKS UP IN MINNESOTA, MAYBE THEY *RAISED* YOU, BUT THEY WEREN'T YOUR BLOOD, WHICH YOU KNOW.
PSS
WHAT YOU *DON'T* KNOW IS THAT YOUR *REAL* FAMILY'S DOWN IN AFRICA, THEY ARE VERY MUCH *ALIVE,* AND I CAN TELL YOU *RIGHT* WHERE THEY ARE.

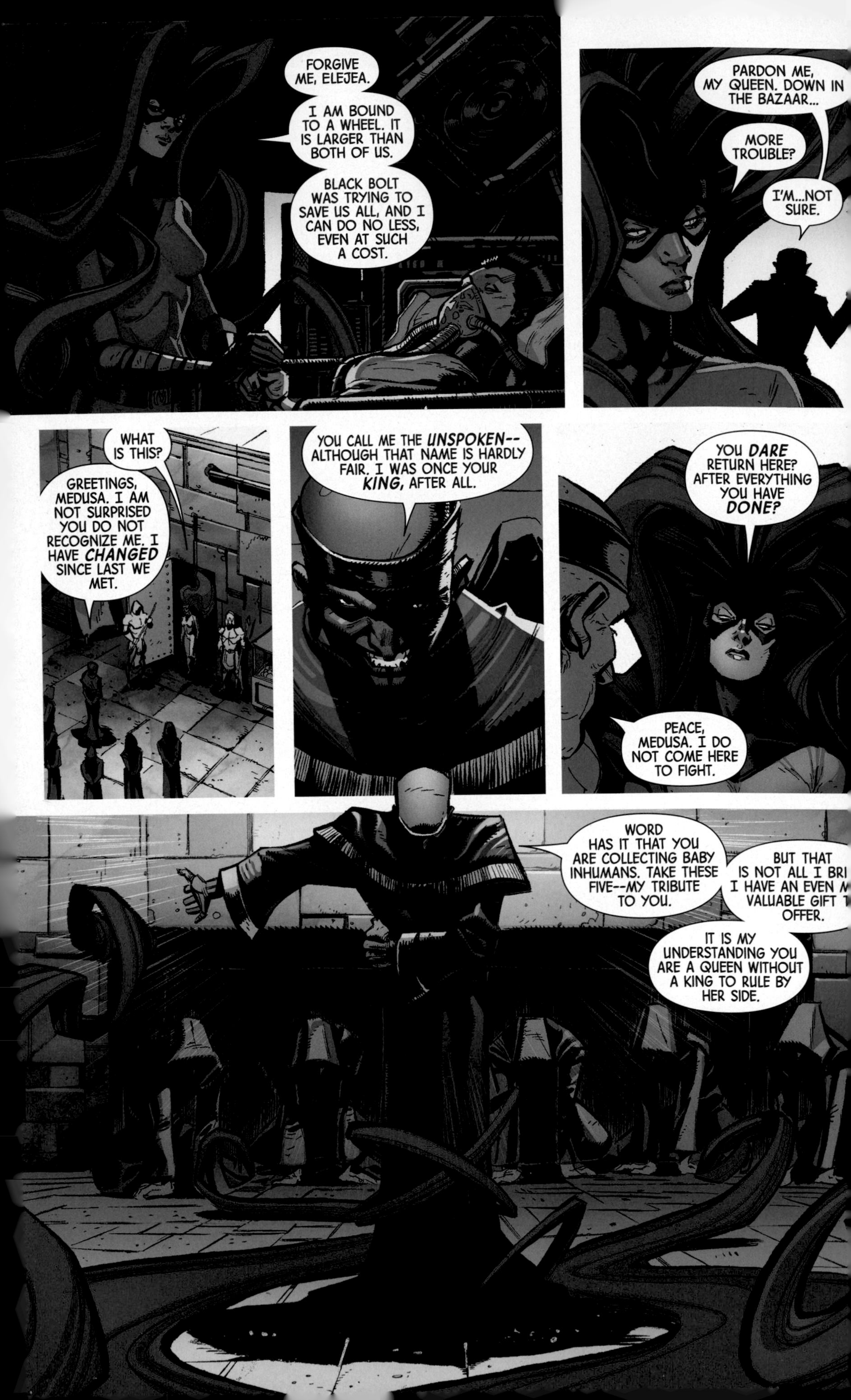
FORGIVE ME, ELEJEA.
I AM BOUND TO A WHEEL. IT IS LARGER THAN BOTH OF US.
BLACK BOLT WAS TRYING TO SAVE US ALL, AND I CAN DO NO LESS, EVEN AT SUCH A COST.
PARDON ME, MY QUEEN. DOWN IN THE BAZAAR...
MORE TROUBLE?
I'M...NOT SURE.
WHAT IS THIS?
GREETINGS, MEDUSA. I AM NOT SURPRISED YOU DO NOT RECOGNIZE ME. I HAVE CHANGED SINCE LAST WE MET.
YOU CALL ME THE UNSPOKEN-- ALTHOUGH THAT NAME IS HARDLY FAIR. I WAS ONCE YOUR KING, AFTER ALL.
YOU DARE RETURN HERE? AFTER EVERYTHING YOU HAVE DONE?
PEACE, MEDUSA. I DO NOT COME HERE TO FIGHT.
WORD HAS IT THAT YOU ARE COLLECTING BABY INHUMANS. TAKE THESE FIVE--MY TRIBUTE TO YOU.
IT IS MY UNDERSTANDING YOU ARE A QUEEN WITHOUT A KING TO RULE BY HER SIDE.

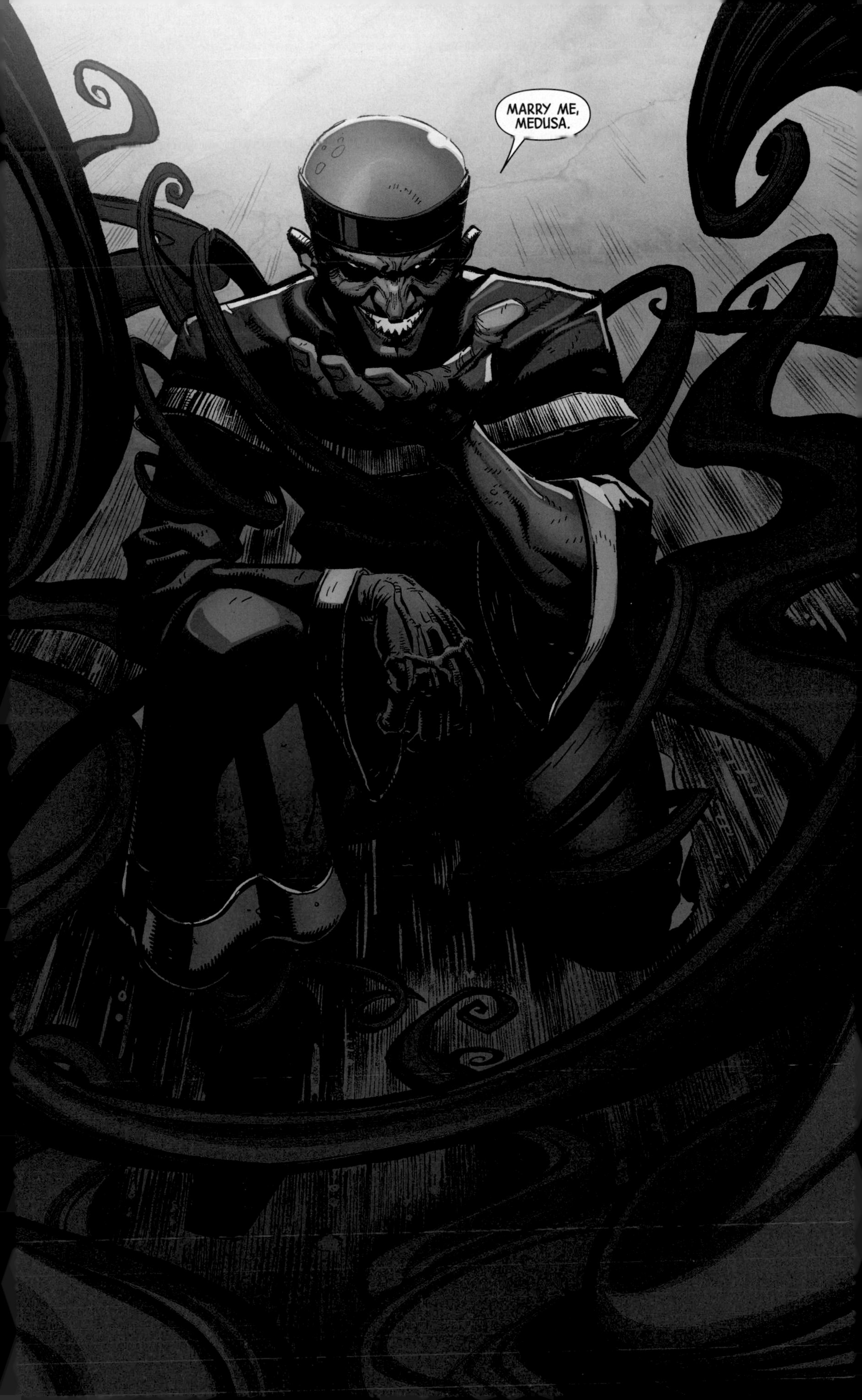
MARRY ME, MEDUSA.

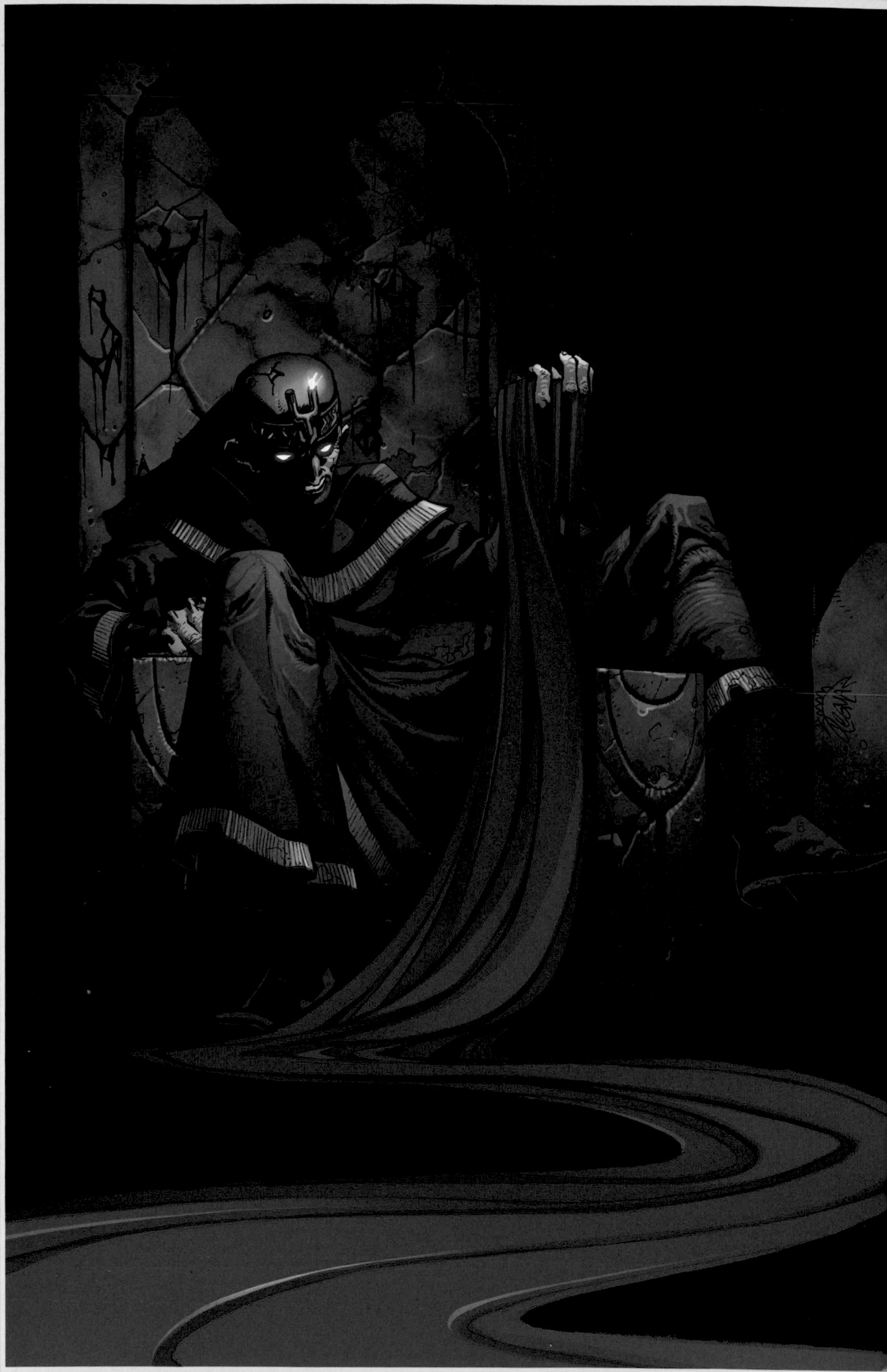

5 PART FIVE: EMPTY THRONE

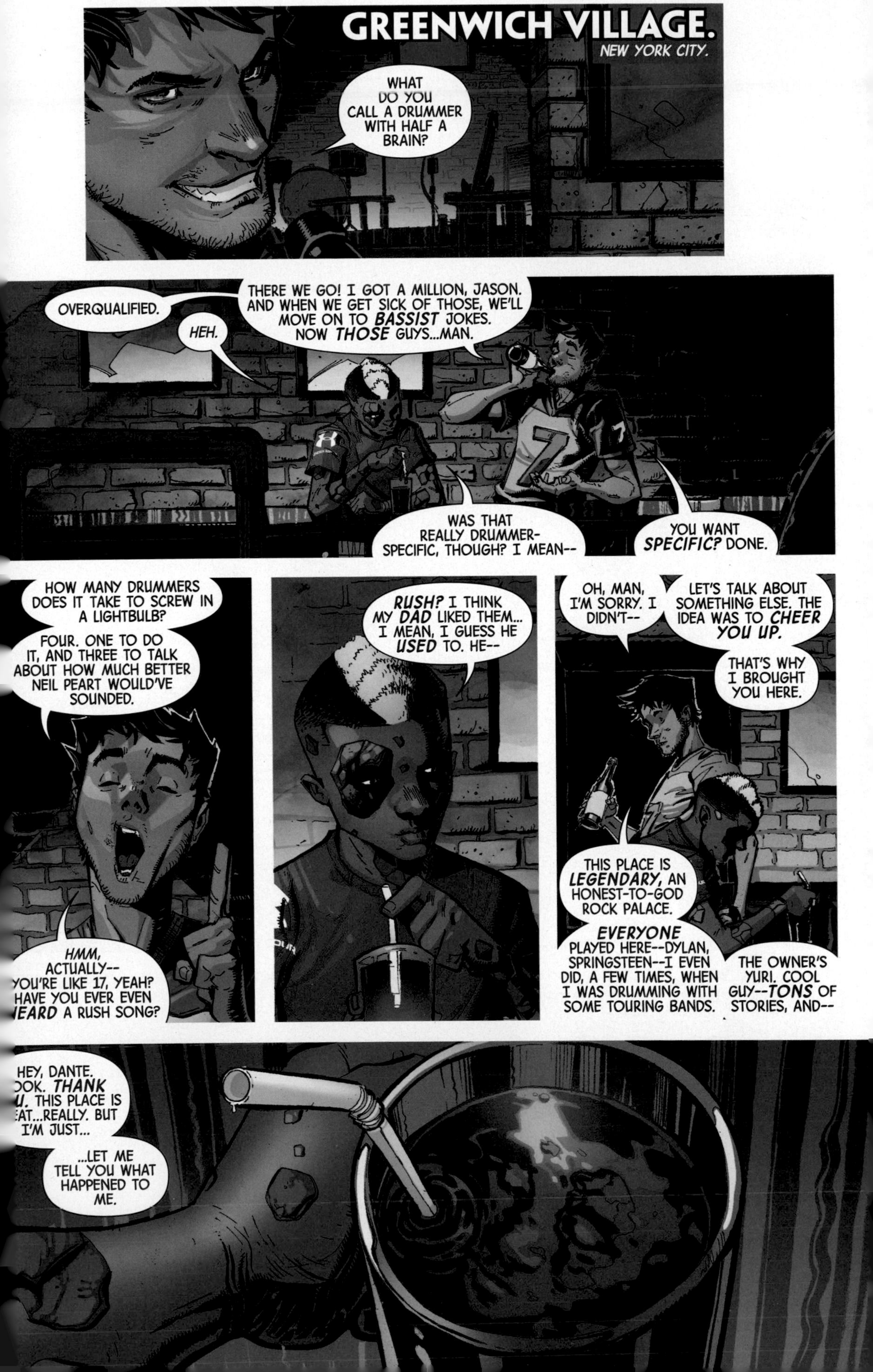
GREENWICH VILLAGE.
NEW YORK CITY.
WHAT DO YOU CALL A DRUMMER WITH HALF A BRAIN?
OVERQUALIFIED.
HEH.
THERE WE GO! I GOT A MILLION, JASON. AND WHEN WE GET SICK OF THOSE, WE'LL MOVE ON TO BASSIST JOKES. NOW THOSE GUYS...MAN.
WAS THAT REALLY DRUMMER-SPECIFIC, THOUGH? I MEAN--
YOU WANT SPECIFIC? DONE.
HOW MANY DRUMMERS DOES IT TAKE TO SCREW IN A LIGHTBULB?
FOUR. ONE TO DO IT, AND THREE TO TALK ABOUT HOW MUCH BETTER NEIL PEART WOULD'VE SOUNDED.
HMM, ACTUALLY-- YOU'RE LIKE 17, YEAH? HAVE YOU EVER EVEN EARD A RUSH SONG?
RUSH? I THINK MY DAD LIKED THEM... I MEAN, I GUESS HE USED TO. HE--
OH, MAN, I'M SORRY. I DIDN'T--
LET'S TALK ABOUT SOMETHING ELSE. THE IDEA WAS TO CHEER YOU UP.
THAT'S WHY I BROUGHT YOU HERE.
THIS PLACE IS LEGENDARY, AN HONEST-TO-GOD ROCK PALACE.
EVERYONE PLAYED HERE--DYLAN, SPRINGSTEEN--I EVEN DID, A FEW TIMES, WHEN I WAS DRUMMING WITH SOME TOURING BANDS.
THE OWNER'S YURI. COOL GUY--TONS OF STORIES, AND--
HEY, DANTE. LOOK. THANK YOU. THIS PLACE IS GREAT...REALLY. BUT I'M JUST...
...LET ME TELL YOU WHAT HAPPENED TO ME.

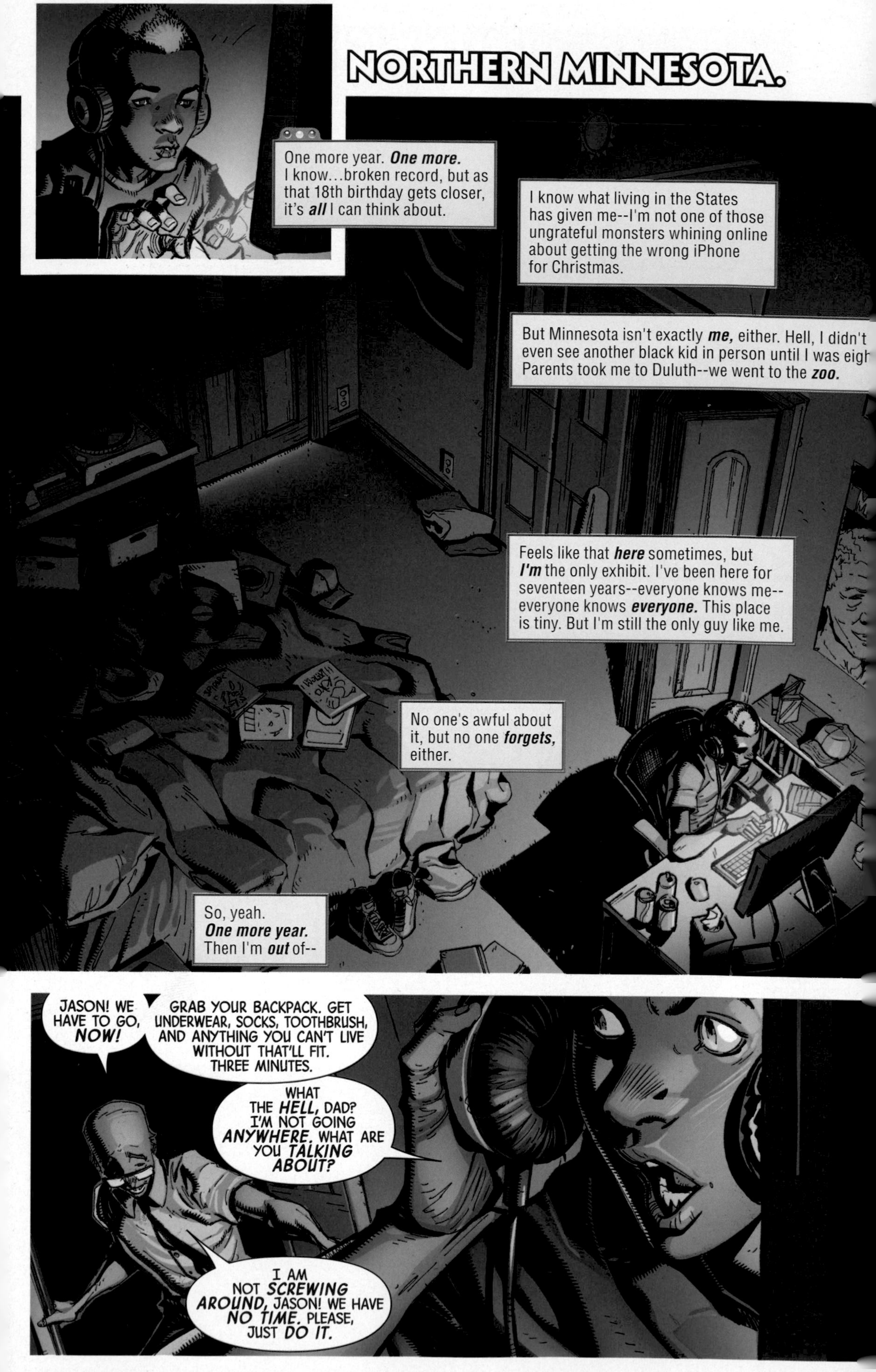
NORTHERN MINNESOTA.
One more year. One more. I know...broken record, but as that 18th birthday gets closer, it's all I can think about.
I know what living in the States has given me--I'm not one of those ungrateful monsters whining online about getting the wrong iPhone for Christmas.
But Minnesota isn't exactly me, either. Hell, I didn't even see another black kid in person until I was eigh Parents took me to Duluth--we went to the zoo.
Feels like that here sometimes, but I'm the only exhibit. I've been here for seventeen years--everyone knows me--everyone knows everyone. This place is tiny. But I'm still the only guy like me.
No one's awful about it, but no one forgets, either.
So, yeah. One more year. Then I'm out of--
JASON! WE HAVE TO GO, NOW!
GRAB YOUR BACKPACK. GET UNDERWEAR, SOCKS, TOOTHBRUSH, AND ANYTHING YOU CAN'T LIVE WITHOUT THAT'LL FIT. THREE MINUTES.
WHAT THE HELL, DAD? I'M NOT GOING ANYWHERE. WHAT ARE YOU TALKING ABOUT?
I AM NOT SCREWING AROUND, JASON! WE HAVE NO TIME. PLEASE, JUST DO IT.

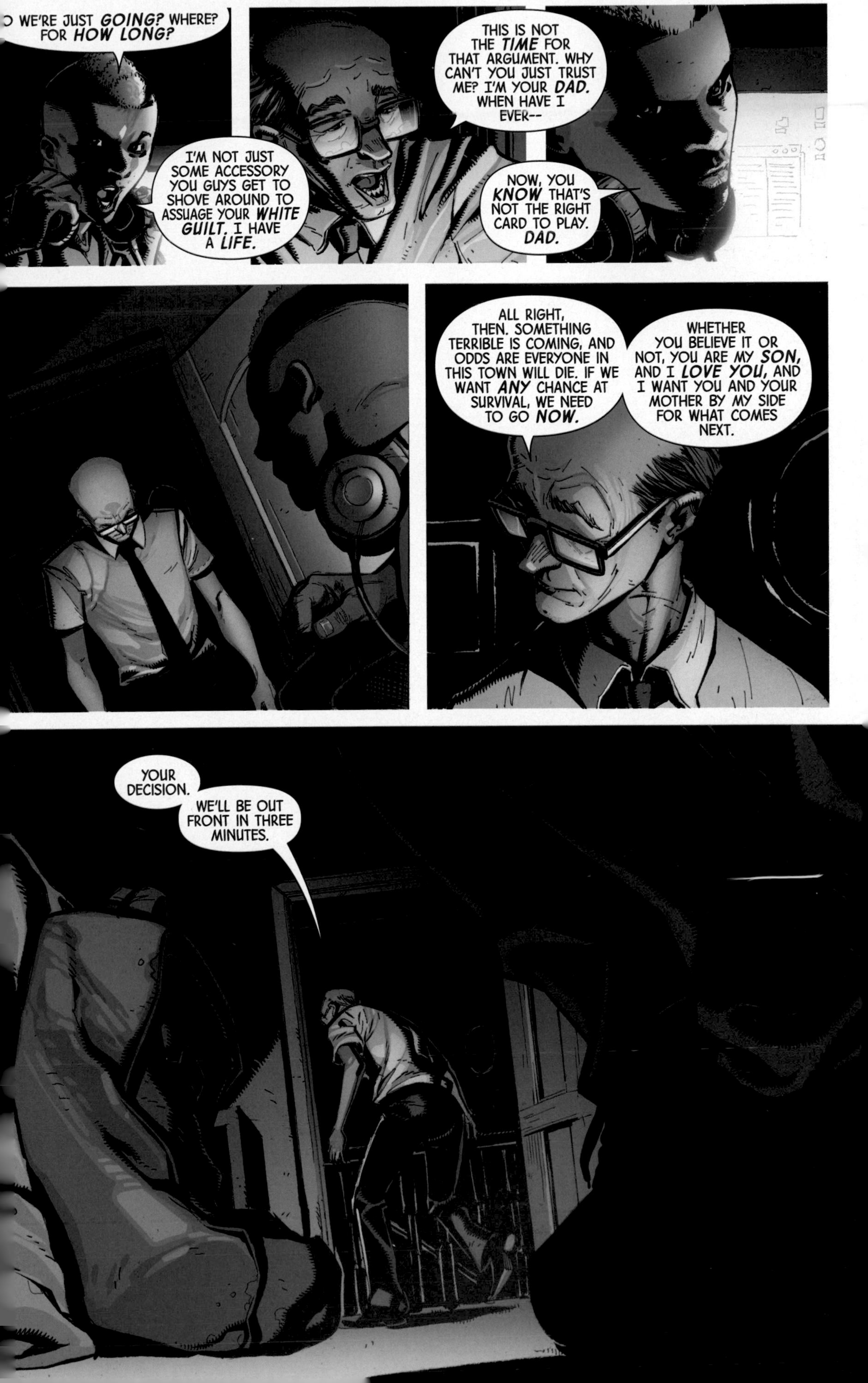
O WE'RE JUST GOING? WHERE? FOR HOW LONG?
THIS IS NOT THE TIME FOR THAT ARGUMENT. WHY CAN'T YOU JUST TRUST ME? I'M YOUR DAD. WHEN HAVE I EVER--
I'M NOT JUST SOME ACCESSORY YOU GUYS GET TO SHOVE AROUND TO ASSUAGE YOUR WHITE GUILT. I HAVE A LIFE.
NOW, YOU KNOW THAT'S NOT THE RIGHT CARD TO PLAY. DAD.
ALL RIGHT, THEN. SOMETHING TERRIBLE IS COMING, AND ODDS ARE EVERYONE IN THIS TOWN WILL DIE. IF WE WANT ANY CHANCE AT SURVIVAL, WE NEED TO GO NOW.
WHETHER YOU BELIEVE IT OR NOT, YOU ARE MY SON, AND I LOVE YOU, AND I WANT YOU AND YOUR MOTHER BY MY SIDE FOR WHAT COMES NEXT.
YOUR DECISION.
WE'LL BE OUT FRONT IN THREE MINUTES.

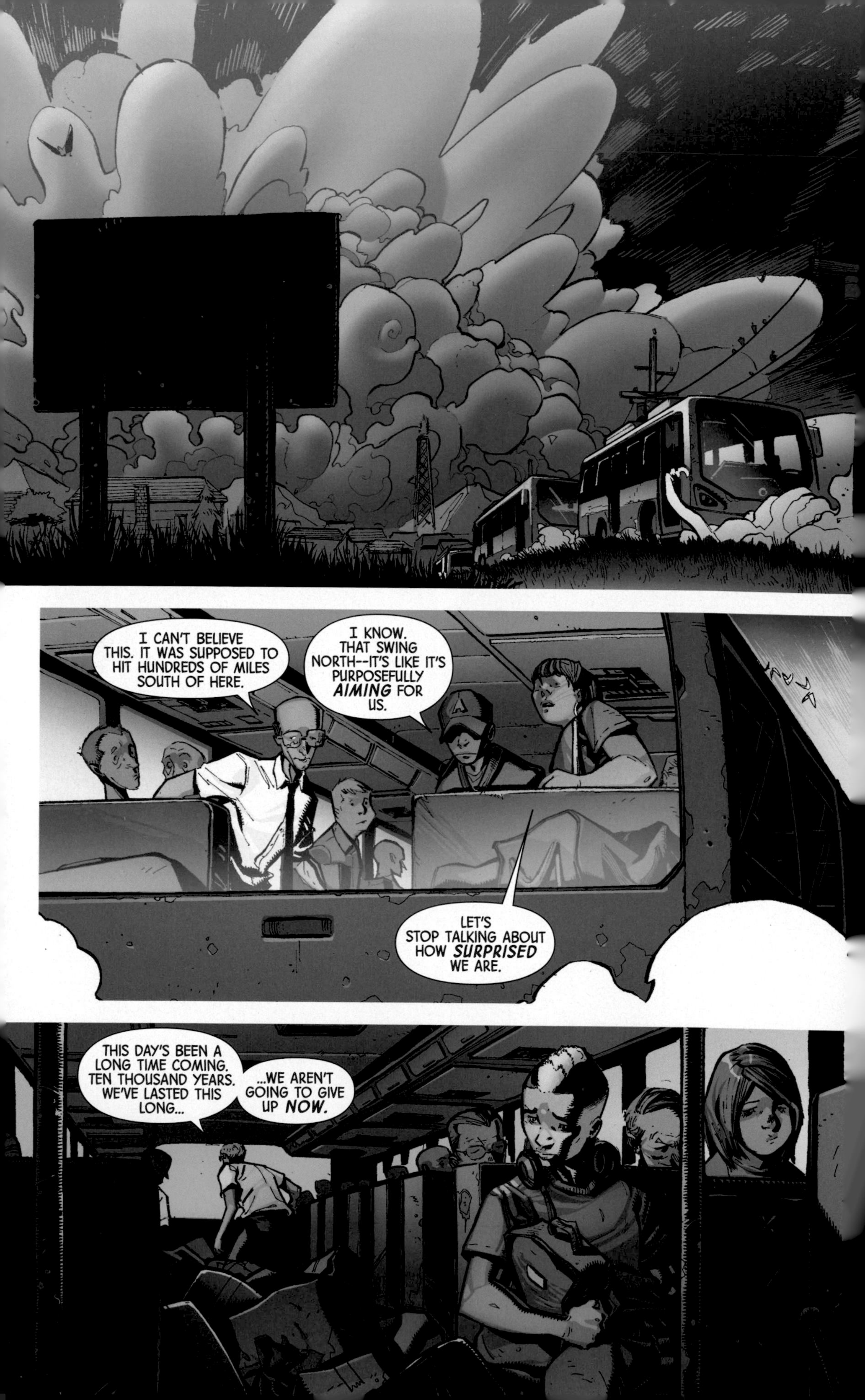
I CAN'T BELIEVE THIS. IT WAS SUPPOSED TO HIT HUNDREDS OF MILES SOUTH OF HERE.
I KNOW. THAT SWING NORTH--IT'S LIKE IT'S PURPOSEFULLY AIMING FOR US.
LET'S STOP TALKING ABOUT HOW SURPRISED WE ARE.
THIS DAY'S BEEN A LONG TIME COMING. TEN THOUSAND YEARS. WE'VE LASTED THIS LONG...
...WE AREN'T GOING TO GIVE UP NOW.

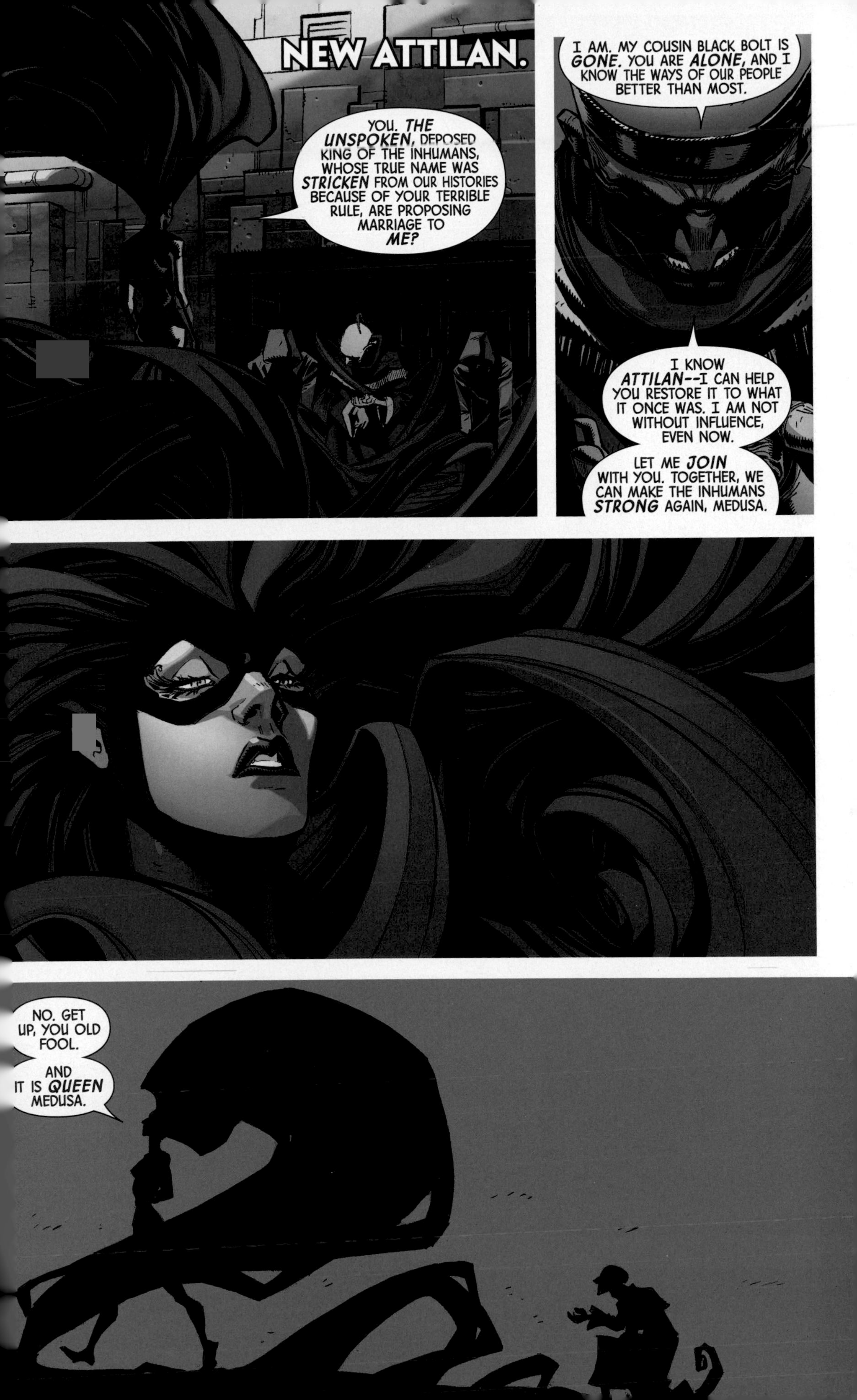
NEW ATTILAN.
YOU. THE UNSPOKEN, DEPOSED KING OF THE INHUMANS, WHOSE TRUE NAME WAS STRICKEN FROM OUR HISTORIES BECAUSE OF YOUR TERRIBLE RULE, ARE PROPOSING MARRIAGE TO ME?
I AM. MY COUSIN BLACK BOLT IS GONE. YOU ARE ALONE, AND I KNOW THE WAYS OF OUR PEOPLE BETTER THAN MOST.
I KNOW ATTILAN--I CAN HELP YOU RESTORE IT TO WHAT IT ONCE WAS. I AM NOT WITHOUT INFLUENCE, EVEN NOW.
LET ME JOIN WITH YOU. TOGETHER, WE CAN MAKE THE INHUMANS STRONG AGAIN, MEDUSA.
NO. GET UP, YOU OLD FOOL.
AND IT IS QUEEN MEDUSA.

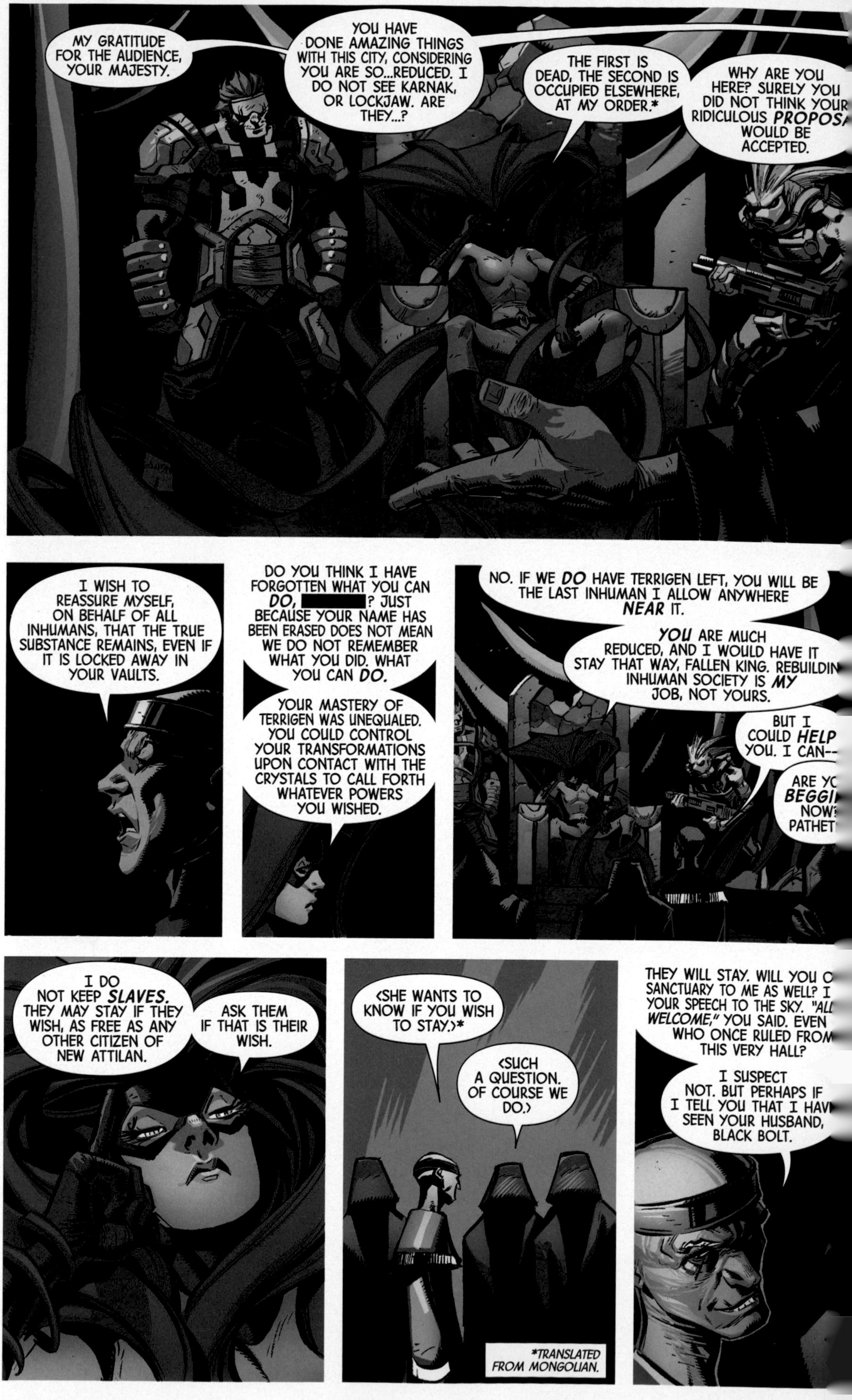

MY GRATITUDE FOR THE AUDIENCE, YOUR MAJESTY.
YOU HAVE DONE AMAZING THINGS WITH THIS CITY, CONSIDERING YOU ARE SO...REDUCED. I DO NOT SEE KARNAK, OR LOCKJAW. ARE THEY...?
THE FIRST IS DEAD, THE SECOND IS OCCUPIED ELSEWHERE, AT MY ORDER.*
WHY ARE YOU HERE? SURELY YOU DID NOT THINK YOUR RIDICULOUS PROPOS WOULD BE ACCEPTED.
I WISH TO REASSURE MYSELF, ON BEHALF OF ALL INHUMANS, THAT THE TRUE SUBSTANCE REMAINS, EVEN IF IT IS LOCKED AWAY IN YOUR VAULTS.
DO YOU THINK I HAVE FORGOTTEN WHAT YOU CAN DO, [redacted]? JUST BECAUSE YOUR NAME HAS BEEN ERASED DOES NOT MEAN WE DO NOT REMEMBER WHAT YOU DID. WHAT YOU CAN DO.
YOUR MASTERY OF TERRIGEN WAS UNEQUALED. YOU COULD CONTROL YOUR TRANSFORMATIONS UPON CONTACT WITH THE CRYSTALS TO CALL FORTH WHATEVER POWERS YOU WISHED.
NO. IF WE DO HAVE TERRIGEN LEFT, YOU WILL BE THE LAST INHUMAN I ALLOW ANYWHERE NEAR IT.
YOU ARE MUCH REDUCED, AND I WOULD HAVE IT STAY THAT WAY, FALLEN KING. REBUILDIN INHUMAN SOCIETY IS MY JOB, NOT YOURS.
BUT I COULD HELP YOU. I CAN--
ARE YO BEGGI NOW? PATHET
I DO NOT KEEP SLAVES. THEY MAY STAY IF THEY WISH, AS FREE AS ANY OTHER CITIZEN OF NEW ATTILAN.
ASK THEM IF THAT IS THEIR WISH.
<SHE WANTS TO KNOW IF YOU WISH TO STAY.>*
<SUCH A QUESTION. OF COURSE WE DO.>
*TRANSLATED FROM MONGOLIAN.
THEY WILL STAY. WILL YOU O SANCTUARY TO ME AS WELL? I YOUR SPEECH TO THE SKY. "ALL WELCOME," YOU SAID. EVEN WHO ONCE RULED FROM THIS VERY HALL?
I SUSPECT NOT. BUT PERHAPS IF I TELL YOU THAT I HAV SEEN YOUR HUSBAND, BLACK BOLT.

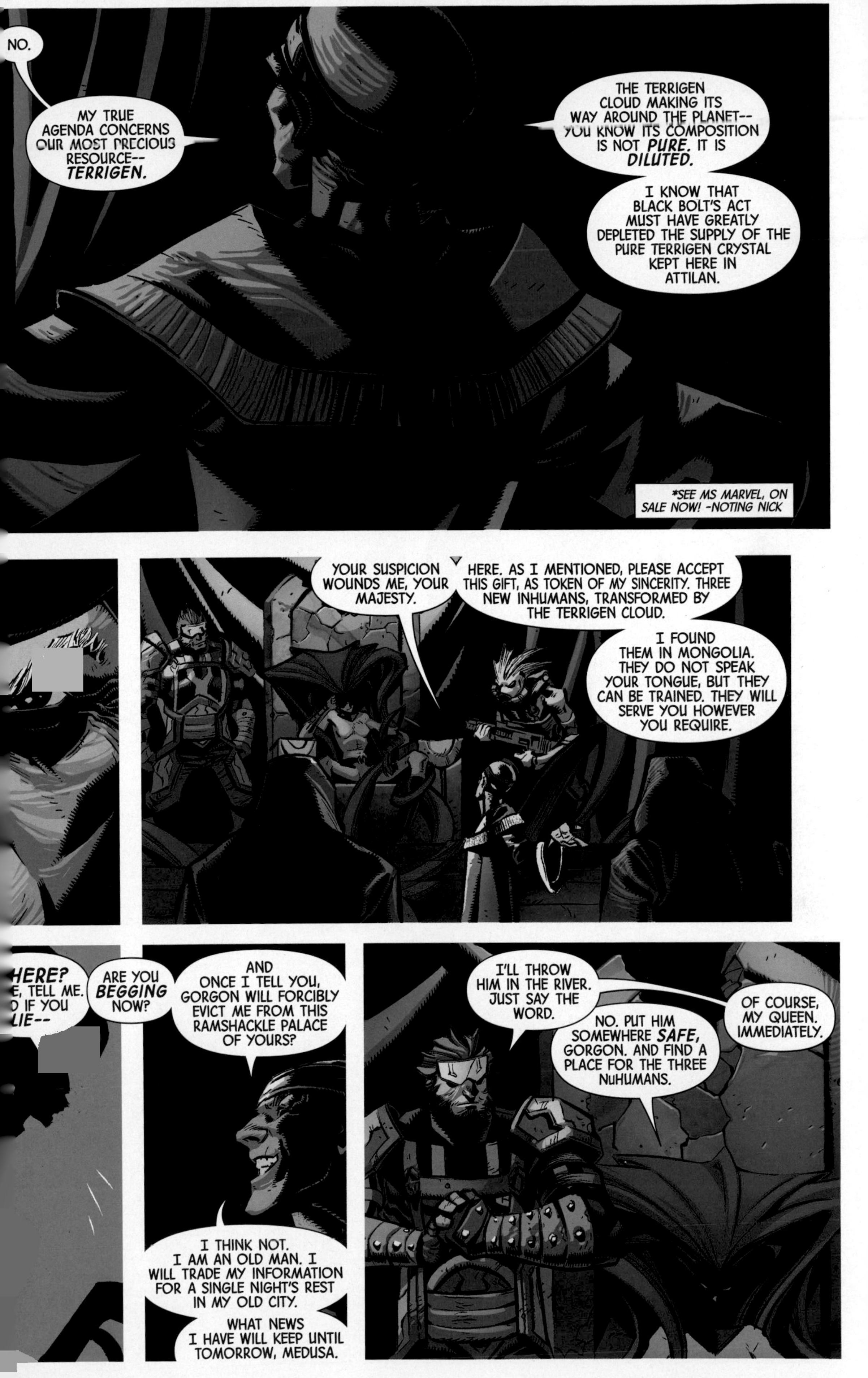
NO.
MY TRUE AGENDA CONCERNS OUR MOST PRECIOUS RESOURCE-- TERRIGEN.
THE TERRIGEN CLOUD MAKING ITS WAY AROUND THE PLANET-- YOU KNOW ITS COMPOSITION IS NOT PURE. IT IS DILUTED.
I KNOW THAT BLACK BOLT'S ACT MUST HAVE GREATLY DEPLETED THE SUPPLY OF THE PURE TERRIGEN CRYSTAL KEPT HERE IN ATTILAN.
*SEE MS MARVEL, ON SALE NOW! -NOTING NICK
YOUR SUSPICION WOUNDS ME, YOUR MAJESTY.
HERE. AS I MENTIONED, PLEASE ACCEPT THIS GIFT, AS TOKEN OF MY SINCERITY. THREE NEW INHUMANS, TRANSFORMED BY THE TERRIGEN CLOUD.
I FOUND THEM IN MONGOLIA. THEY DO NOT SPEAK YOUR TONGUE, BUT THEY CAN BE TRAINED. THEY WILL SERVE YOU HOWEVER YOU REQUIRE.
ARE YOU BEGGING NOW?
AND ONCE I TELL YOU, GORGON WILL FORCIBLY EVICT ME FROM THIS RAMSHACKLE PALACE OF YOURS?
I THINK NOT. I AM AN OLD MAN. I WILL TRADE MY INFORMATION FOR A SINGLE NIGHT'S REST IN MY OLD CITY.
WHAT NEWS I HAVE WILL KEEP UNTIL TOMORROW, MEDUSA.
I'LL THROW HIM IN THE RIVER. JUST SAY THE WORD.
NO. PUT HIM SOMEWHERE SAFE, GORGON. AND FIND A PLACE FOR THE THREE NUHUMANS.
OF COURSE, MY QUEEN. IMMEDIATELY.

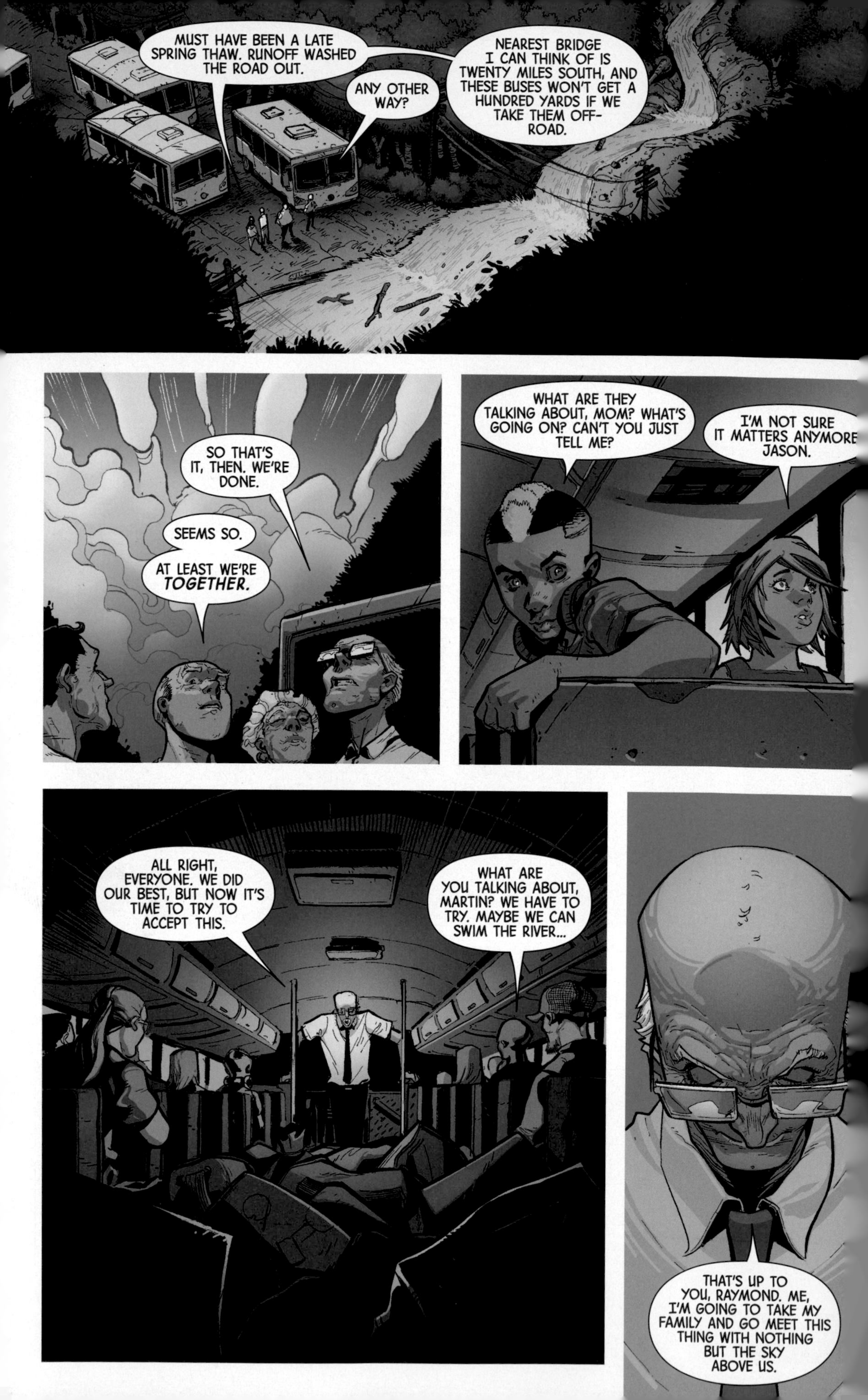
MUST HAVE BEEN A LATE SPRING THAW. RUNOFF WASHED THE ROAD OUT.
ANY OTHER WAY?
NEAREST BRIDGE I CAN THINK OF IS TWENTY MILES SOUTH, AND THESE BUSES WON'T GET A HUNDRED YARDS IF WE TAKE THEM OFF-ROAD.
SO THAT'S IT, THEN. WE'RE DONE.
SEEMS SO.
AT LEAST WE'RE *TOGETHER.*
WHAT ARE THEY TALKING ABOUT, MOM? WHAT'S GOING ON? CAN'T YOU JUST TELL ME?
I'M NOT SURE IT MATTERS ANYMORE JASON.
ALL RIGHT, EVERYONE. WE DID OUR BEST, BUT NOW IT'S TIME TO TRY TO ACCEPT THIS.
WHAT ARE YOU TALKING ABOUT, MARTIN? WE HAVE TO TRY. MAYBE WE CAN SWIM THE RIVER...
THAT'S UP TO YOU, RAYMOND. ME, I'M GOING TO TAKE MY FAMILY AND GO MEET THIS THING WITH NOTHING BUT THE SKY ABOVE US.

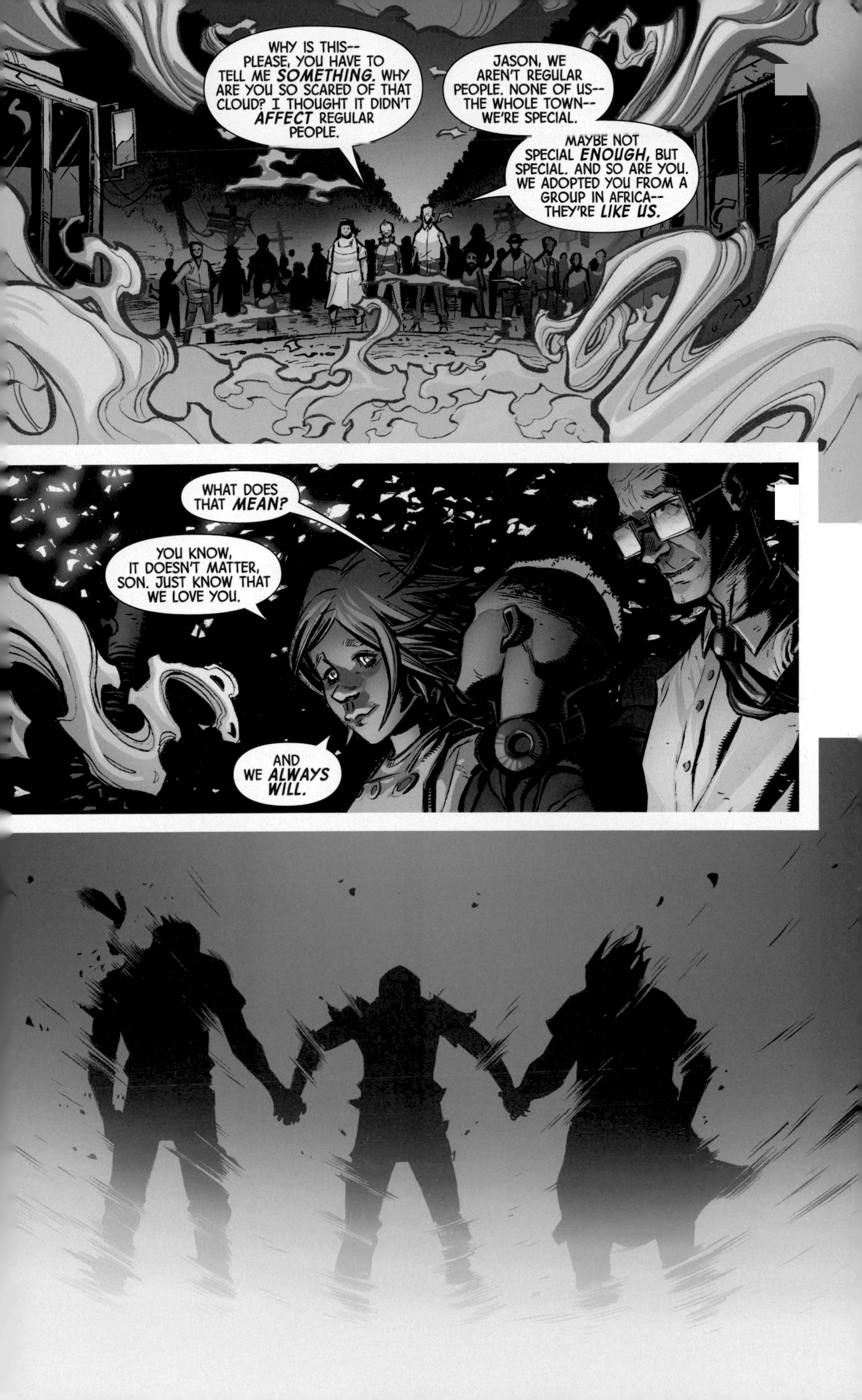
WHY IS THIS-- PLEASE, YOU HAVE TO TELL ME SOMETHING. WHY ARE YOU SO SCARED OF THAT CLOUD? I THOUGHT IT DIDN'T AFFECT REGULAR PEOPLE.
JASON, WE AREN'T REGULAR PEOPLE. NONE OF US-- THE WHOLE TOWN-- WE'RE SPECIAL.
MAYBE NOT SPECIAL ENOUGH, BUT SPECIAL. AND SO ARE YOU. WE ADOPTED YOU FROM A GROUP IN AFRICA-- THEY'RE LIKE US.
WHAT DOES THAT MEAN?
YOU KNOW, IT DOESN'T MATTER, SON. JUST KNOW THAT WE LOVE YOU.
AND WE ALWAYS WILL.

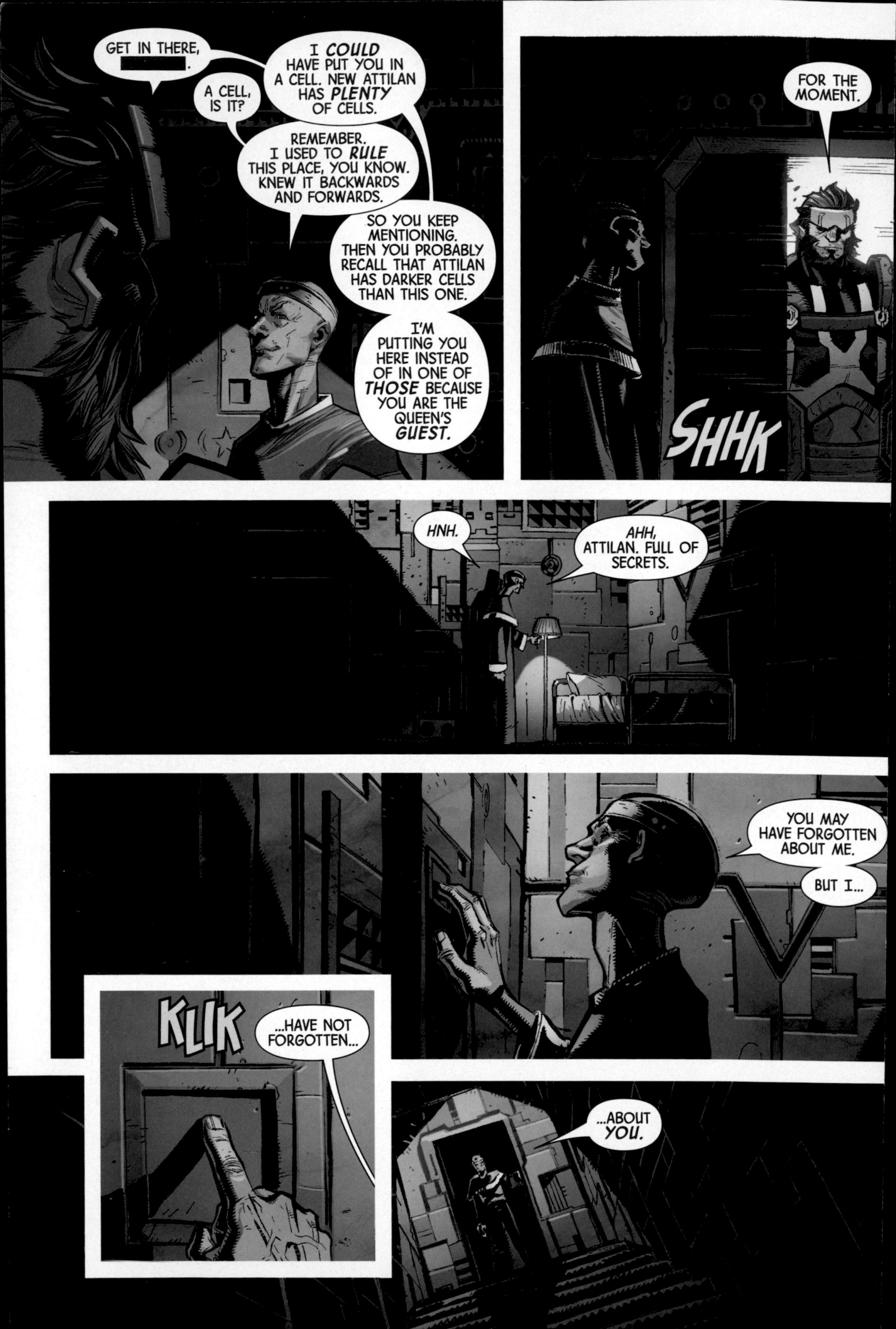
GET IN THERE, [redacted].
A CELL, IS IT?
I COULD HAVE PUT YOU IN A CELL. NEW ATTILAN HAS PLENTY OF CELLS.
REMEMBER. I USED TO RULE THIS PLACE, YOU KNOW. KNEW IT BACKWARDS AND FORWARDS.
SO YOU KEEP MENTIONING. THEN YOU PROBABLY RECALL THAT ATTILAN HAS DARKER CELLS THAN THIS ONE.
I'M PUTTING YOU HERE INSTEAD OF IN ONE OF THOSE BECAUSE YOU ARE THE QUEEN'S GUEST.
FOR THE MOMENT.
SHHK
HNH.
AHH, ATTILAN. FULL OF SECRETS.
YOU MAY HAVE FORGOTTEN ABOUT ME.
BUT I...
KLIK
...HAVE NOT FORGOTTEN...
...ABOUT YOU.

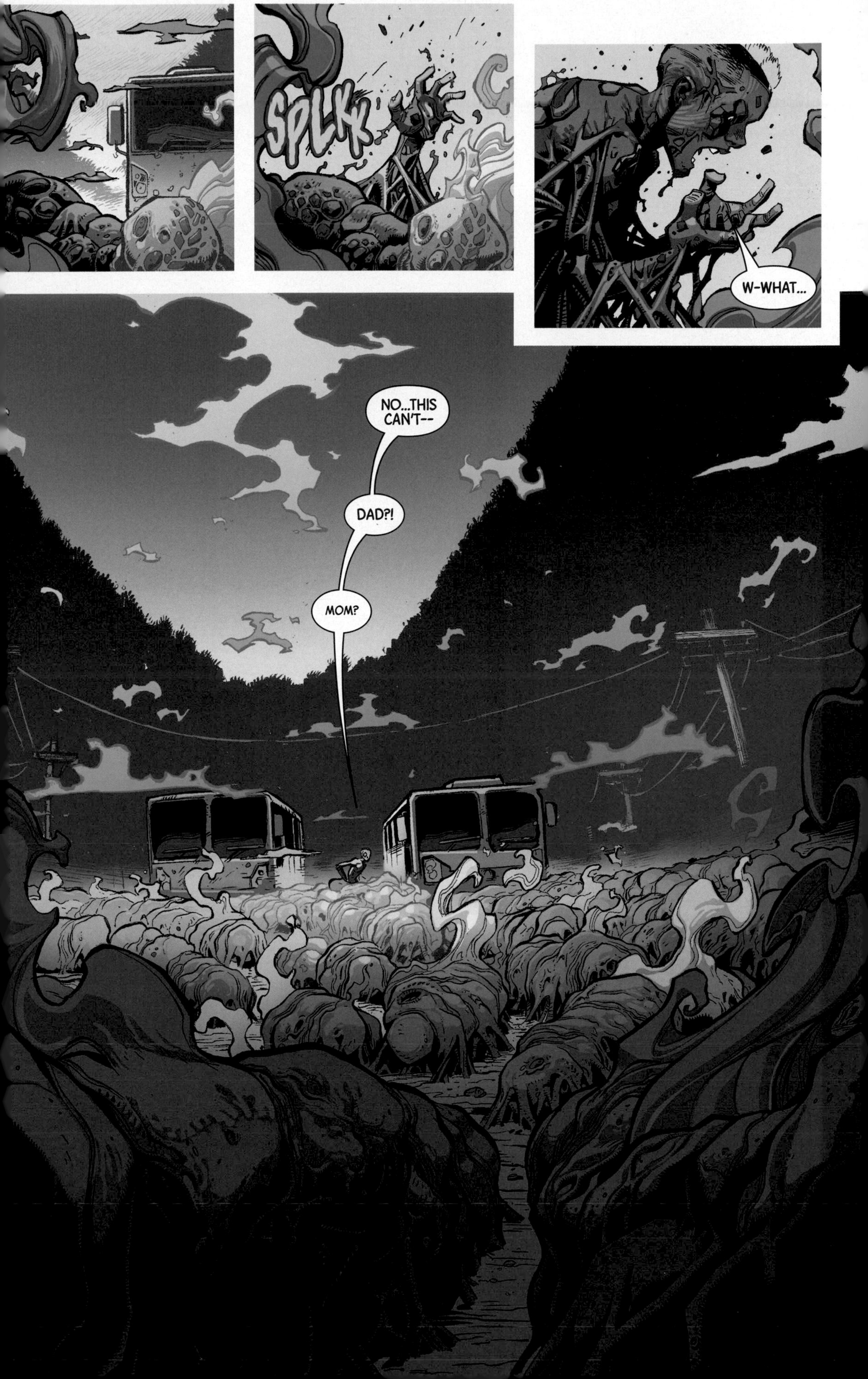
SPLKK
W-WHAT...
NO...THIS CAN'T--
DAD?!
MOM?

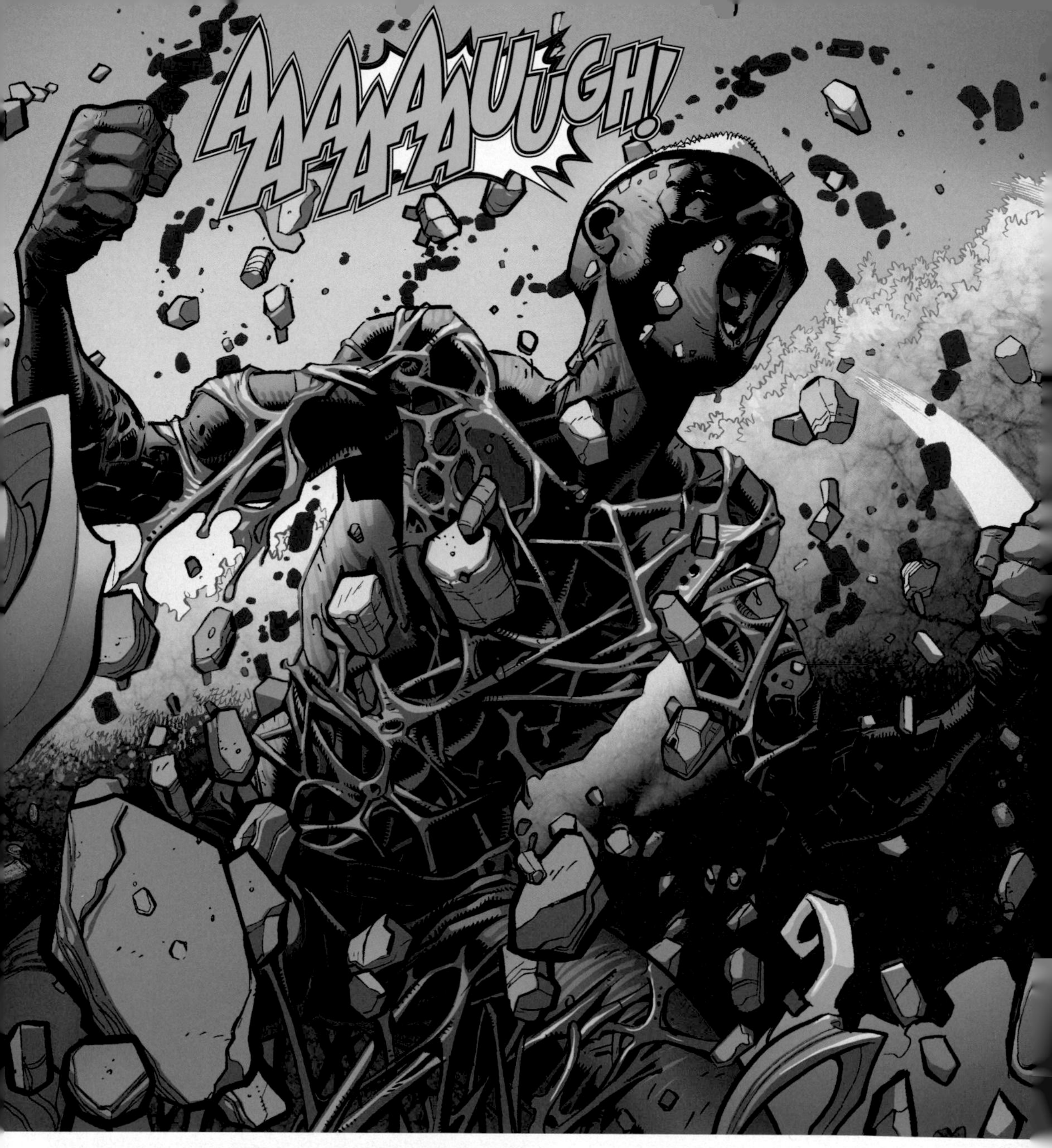
AAAAAUUGH!

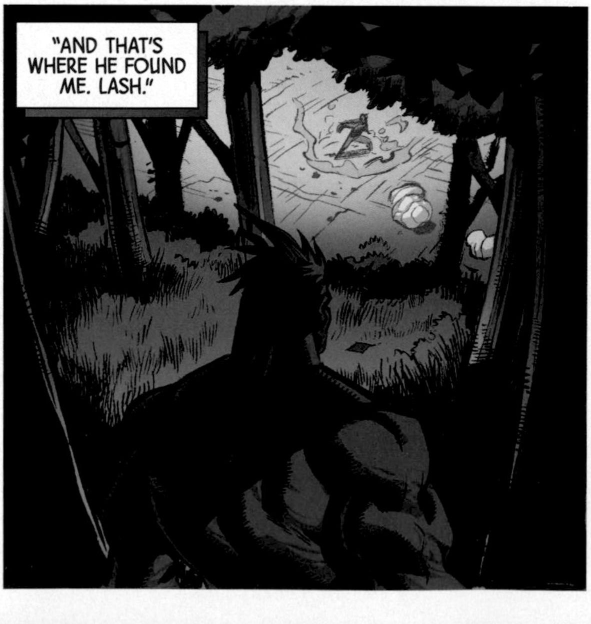
"AND THAT'S WHERE HE FOUND ME. LASH."

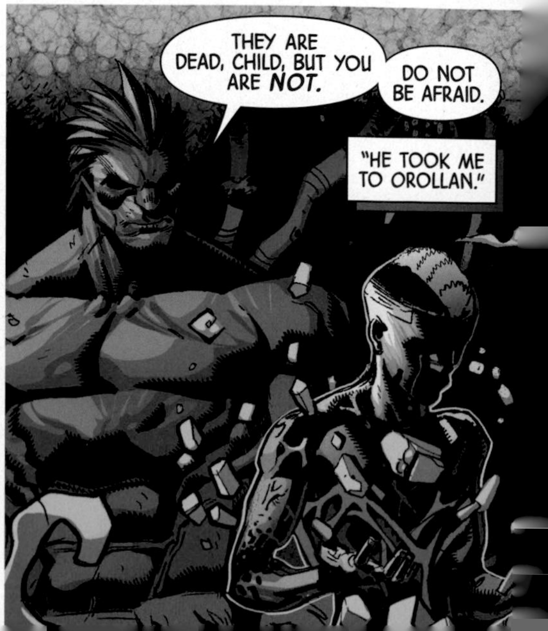
THEY ARE DEAD, CHILD, BUT YOU ARE NOT.
DO NOT BE AFRAID.
"HE TOOK ME TO OROLLAN."

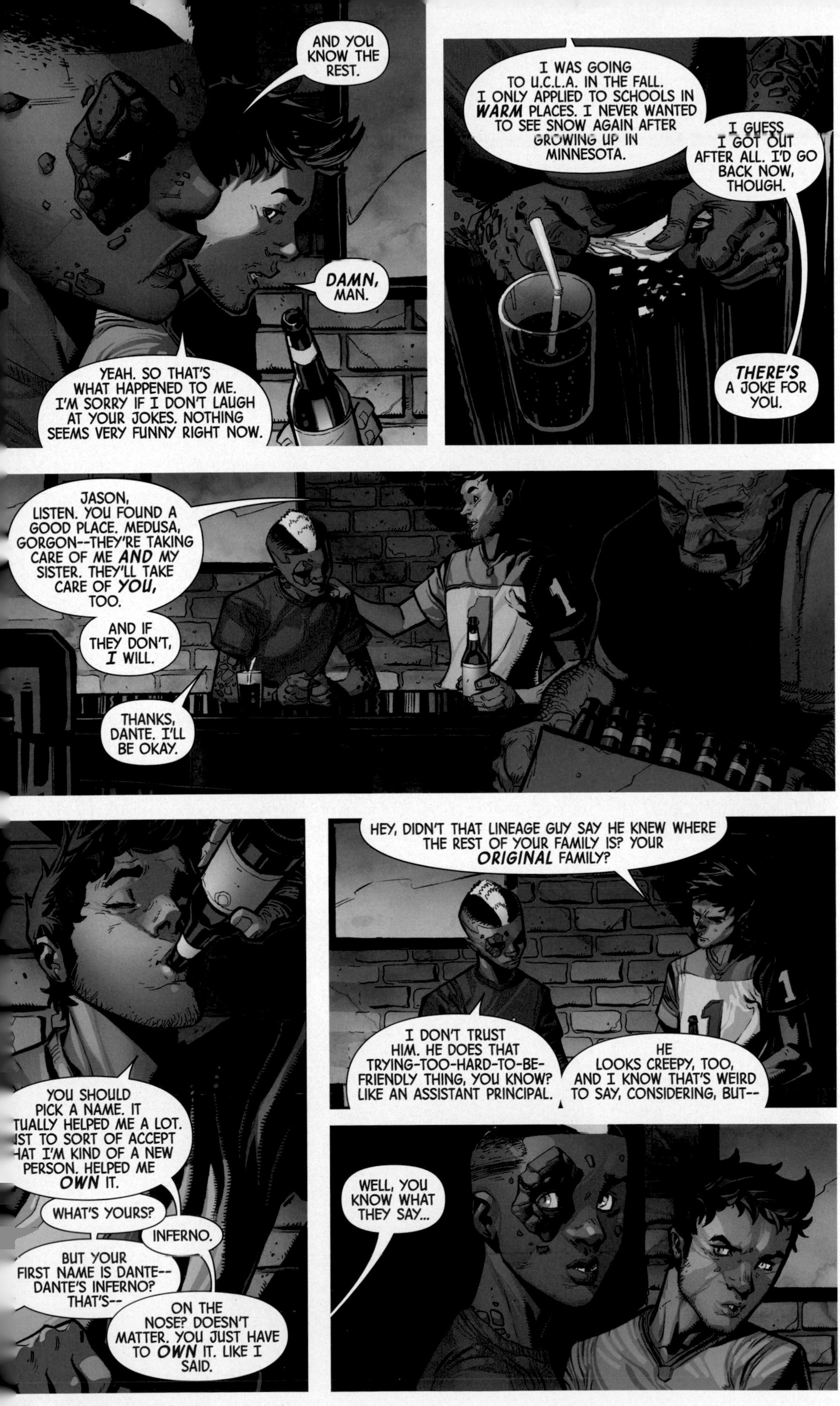
AND YOU KNOW THE REST.
DAMN, MAN.
YEAH. SO THAT'S WHAT HAPPENED TO ME. I'M SORRY IF I DON'T LAUGH AT YOUR JOKES. NOTHING SEEMS VERY FUNNY RIGHT NOW.
I WAS GOING TO U.C.L.A. IN THE FALL. I ONLY APPLIED TO SCHOOLS IN WARM PLACES. I NEVER WANTED TO SEE SNOW AGAIN AFTER GROWING UP IN MINNESOTA.
I GUESS I GOT OUT AFTER ALL. I'D GO BACK NOW, THOUGH.
THERE'S A JOKE FOR YOU.
JASON, LISTEN. YOU FOUND A GOOD PLACE. MEDUSA, GORGON--THEY'RE TAKING CARE OF ME AND MY SISTER. THEY'LL TAKE CARE OF YOU, TOO.
AND IF THEY DON'T, I WILL.
THANKS, DANTE. I'LL BE OKAY.
YOU SHOULD PICK A NAME. IT TUALLY HELPED ME A LOT. IST TO SORT OF ACCEPT HAT I'M KIND OF A NEW PERSON. HELPED ME OWN IT.
WHAT'S YOURS?
INFERNO.
BUT YOUR FIRST NAME IS DANTE-- DANTE'S INFERNO? THAT'S--
ON THE NOSE? DOESN'T MATTER. YOU JUST HAVE TO OWN IT. LIKE I SAID.
HEY, DIDN'T THAT LINEAGE GUY SAY HE KNEW WHERE THE REST OF YOUR FAMILY IS? YOUR ORIGINAL FAMILY?
I DON'T TRUST HIM. HE DOES THAT TRYING-TOO-HARD-TO-BE-FRIENDLY THING, YOU KNOW? LIKE AN ASSISTANT PRINCIPAL.
HE LOOKS CREEPY, TOO, AND I KNOW THAT'S WEIRD TO SAY, CONSIDERING, BUT--
WELL, YOU KNOW WHAT THEY SAY...

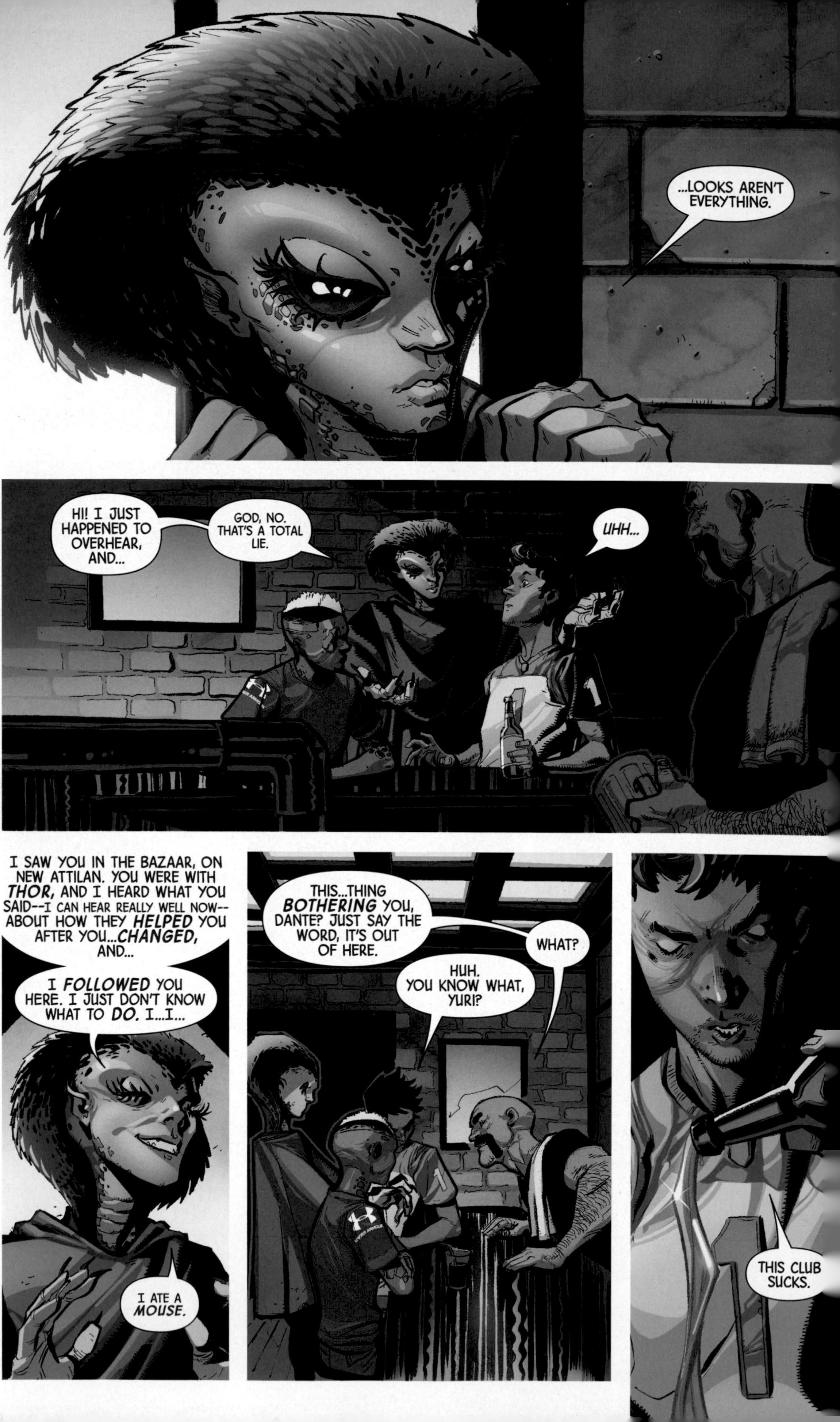
...LOOKS AREN'T EVERYTHING.
HI! I JUST HAPPENED TO OVERHEAR, AND...
GOD, NO. THAT'S A TOTAL LIE.
UHH...
I SAW YOU IN THE BAZAAR, ON NEW ATTILAN. YOU WERE WITH THOR, AND I HEARD WHAT YOU SAID--I CAN HEAR REALLY WELL NOW--ABOUT HOW THEY HELPED YOU AFTER YOU...CHANGED, AND...
I FOLLOWED YOU HERE. I JUST DON'T KNOW WHAT TO DO. I...I...
I ATE A MOUSE.
THIS...THING BOTHERING YOU, DANTE? JUST SAY THE WORD, IT'S OUT OF HERE.
WHAT?
HUH. YOU KNOW WHAT, YURI?
THIS CLUB SUCKS.

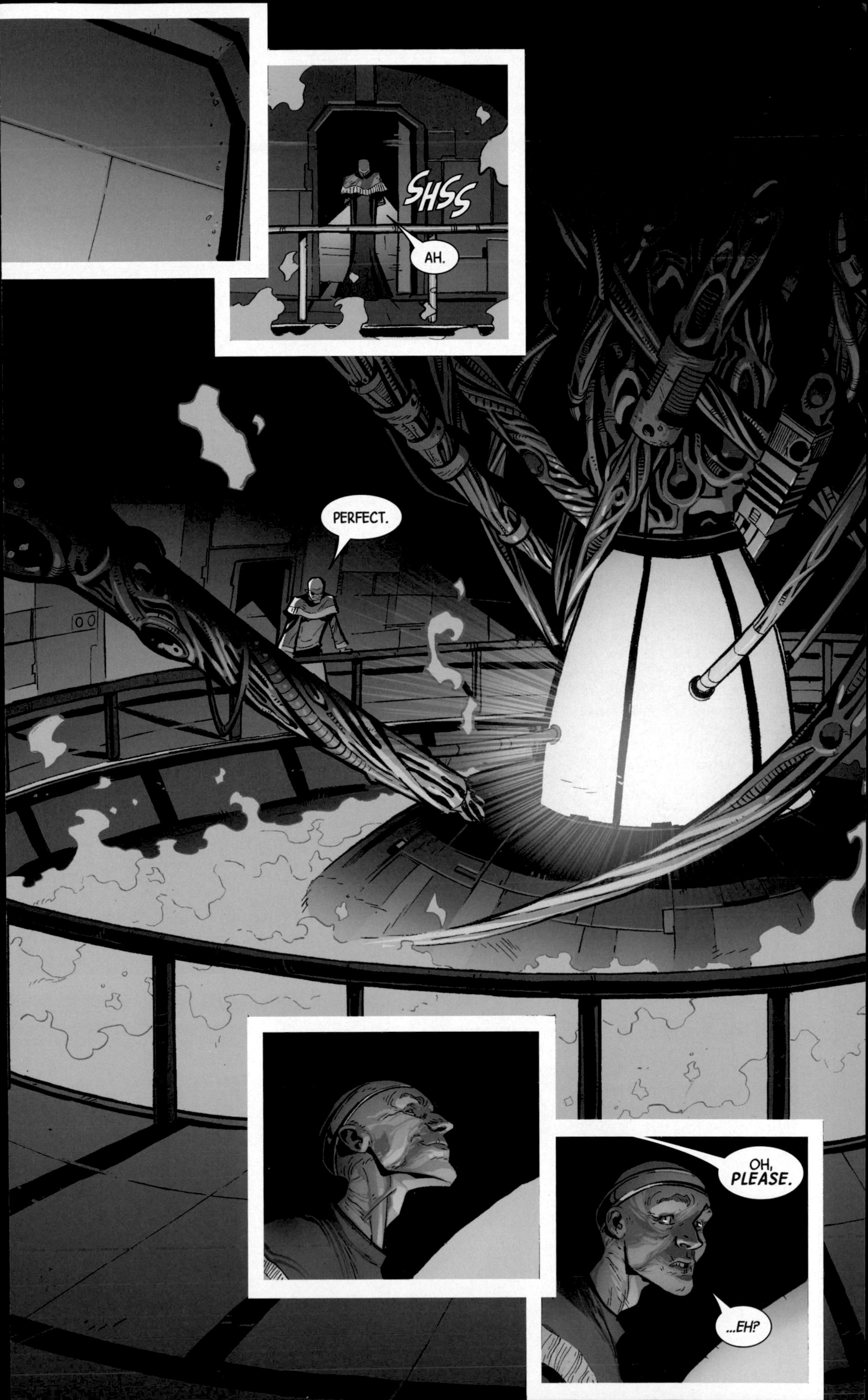
SHSS
AH.
PERFECT.
OH, PLEASE.
...EH?

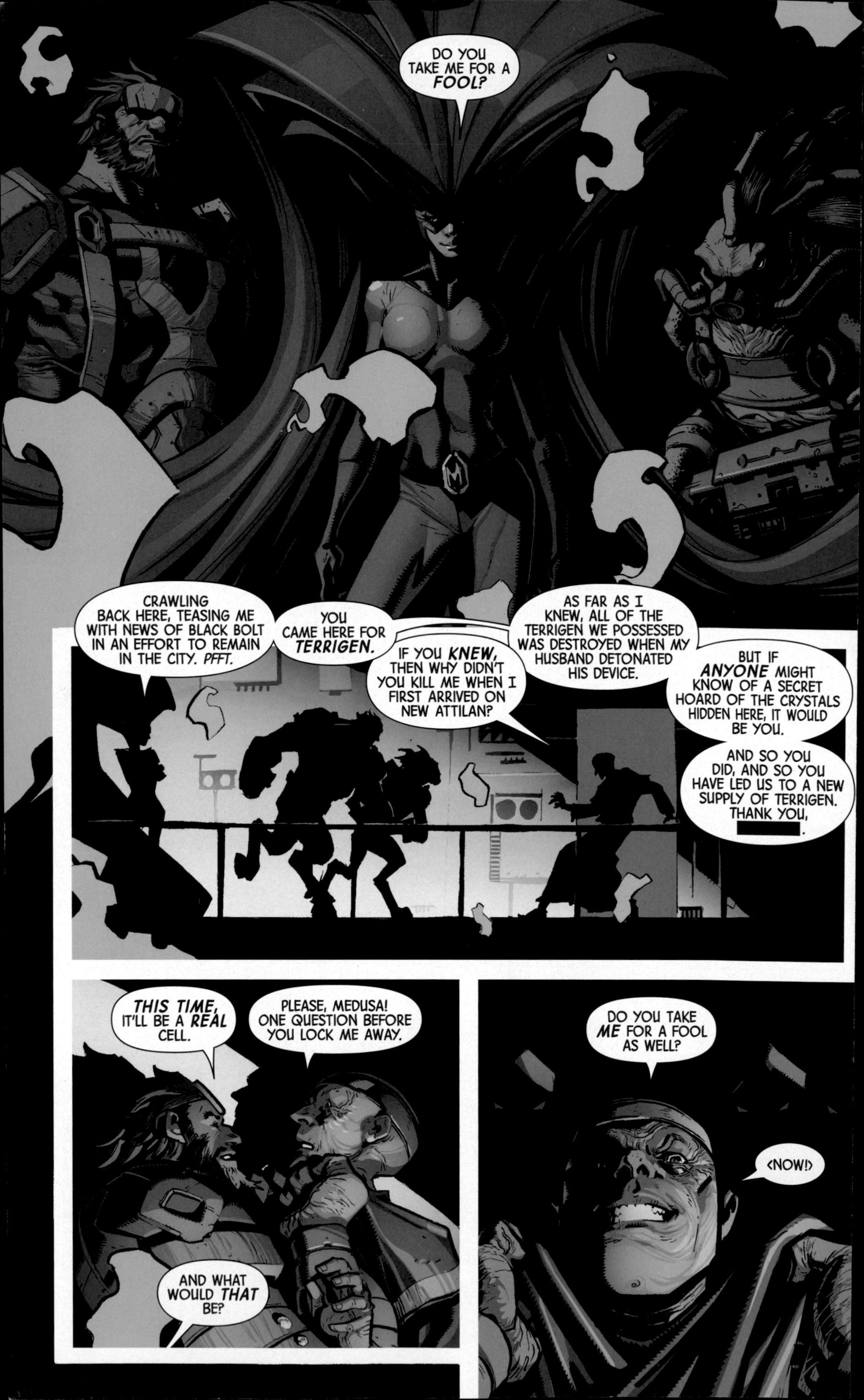
DO YOU TAKE ME FOR A FOOL?
CRAWLING BACK HERE, TEASING ME WITH NEWS OF BLACK BOLT IN AN EFFORT TO REMAIN IN THE CITY. PFFT.
YOU CAME HERE FOR TERRIGEN.
IF YOU KNEW, THEN WHY DIDN'T YOU KILL ME WHEN I FIRST ARRIVED ON NEW ATTILAN?
AS FAR AS I KNEW, ALL OF THE TERRIGEN WE POSSESSED WAS DESTROYED WHEN MY HUSBAND DETONATED HIS DEVICE.
BUT IF ANYONE MIGHT KNOW OF A SECRET HOARD OF THE CRYSTALS HIDDEN HERE, IT WOULD BE YOU.
AND SO YOU DID, AND SO YOU HAVE LED US TO A NEW SUPPLY OF TERRIGEN. THANK YOU, [redacted].
THIS TIME, IT'LL BE A REAL CELL.
PLEASE, MEDUSA! ONE QUESTION BEFORE YOU LOCK ME AWAY.
AND WHAT WOULD THAT BE?
DO YOU TAKE ME FOR A FOOL AS WELL?
<NOW!>

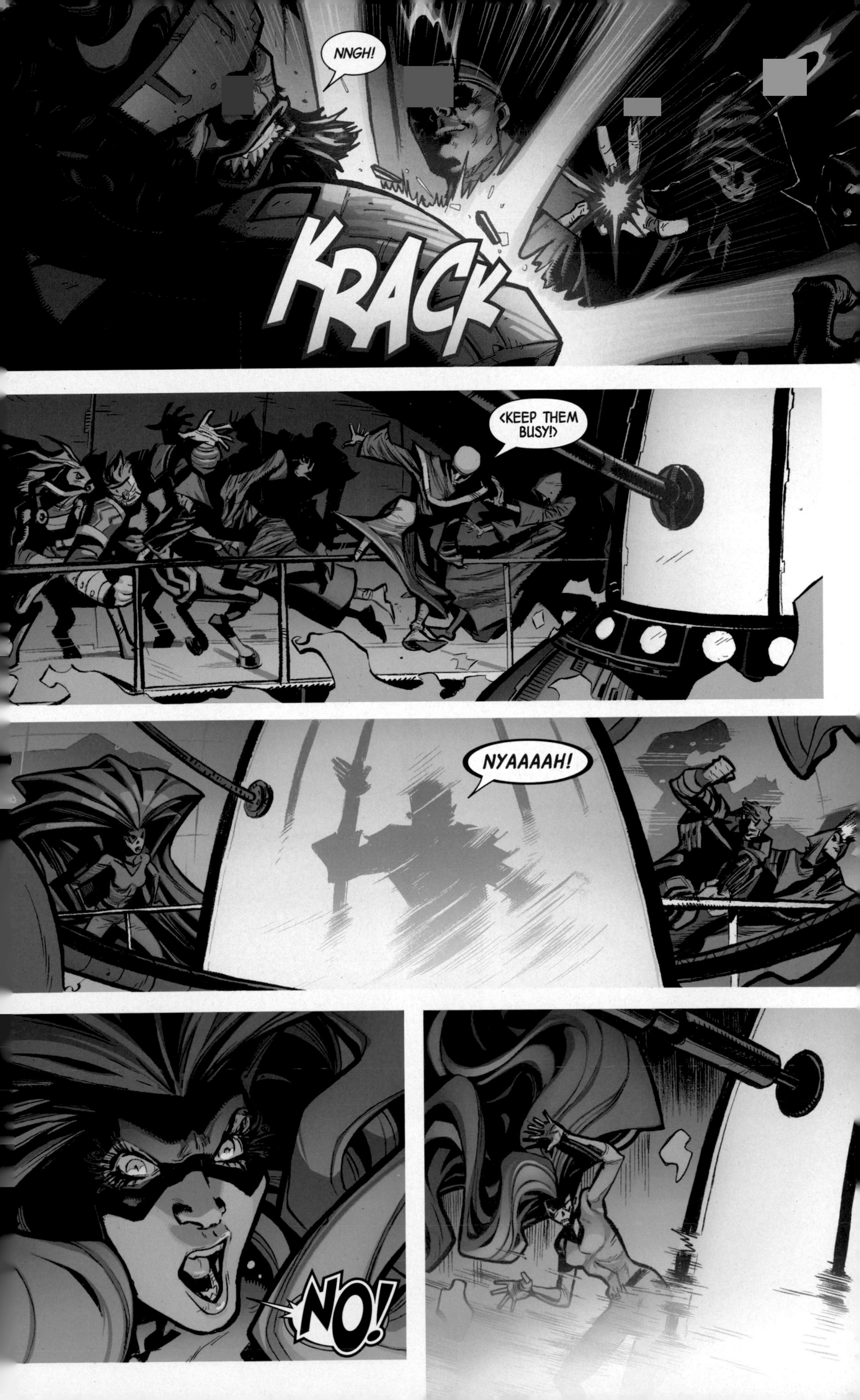
NNGH!
KRACK
<KEEP THEM BUSY!>
NYAAAAH!
NO!

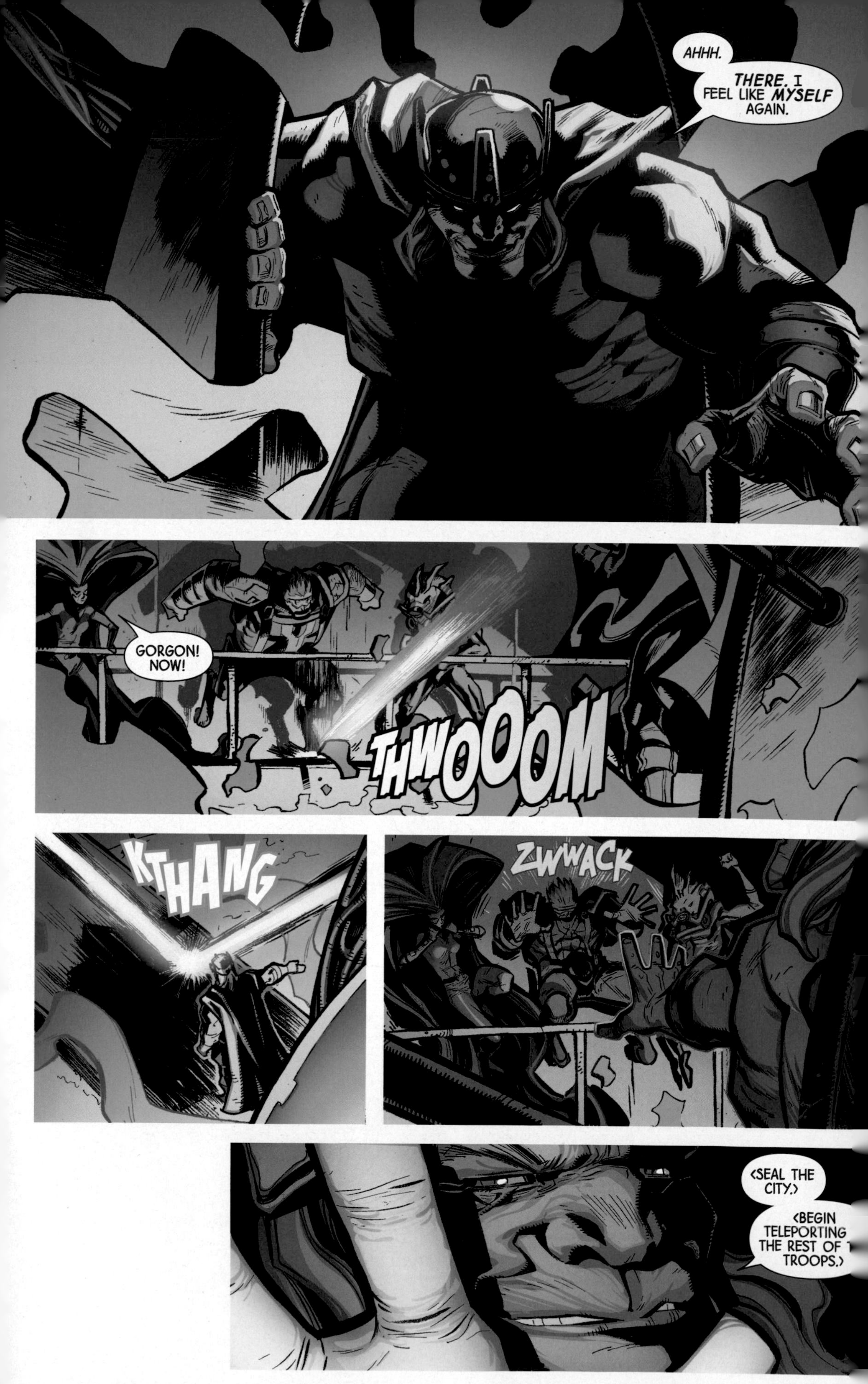
AHHH.
THERE. I FEEL LIKE MYSELF AGAIN.
GORGON! NOW!
THWOOOM
KTHANG
ZWWACK
<SEAL THE CITY.>
<BEGIN TELEPORTING THE REST OF T TROOPS.>

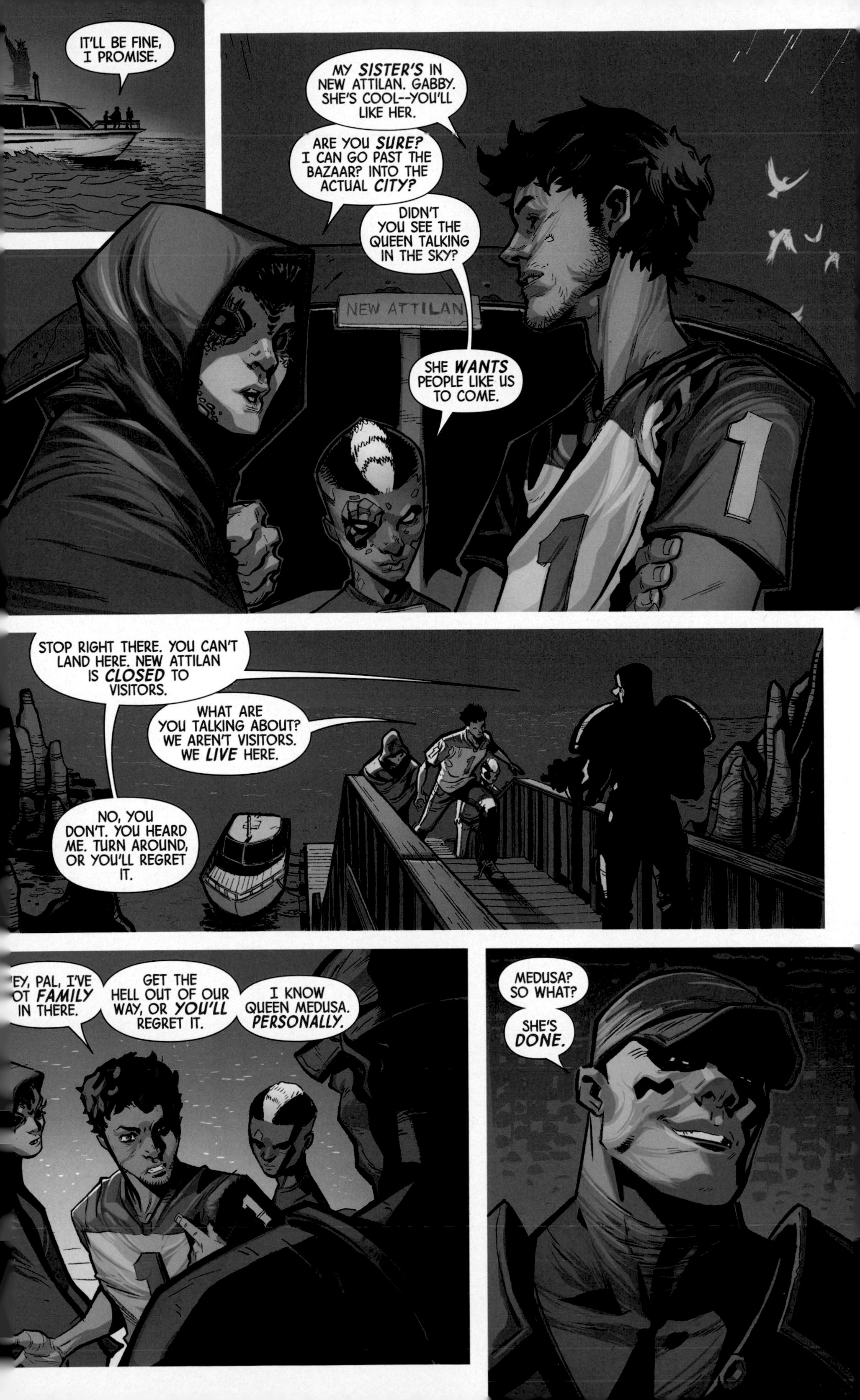
IT'LL BE FINE, I PROMISE.
MY SISTER'S IN NEW ATTILAN. GABBY. SHE'S COOL--YOU'LL LIKE HER.
ARE YOU SURE? I CAN GO PAST THE BAZAAR? INTO THE ACTUAL CITY?
DIDN'T YOU SEE THE QUEEN TALKING IN THE SKY?
NEW ATTILAN
SHE WANTS PEOPLE LIKE US TO COME.
STOP RIGHT THERE. YOU CAN'T LAND HERE. NEW ATTILAN IS CLOSED TO VISITORS.
WHAT ARE YOU TALKING ABOUT? WE AREN'T VISITORS. WE LIVE HERE.
NO, YOU DON'T. YOU HEARD ME. TURN AROUND, OR YOU'LL REGRET IT.
EY, PAL, I'VE OT FAMILY IN THERE.
GET THE HELL OUT OF OUR WAY, OR YOU'LL REGRET IT.
I KNOW QUEEN MEDUSA. PERSONALLY.
MEDUSA? SO WHAT?
SHE'S DONE.

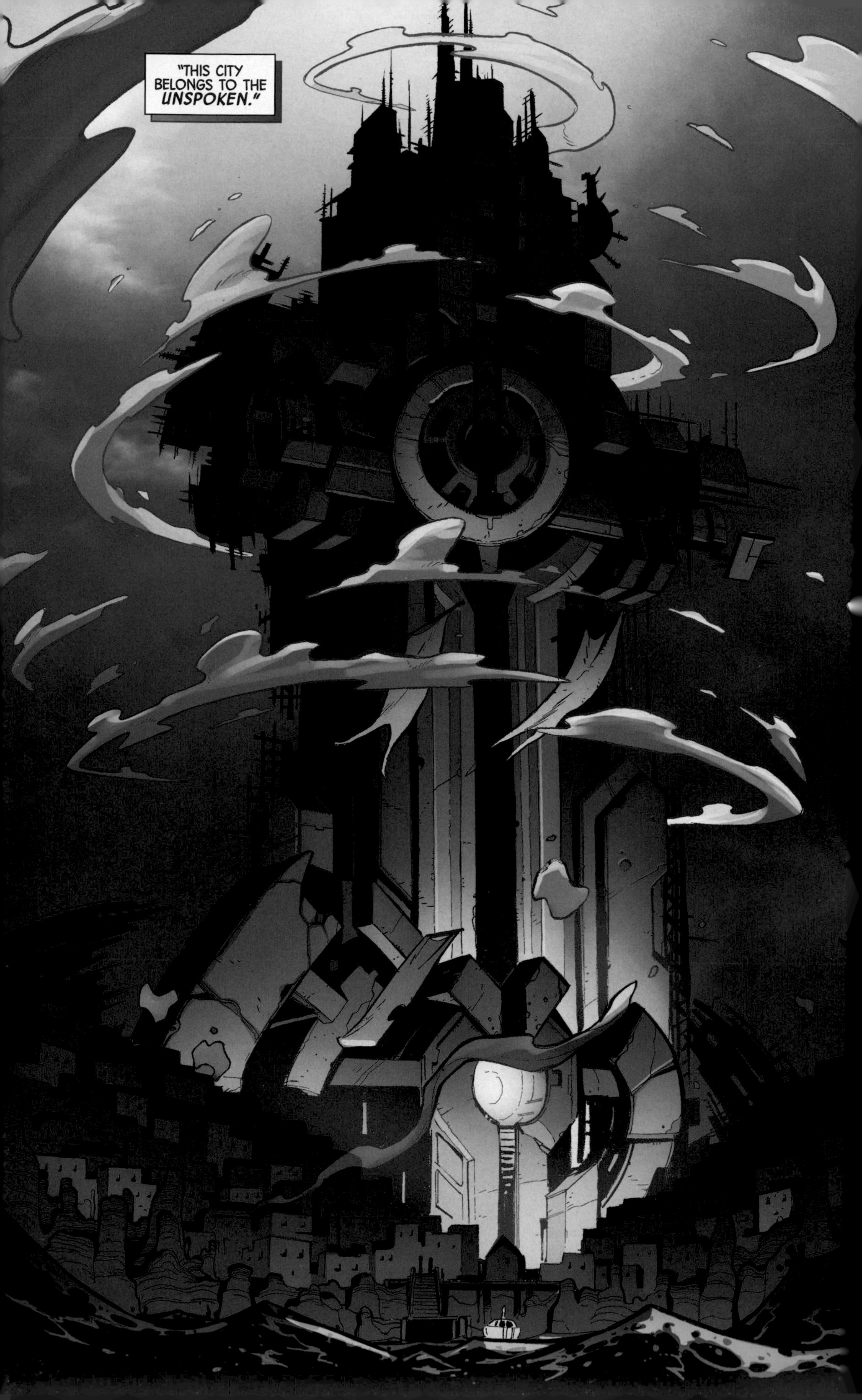
"THIS CITY BELONGS TO THE UNSPOKEN."

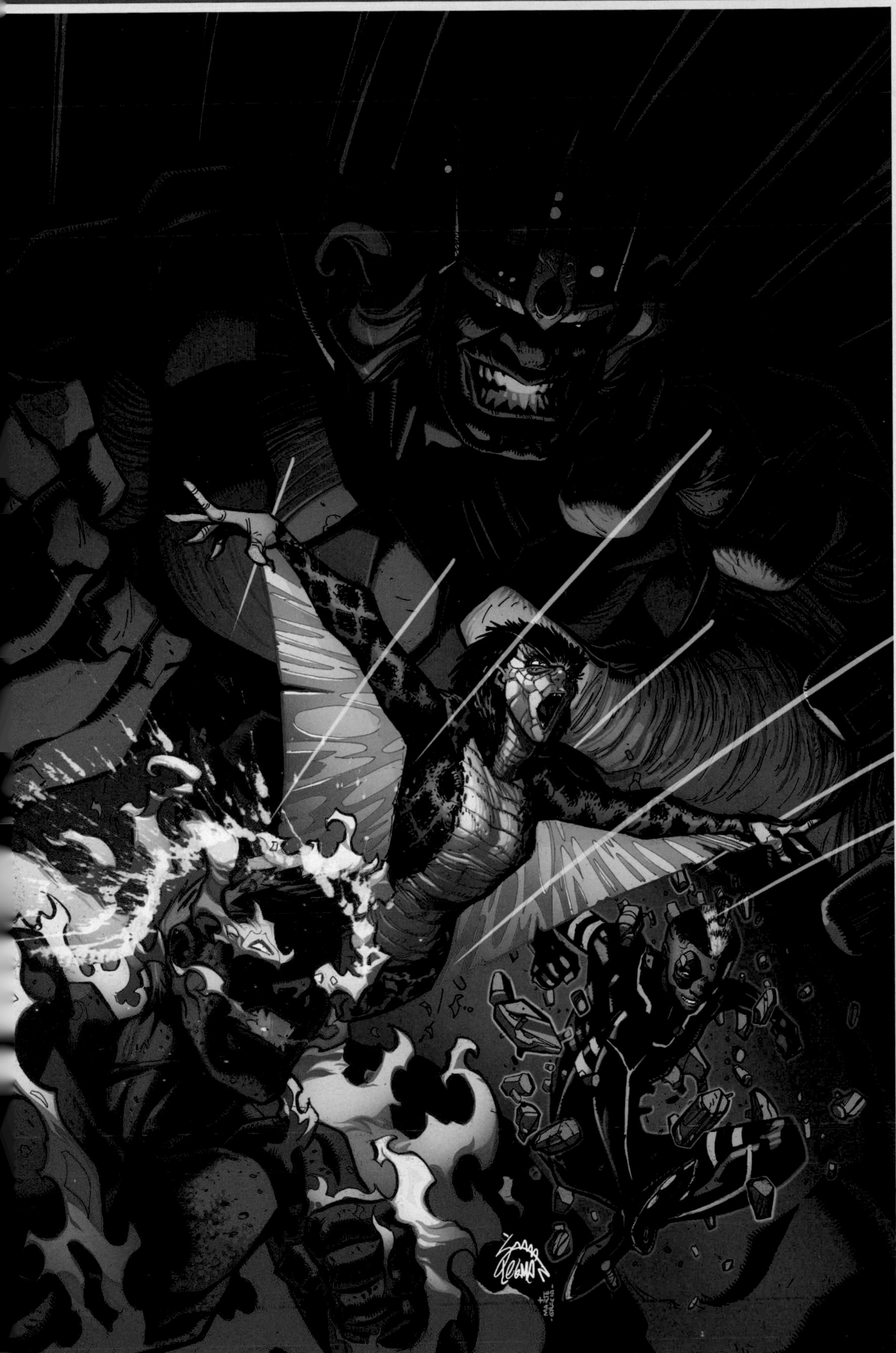

6

PART SIX: TRIAL BY FIRE

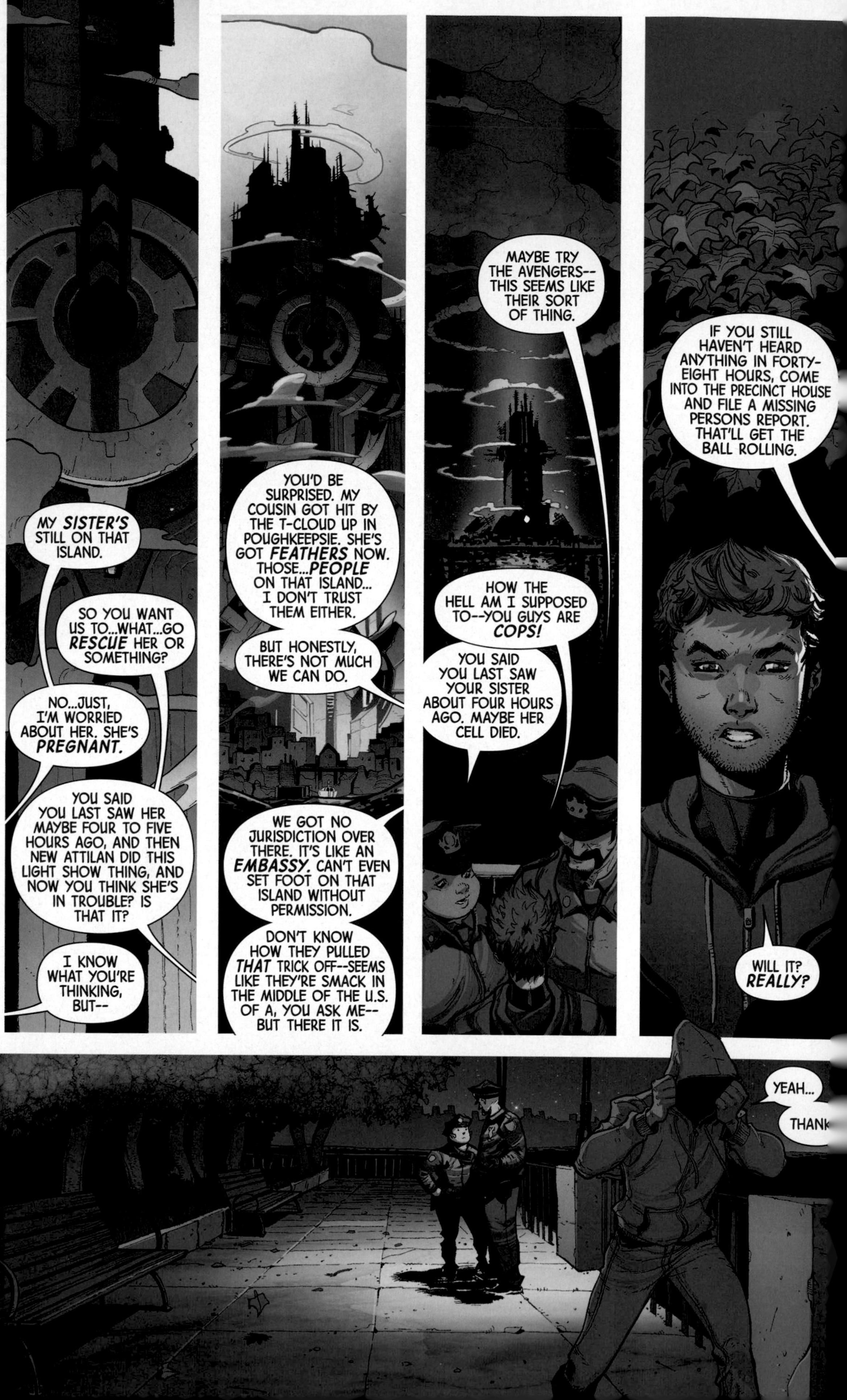

MY SISTER'S STILL ON THAT ISLAND.
SO YOU WANT US TO...WHAT...GO RESCUE HER OR SOMETHING?
NO...JUST, I'M WORRIED ABOUT HER. SHE'S PREGNANT.
YOU SAID YOU LAST SAW HER MAYBE FOUR TO FIVE HOURS AGO, AND THEN NEW ATTILAN DID THIS LIGHT SHOW THING, AND NOW YOU THINK SHE'S IN TROUBLE? IS THAT IT?
I KNOW WHAT YOU'RE THINKING, BUT--
YOU'D BE SURPRISED. MY COUSIN GOT HIT BY THE T-CLOUD UP IN POUGHKEEPSIE. SHE'S GOT FEATHERS NOW. THOSE...PEOPLE ON THAT ISLAND... I DON'T TRUST THEM EITHER.
BUT HONESTLY, THERE'S NOT MUCH WE CAN DO.
WE GOT NO JURISDICTION OVER THERE. IT'S LIKE AN EMBASSY. CAN'T EVEN SET FOOT ON THAT ISLAND WITHOUT PERMISSION.
DON'T KNOW HOW THEY PULLED THAT TRICK OFF--SEEMS LIKE THEY'RE SMACK IN THE MIDDLE OF THE U.S. OF A, YOU ASK ME-- BUT THERE IT IS.
MAYBE TRY THE AVENGERS-- THIS SEEMS LIKE THEIR SORT OF THING.
HOW THE HELL AM I SUPPOSED TO--YOU GUYS ARE COPS!
YOU SAID YOU LAST SAW YOUR SISTER ABOUT FOUR HOURS AGO. MAYBE HER CELL DIED.
IF YOU STILL HAVEN'T HEARD ANYTHING IN FORTY-EIGHT HOURS, COME INTO THE PRECINCT HOUSE AND FILE A MISSING PERSONS REPORT. THAT'LL GET THE BALL ROLLING.
WILL IT? REALLY?
YEAH...
THANK

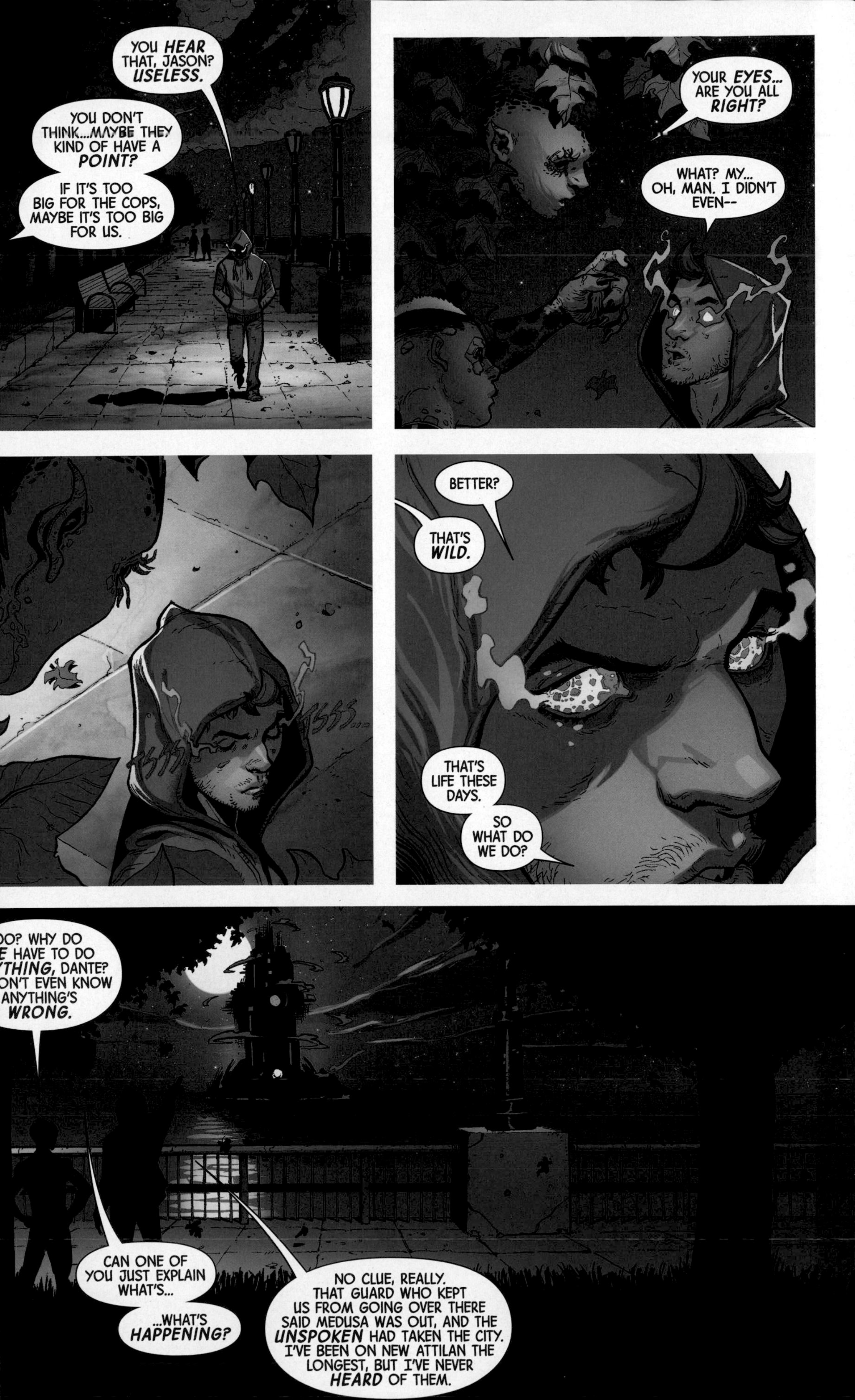
YOU HEAR THAT, JASON? USELESS.
YOU DON'T THINK...MAYBE THEY KIND OF HAVE A POINT?
IF IT'S TOO BIG FOR THE COPS, MAYBE IT'S TOO BIG FOR US.
YOUR EYES... ARE YOU ALL RIGHT?
WHAT? MY... OH, MAN. I DIDN'T EVEN--
TSSSS...
BETTER?
THAT'S WILD.
THAT'S LIFE THESE DAYS.
SO WHAT DO WE DO?
DO? WHY DO WE HAVE TO DO ANYTHING, DANTE? DON'T EVEN KNOW ANYTHING'S WRONG.
CAN ONE OF YOU JUST EXPLAIN WHAT'S...
...WHAT'S HAPPENING?
NO CLUE, REALLY. THAT GUARD WHO KEPT US FROM GOING OVER THERE SAID MEDUSA WAS OUT, AND THE UNSPOKEN HAD TAKEN THE CITY. I'VE BEEN ON NEW ATTILAN THE LONGEST, BUT I'VE NEVER HEARD OF THEM.

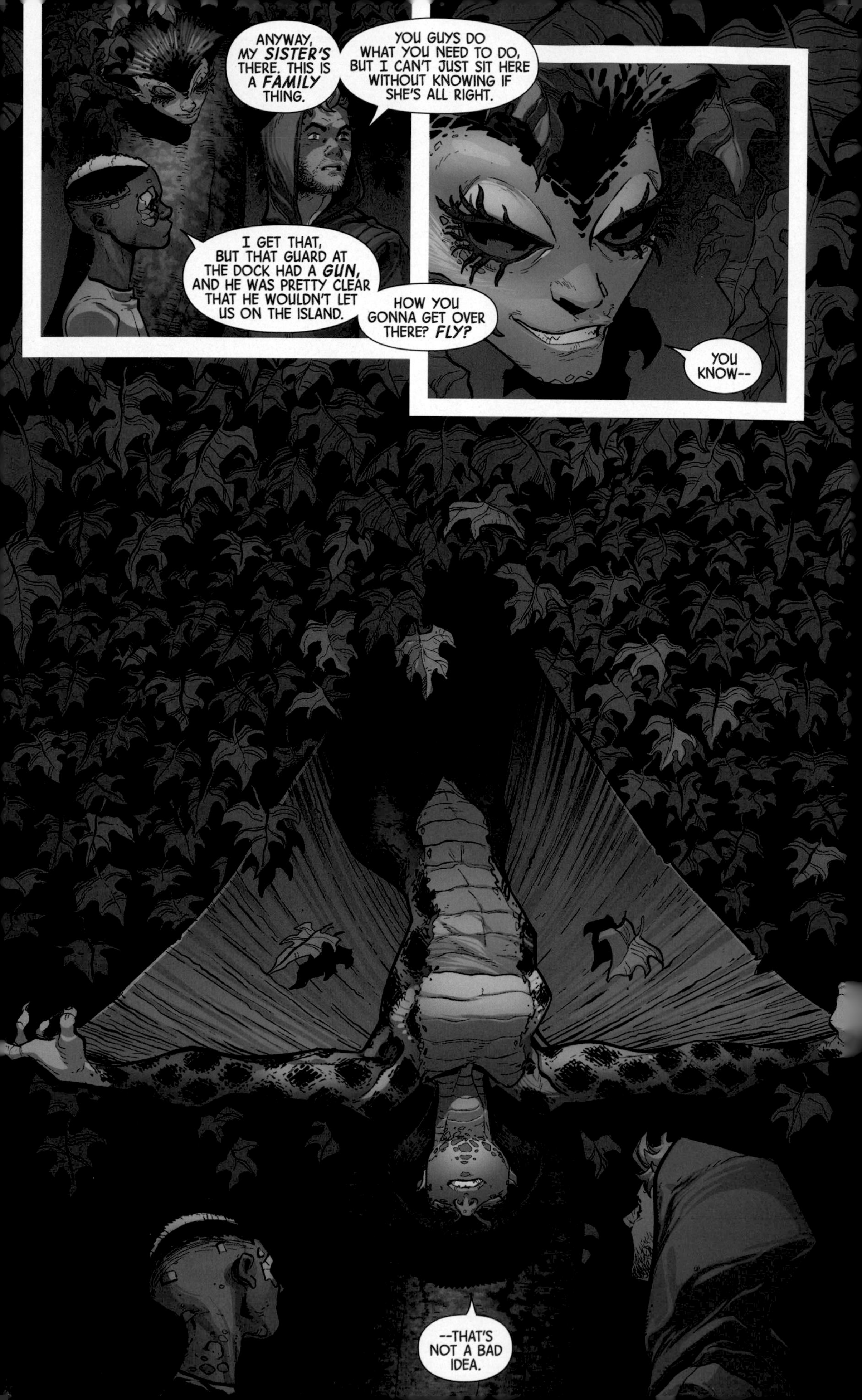
ANYWAY, MY SISTER'S THERE. THIS IS A FAMILY THING.
YOU GUYS DO WHAT YOU NEED TO DO, BUT I CAN'T JUST SIT HERE WITHOUT KNOWING IF SHE'S ALL RIGHT.
I GET THAT, BUT THAT GUARD AT THE DOCK HAD A GUN, AND HE WAS PRETTY CLEAR THAT HE WOULDN'T LET US ON THE ISLAND.
HOW YOU GONNA GET OVER THERE? FLY?
YOU KNOW--
--THAT'S NOT A BAD IDEA.

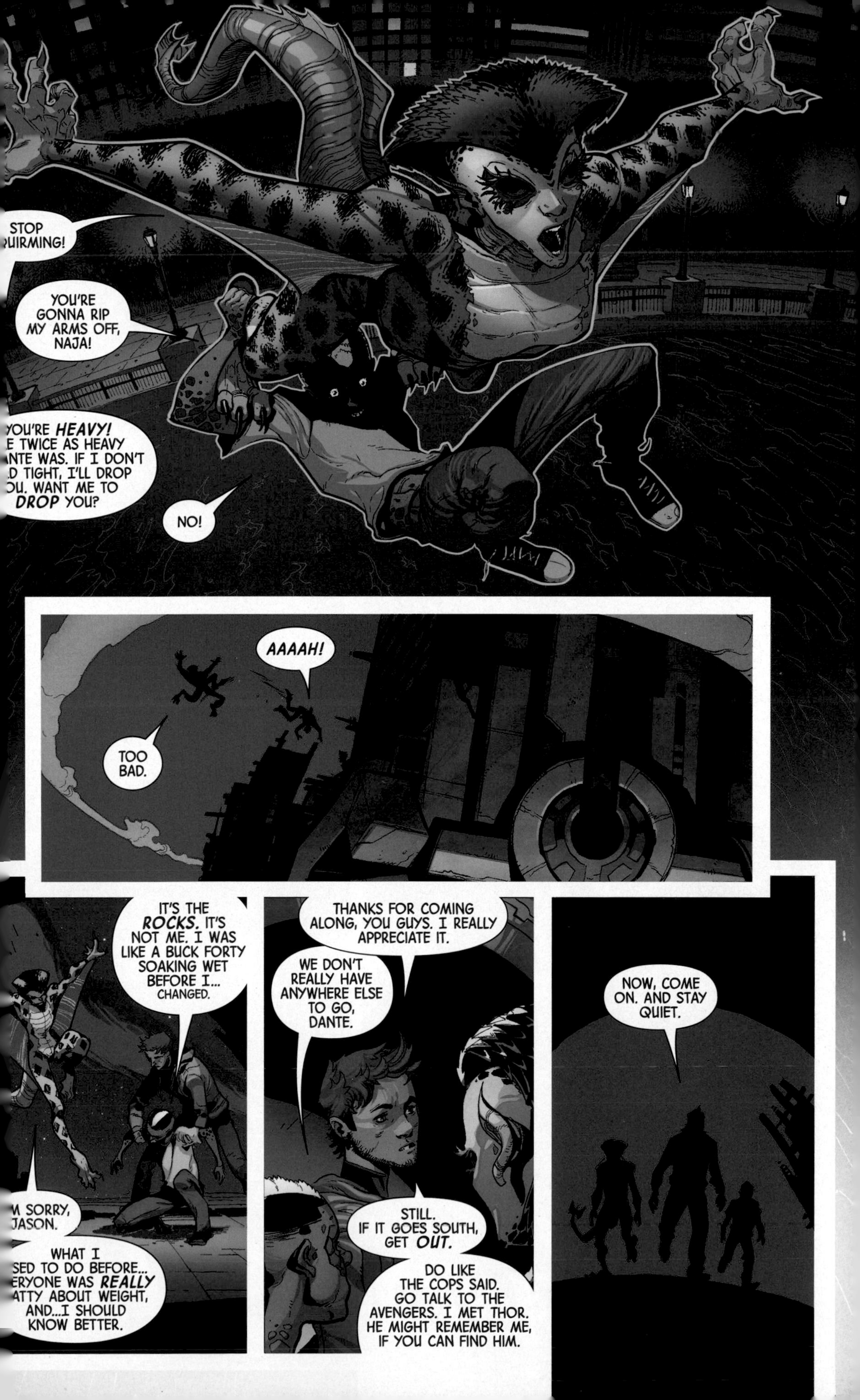
STOP
UIRMING!
YOU'RE GONNA RIP MY ARMS OFF, NAJA!
YOU'RE HEAVY! E TWICE AS HEAVY NTE WAS. IF I DON'T D TIGHT, I'LL DROP U. WANT ME TO DROP YOU?
NO!
AAAAH!
TOO BAD.
IT'S THE ROCKS. IT'S NOT ME. I WAS LIKE A BUCK FORTY SOAKING WET BEFORE I... CHANGED.
M SORRY, JASON.
WHAT I SED TO DO BEFORE... ERYONE WAS REALLY ATTY ABOUT WEIGHT, AND...I SHOULD KNOW BETTER.
THANKS FOR COMING ALONG, YOU GUYS. I REALLY APPRECIATE IT.
WE DON'T REALLY HAVE ANYWHERE ELSE TO GO, DANTE.
STILL. IF IT GOES SOUTH, GET OUT.
DO LIKE THE COPS SAID. GO TALK TO THE AVENGERS. I MET THOR. HE MIGHT REMEMBER ME, IF YOU CAN FIND HIM.
NOW, COME ON. AND STAY QUIET.

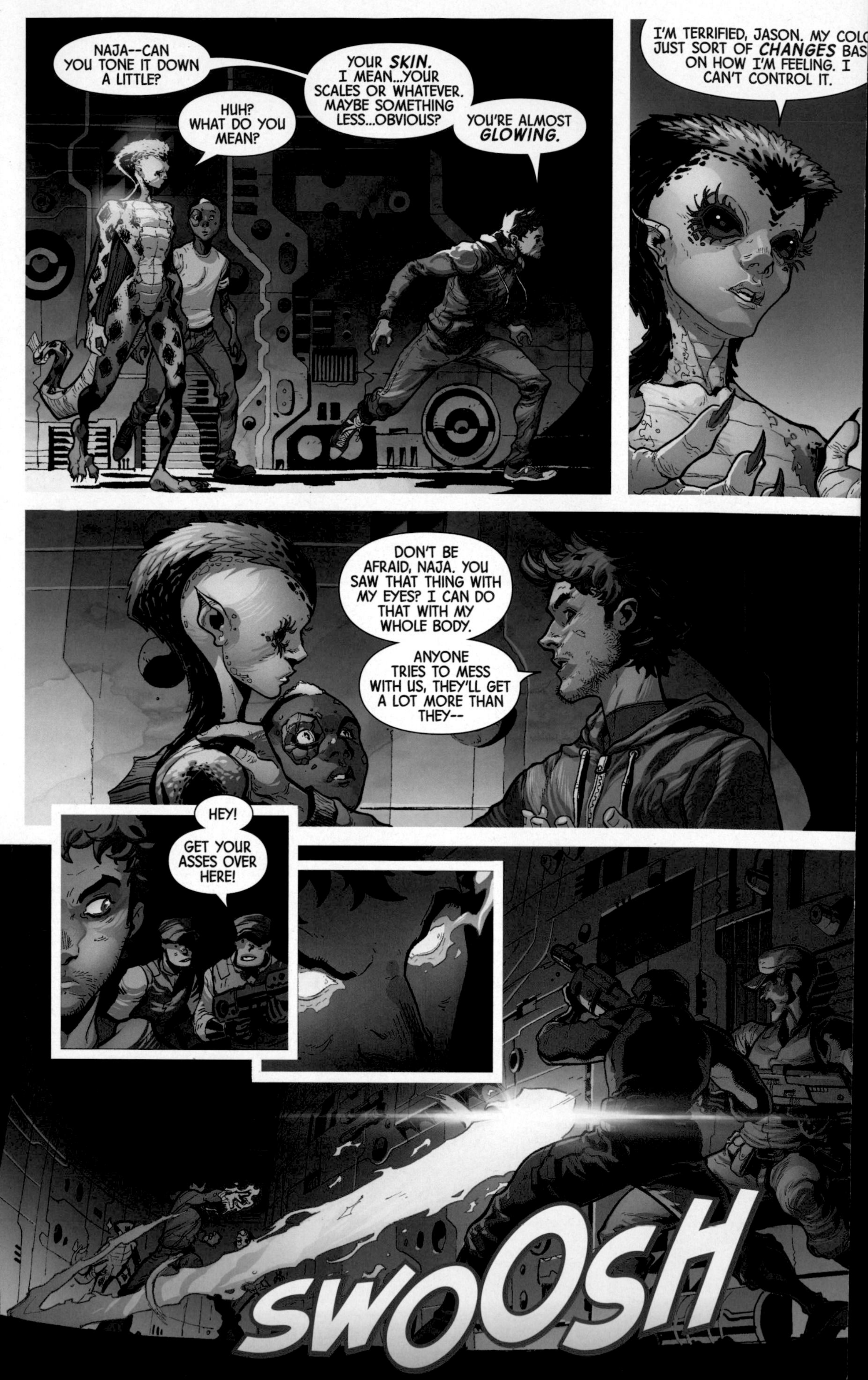
NAJA--CAN YOU TONE IT DOWN A LITTLE?
HUH? WHAT DO YOU MEAN?
YOUR SKIN. I MEAN...YOUR SCALES OR WHATEVER. MAYBE SOMETHING LESS...OBVIOUS?
YOU'RE ALMOST GLOWING.
DON'T BE AFRAID, NAJA. YOU SAW THAT THING WITH MY EYES? I CAN DO THAT WITH MY WHOLE BODY.
ANYONE TRIES TO MESS WITH US, THEY'LL GET A LOT MORE THAN THEY--
HEY!
GET YOUR ASSES OVER HERE!
SWOOSH

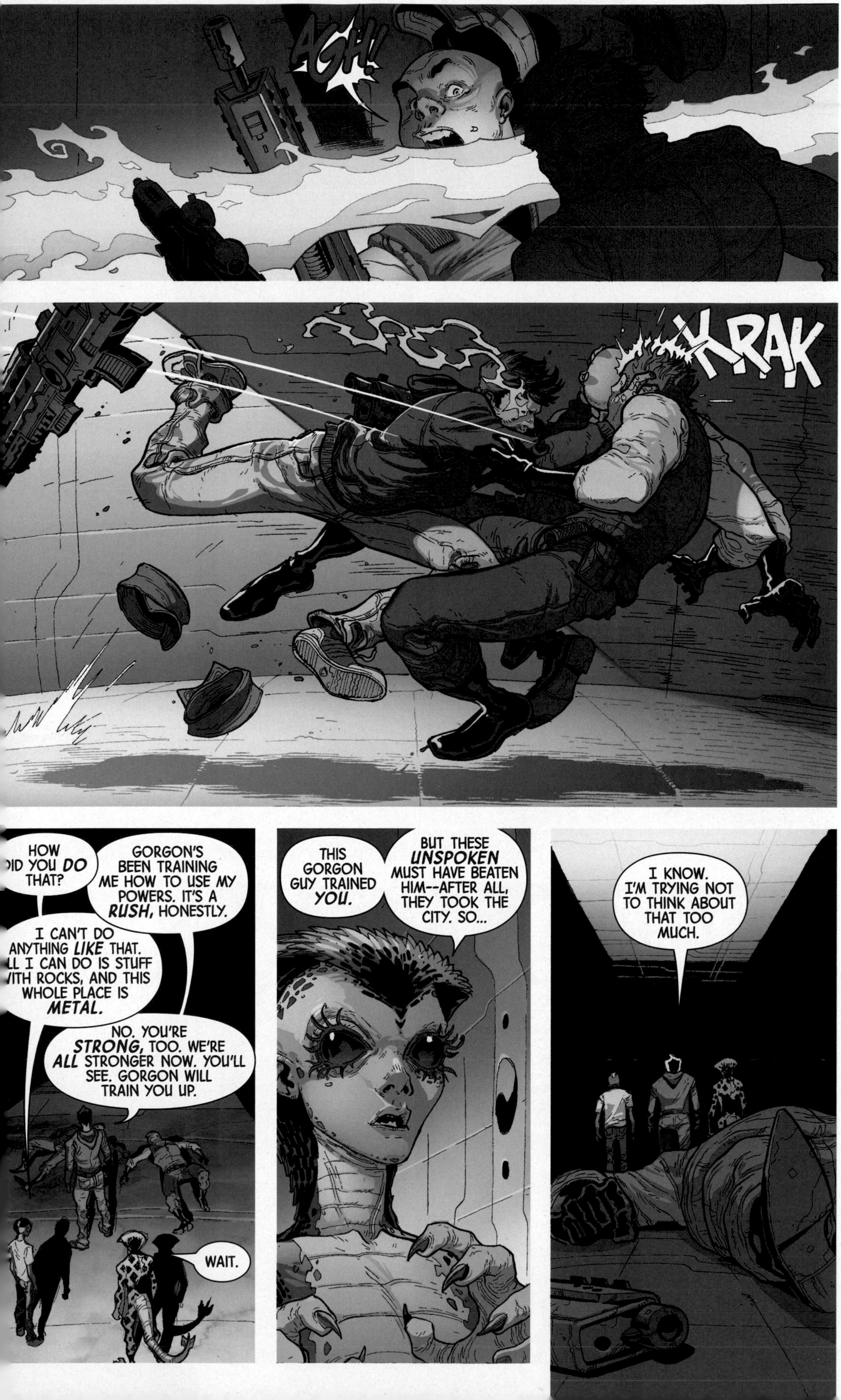
AGH!
KRAK
HOW DID YOU DO THAT?
GORGON'S BEEN TRAINING ME HOW TO USE MY POWERS. IT'S A RUSH, HONESTLY.
I CAN'T DO ANYTHING LIKE THAT. LL I CAN DO IS STUFF WITH ROCKS, AND THIS WHOLE PLACE IS METAL.
NO. YOU'RE STRONG, TOO. WE'RE ALL STRONGER NOW. YOU'LL SEE. GORGON WILL TRAIN YOU UP.
WAIT.
THIS GORGON GUY TRAINED YOU.
BUT THESE UNSPOKEN MUST HAVE BEATEN HIM--AFTER ALL, THEY TOOK THE CITY. SO...
I KNOW. I'M TRYING NOT TO THINK ABOUT THAT TOO MUCH.

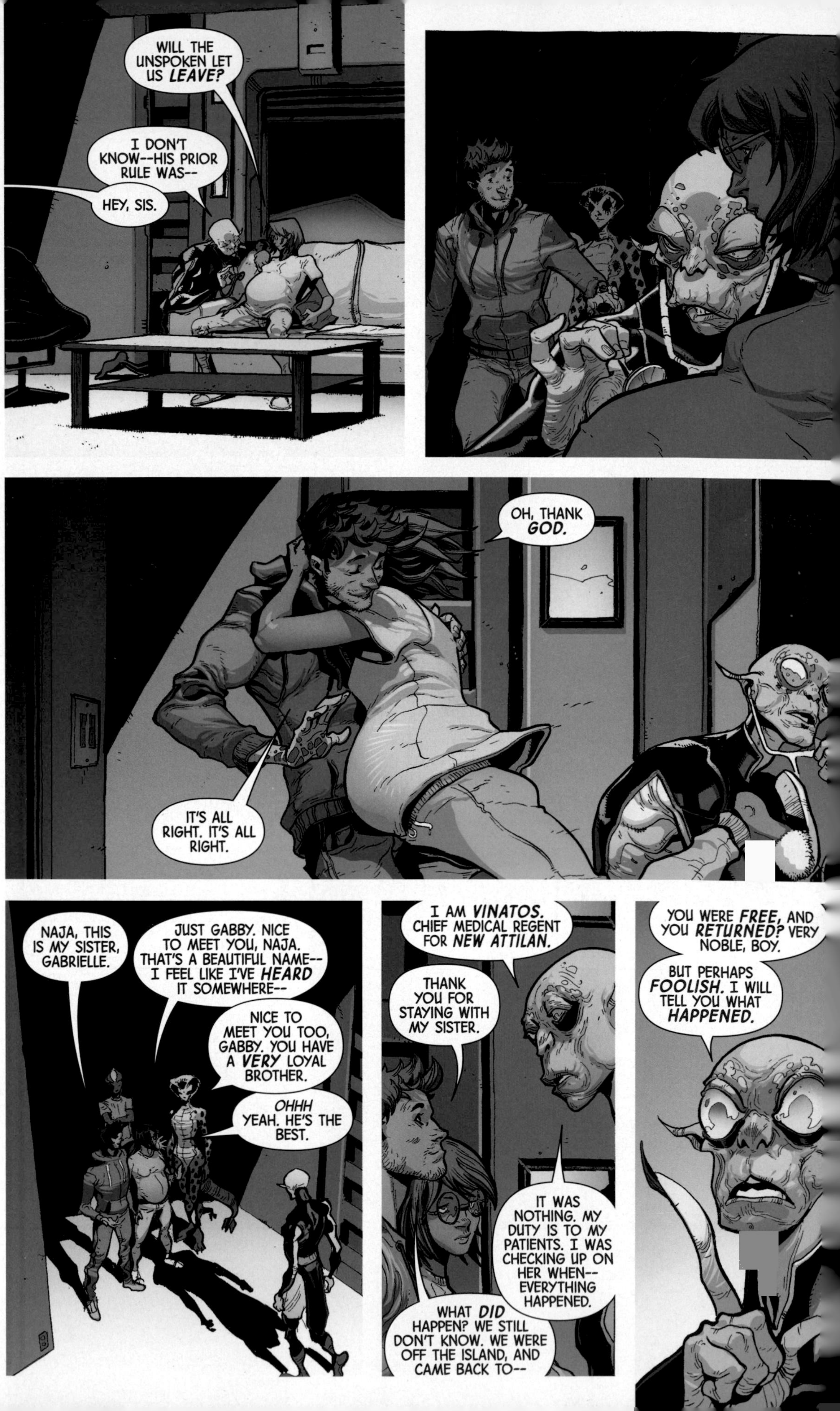
WILL THE UNSPOKEN LET US *LEAVE?*
I DON'T KNOW--HIS PRIOR RULE WAS--
HEY, SIS.
OH, THANK *GOD.*
IT'S ALL RIGHT. IT'S ALL RIGHT.
NAJA, THIS IS MY SISTER, GABRIELLE.
JUST GABBY. NICE TO MEET YOU, NAJA. THAT'S A BEAUTIFUL NAME--I FEEL LIKE I'VE *HEARD* IT SOMEWHERE--
NICE TO MEET YOU TOO, GABBY. YOU HAVE A *VERY* LOYAL BROTHER.
OHHH YEAH. HE'S THE BEST.
I AM *VINATOS.* CHIEF MEDICAL REGENT FOR *NEW ATTILAN.*
THANK YOU FOR STAYING WITH MY SISTER.
IT WAS NOTHING. MY DUTY IS TO MY PATIENTS. I WAS CHECKING UP ON HER WHEN--EVERYTHING HAPPENED.
WHAT *DID* HAPPEN? WE STILL DON'T KNOW. WE WERE OFF THE ISLAND, AND CAME BACK TO--
YOU WERE *FREE,* AND YOU *RETURNED?* VERY NOBLE, BOY.
BUT PERHAPS *FOOLISH.* I WILL TELL YOU WHAT *HAPPENED.*

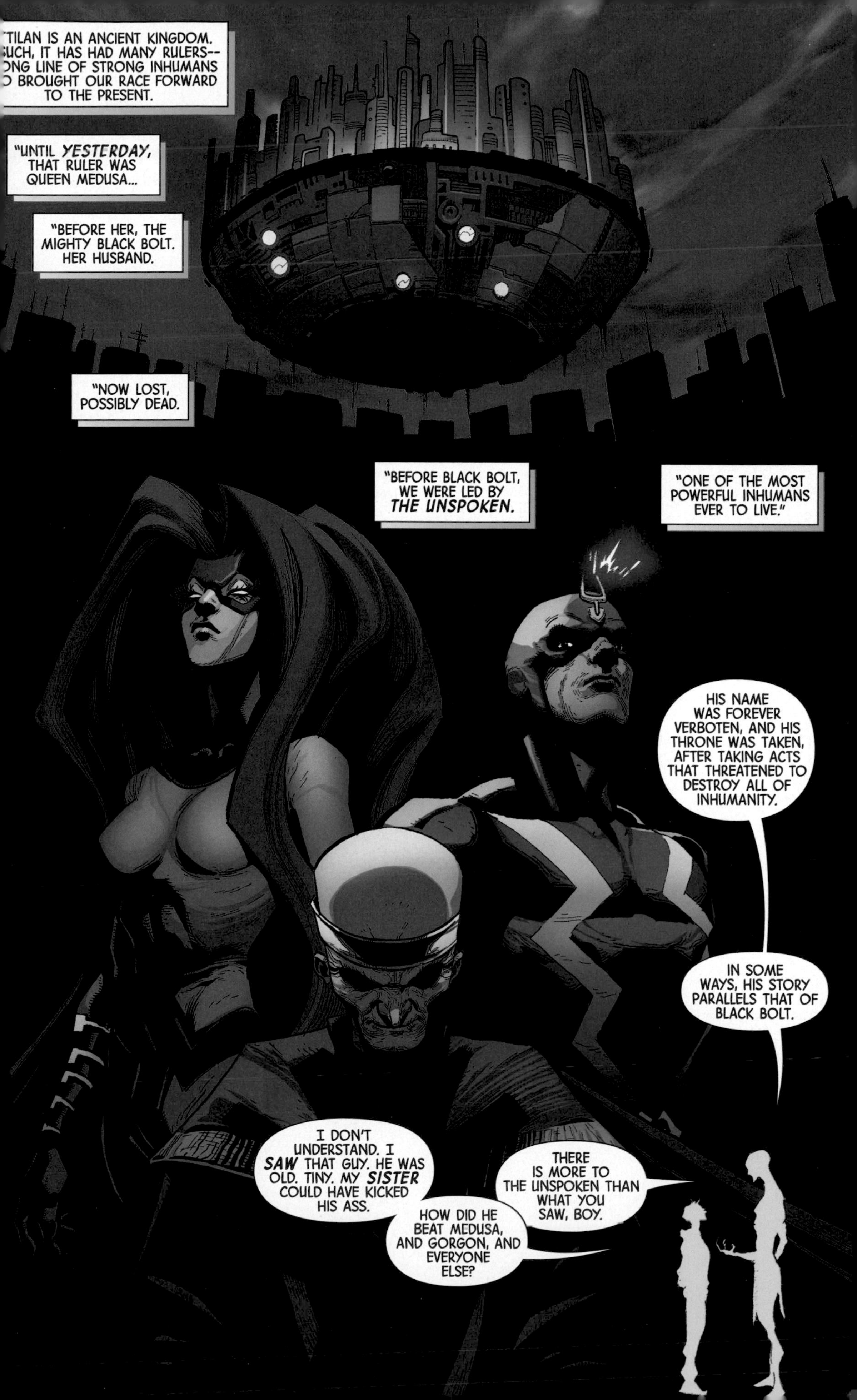
TILAN IS AN ANCIENT KINGDOM. UCH, IT HAS HAD MANY RULERS-- ONG LINE OF STRONG INHUMANS O BROUGHT OUR RACE FORWARD TO THE PRESENT.
"UNTIL YESTERDAY, THAT RULER WAS QUEEN MEDUSA...
"BEFORE HER, THE MIGHTY BLACK BOLT. HER HUSBAND.
"NOW LOST, POSSIBLY DEAD.
"BEFORE BLACK BOLT, WE WERE LED BY THE UNSPOKEN.
"ONE OF THE MOST POWERFUL INHUMANS EVER TO LIVE."
HIS NAME WAS FOREVER VERBOTEN, AND HIS THRONE WAS TAKEN, AFTER TAKING ACTS THAT THREATENED TO DESTROY ALL OF INHUMANITY.
IN SOME WAYS, HIS STORY PARALLELS THAT OF BLACK BOLT.
I DON'T UNDERSTAND. I SAW THAT GUY. HE WAS OLD. TINY. MY SISTER COULD HAVE KICKED HIS ASS.
HOW DID HE BEAT MEDUSA, AND GORGON, AND EVERYONE ELSE?
THERE IS MORE TO THE UNSPOKEN THAN WHAT YOU SAW, BOY.

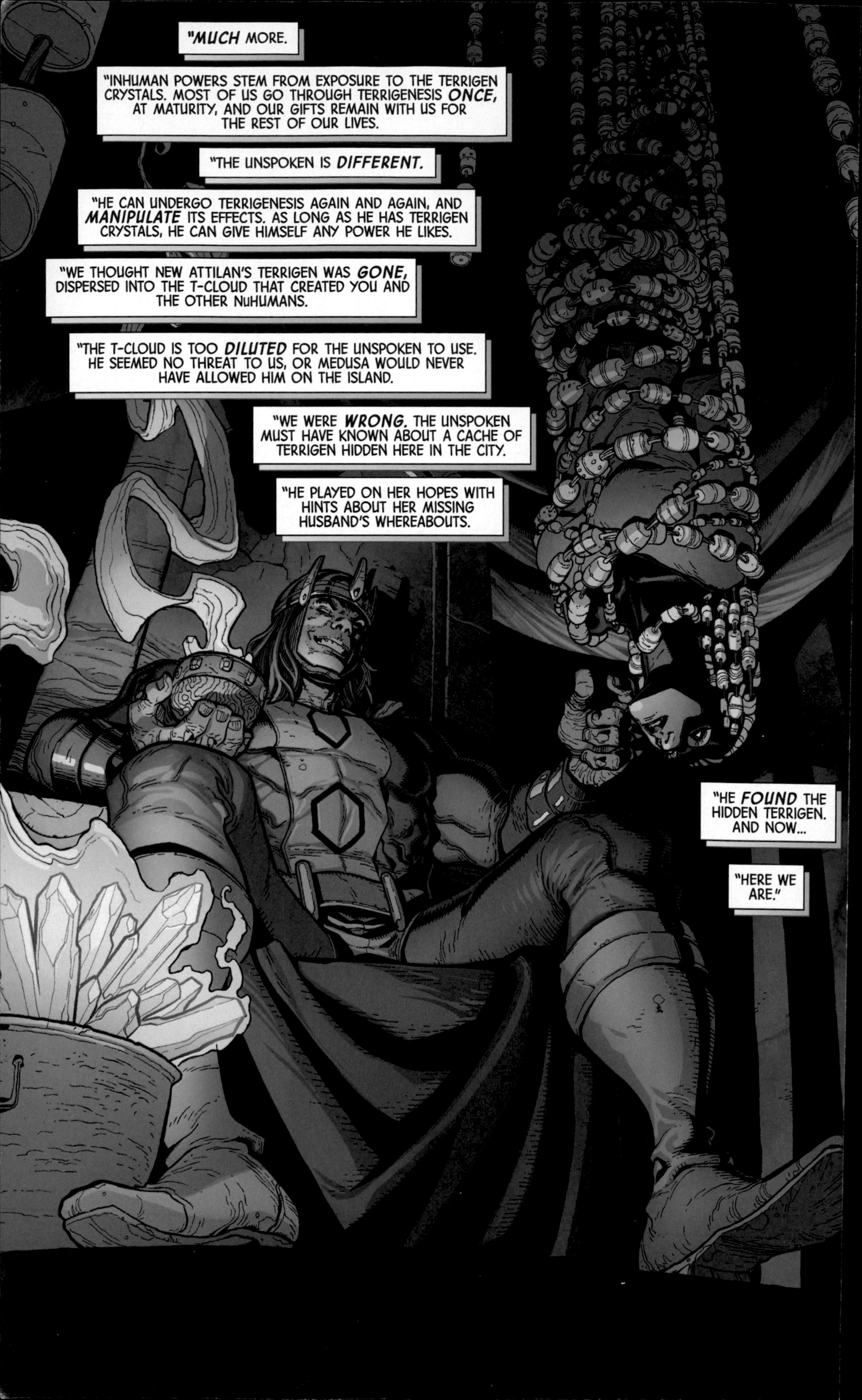
"MUCH MORE.
"INHUMAN POWERS STEM FROM EXPOSURE TO THE TERRIGEN CRYSTALS. MOST OF US GO THROUGH TERRIGENESIS ONCE, AT MATURITY, AND OUR GIFTS REMAIN WITH US FOR THE REST OF OUR LIVES.
"THE UNSPOKEN IS DIFFERENT.
"HE CAN UNDERGO TERRIGENESIS AGAIN AND AGAIN, AND MANIPULATE ITS EFFECTS. AS LONG AS HE HAS TERRIGEN CRYSTALS, HE CAN GIVE HIMSELF ANY POWER HE LIKES.
"WE THOUGHT NEW ATTILAN'S TERRIGEN WAS GONE, DISPERSED INTO THE T-CLOUD THAT CREATED YOU AND THE OTHER NuHUMANS.
"THE T-CLOUD IS TOO DILUTED FOR THE UNSPOKEN TO USE. HE SEEMED NO THREAT TO US, OR MEDUSA WOULD NEVER HAVE ALLOWED HIM ON THE ISLAND.
"WE WERE WRONG. THE UNSPOKEN MUST HAVE KNOWN ABOUT A CACHE OF TERRIGEN HIDDEN HERE IN THE CITY.
"HE PLAYED ON HER HOPES WITH HINTS ABOUT HER MISSING HUSBAND'S WHEREABOUTS.
"HE FOUND THE HIDDEN TERRIGEN. AND NOW...
"HERE WE ARE."

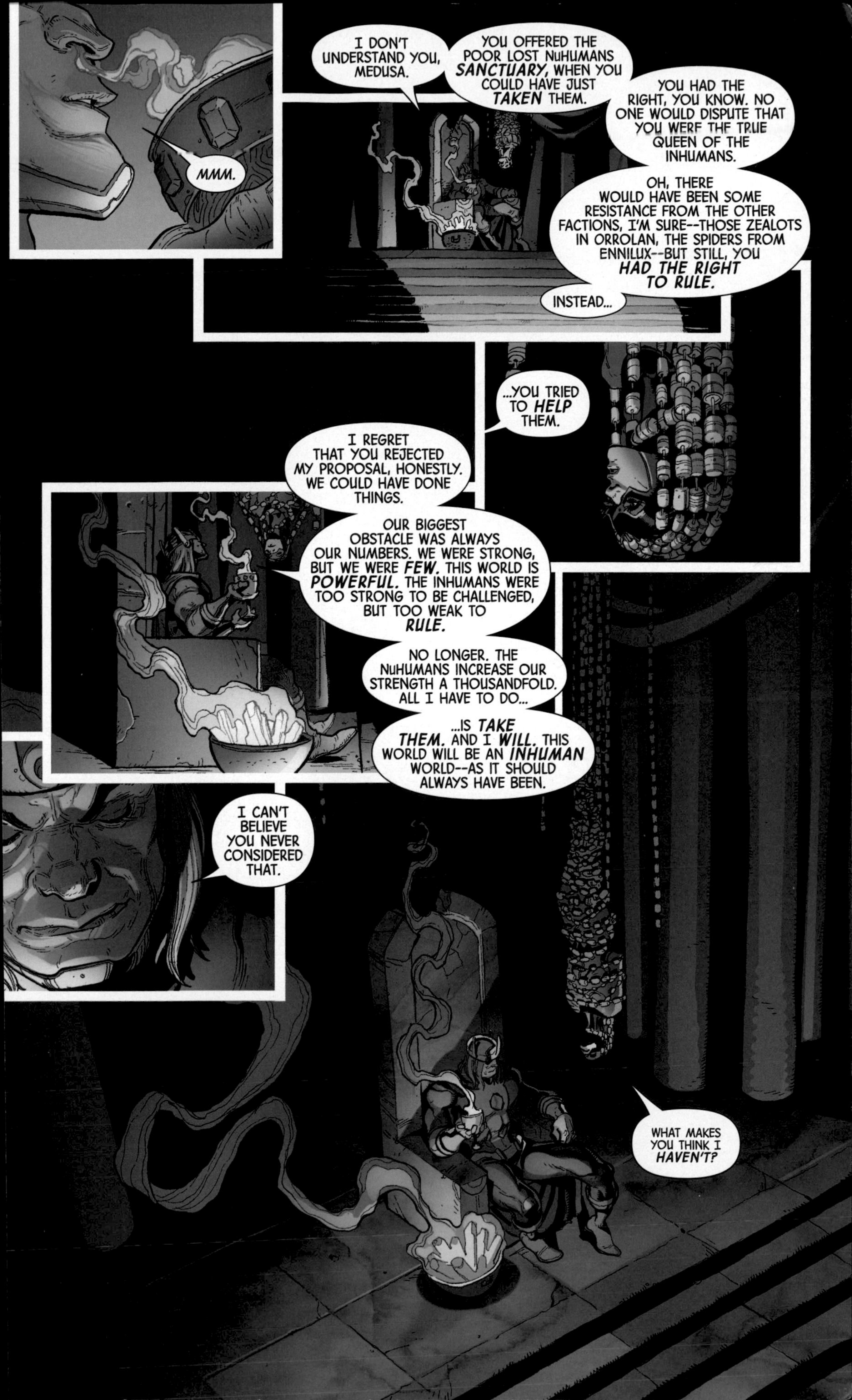
MMM.
I DON'T UNDERSTAND YOU, MEDUSA.
YOU OFFERED THE POOR LOST NuHUMANS SANCTUARY, WHEN YOU COULD HAVE JUST TAKEN THEM.
YOU HAD THE RIGHT, YOU KNOW. NO ONE WOULD DISPUTE THAT YOU WERE THE TRUE QUEEN OF THE INHUMANS.
OH, THERE WOULD HAVE BEEN SOME RESISTANCE FROM THE OTHER FACTIONS, I'M SURE--THOSE ZEALOTS IN ORROLAN, THE SPIDERS FROM ENNILUX--BUT STILL, YOU HAD THE RIGHT TO RULE.
INSTEAD...
...YOU TRIED TO HELP THEM.
I REGRET THAT YOU REJECTED MY PROPOSAL, HONESTLY. WE COULD HAVE DONE THINGS.
OUR BIGGEST OBSTACLE WAS ALWAYS OUR NUMBERS. WE WERE STRONG, BUT WE WERE FEW. THIS WORLD IS POWERFUL. THE INHUMANS WERE TOO STRONG TO BE CHALLENGED, BUT TOO WEAK TO RULE.
NO LONGER. THE NuHUMANS INCREASE OUR STRENGTH A THOUSANDFOLD. ALL I HAVE TO DO...
...IS TAKE THEM. AND I WILL. THIS WORLD WILL BE AN INHUMAN WORLD--AS IT SHOULD ALWAYS HAVE BEEN.
I CAN'T BELIEVE YOU NEVER CONSIDERED THAT.
WHAT MAKES YOU THINK I HAVEN'T?

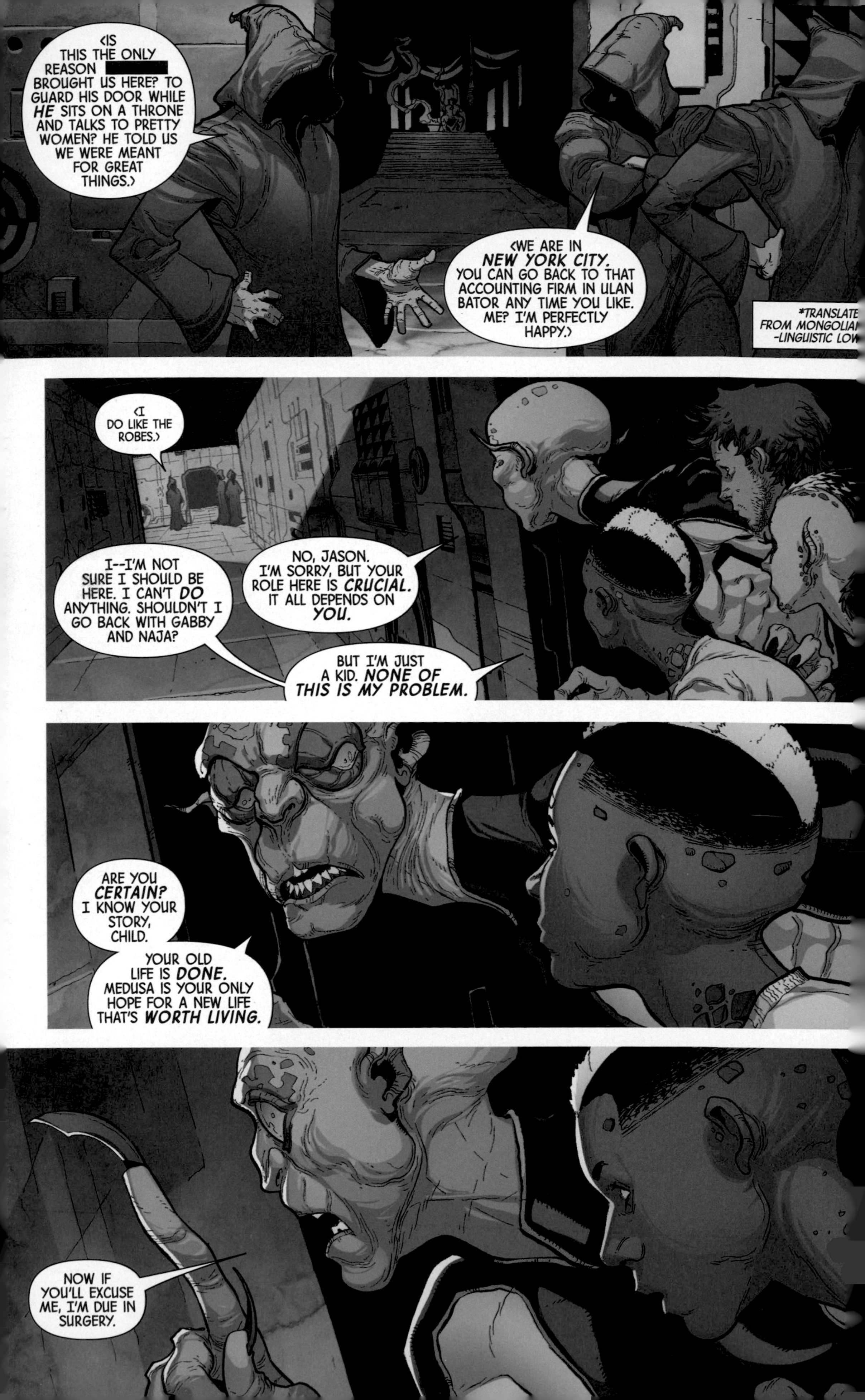
‹IS THIS THE ONLY REASON [redacted] BROUGHT US HERE? TO GUARD HIS DOOR WHILE HE SITS ON A THRONE AND TALKS TO PRETTY WOMEN? HE TOLD US WE WERE MEANT FOR GREAT THINGS.›
‹WE ARE IN NEW YORK CITY. YOU CAN GO BACK TO THAT ACCOUNTING FIRM IN ULAN BATOR ANY TIME YOU LIKE. ME? I'M PERFECTLY HAPPY.›
*TRANSLATE
FROM MONGOLIA
-LINGUISTIC LOW
‹I DO LIKE THE ROBES.›
I--I'M NOT SURE I SHOULD BE HERE. I CAN'T DO ANYTHING. SHOULDN'T I GO BACK WITH GABBY AND NAJA?
NO, JASON. I'M SORRY, BUT YOUR ROLE HERE IS CRUCIAL. IT ALL DEPENDS ON YOU.
BUT I'M JUST A KID. NONE OF THIS IS MY PROBLEM.
ARE YOU CERTAIN? I KNOW YOUR STORY, CHILD.
YOUR OLD LIFE IS DONE. MEDUSA IS YOUR ONLY HOPE FOR A NEW LIFE THAT'S WORTH LIVING.
NOW IF YOU'LL EXCUSE ME, I'M DUE IN SURGERY.

〈STOP THERE.〉

〈I ALLOWED IN. I DOCTOR. YOU REMEMBER. I NEED CHECK QUEEN.〉

〈YOUR SPEECH IS PATHETIC. YOU SOUND LIKE AN INFANT.〉

〈AGREE. STILL MUST DO JOB. UNSPOKEN KING ASK ME.〉

〈I'LL CHECK WITH THE KING.〉

〈GOOD IDEA.〉

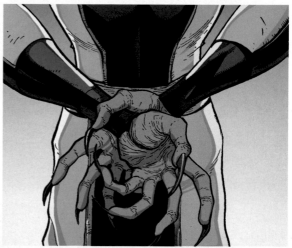

T

SLSH

PPPHHH

SLSH

〈INFANT? INFANT? I HAVE COMPOSED EPIC POEMS IN YOUR LANGUAGE, YOU PHILISTINES!〉

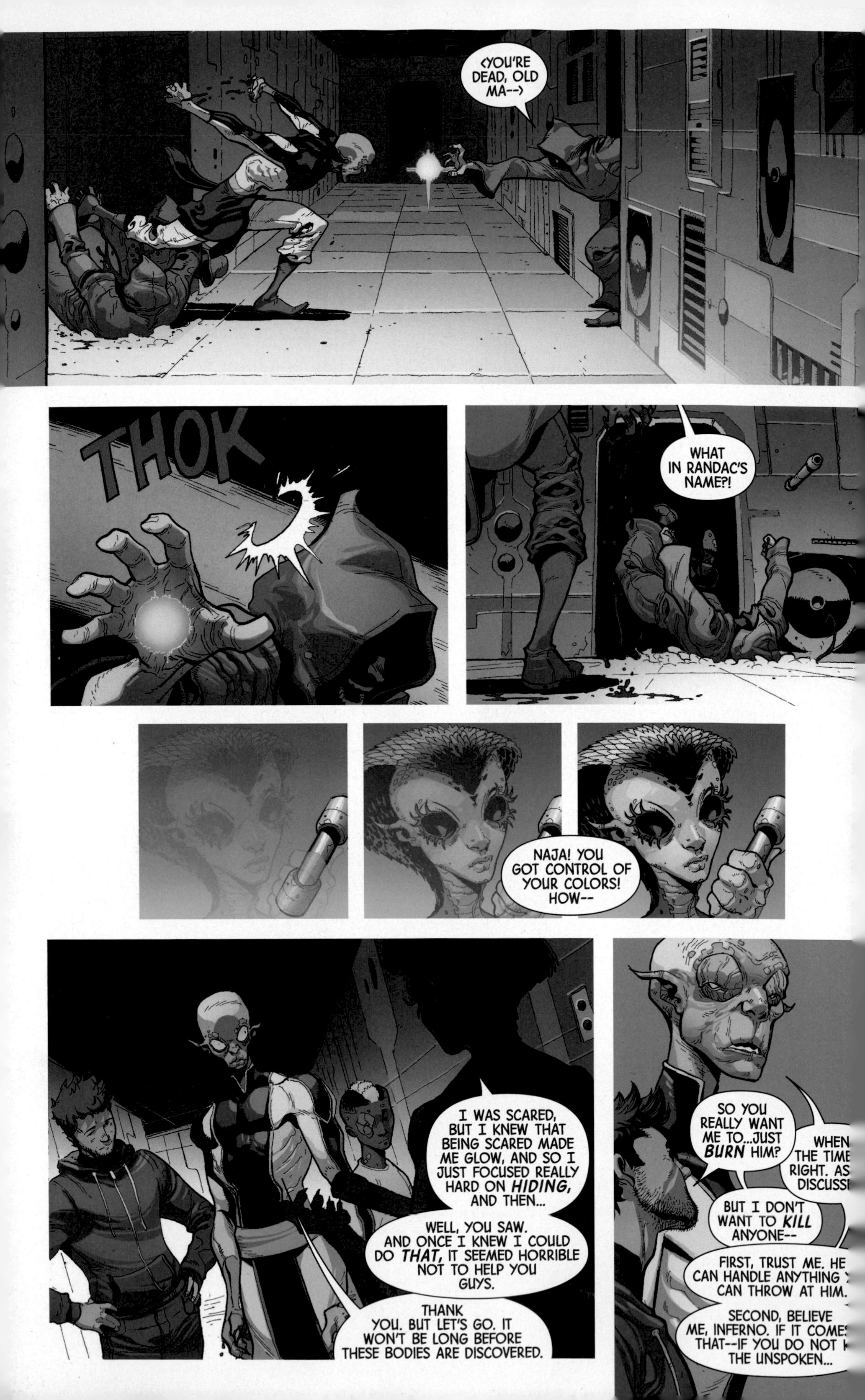
<YOU'RE DEAD, OLD MA-->
THOK
WHAT IN RANDAC'S NAME?!
NAJA! YOU GOT CONTROL OF YOUR COLORS! HOW--
I WAS SCARED, BUT I KNEW THAT BEING SCARED MADE ME GLOW, AND SO I JUST FOCUSED REALLY HARD ON HIDING, AND THEN...
WELL, YOU SAW. AND ONCE I KNEW I COULD DO THAT, IT SEEMED HORRIBLE NOT TO HELP YOU GUYS.
THANK YOU. BUT LET'S GO. IT WON'T BE LONG BEFORE THESE BODIES ARE DISCOVERED.
SO YOU REALLY WANT ME TO...JUST BURN HIM?
WHEN THE TIME RIGHT. AS DISCUSS
BUT I DON'T WANT TO KILL ANYONE--
FIRST, TRUST ME. HE CAN HANDLE ANYTHING CAN THROW AT HIM.
SECOND, BELIEVE ME, INFERNO. IF IT COME THAT--IF YOU DO NOT THE UNSPOKEN...

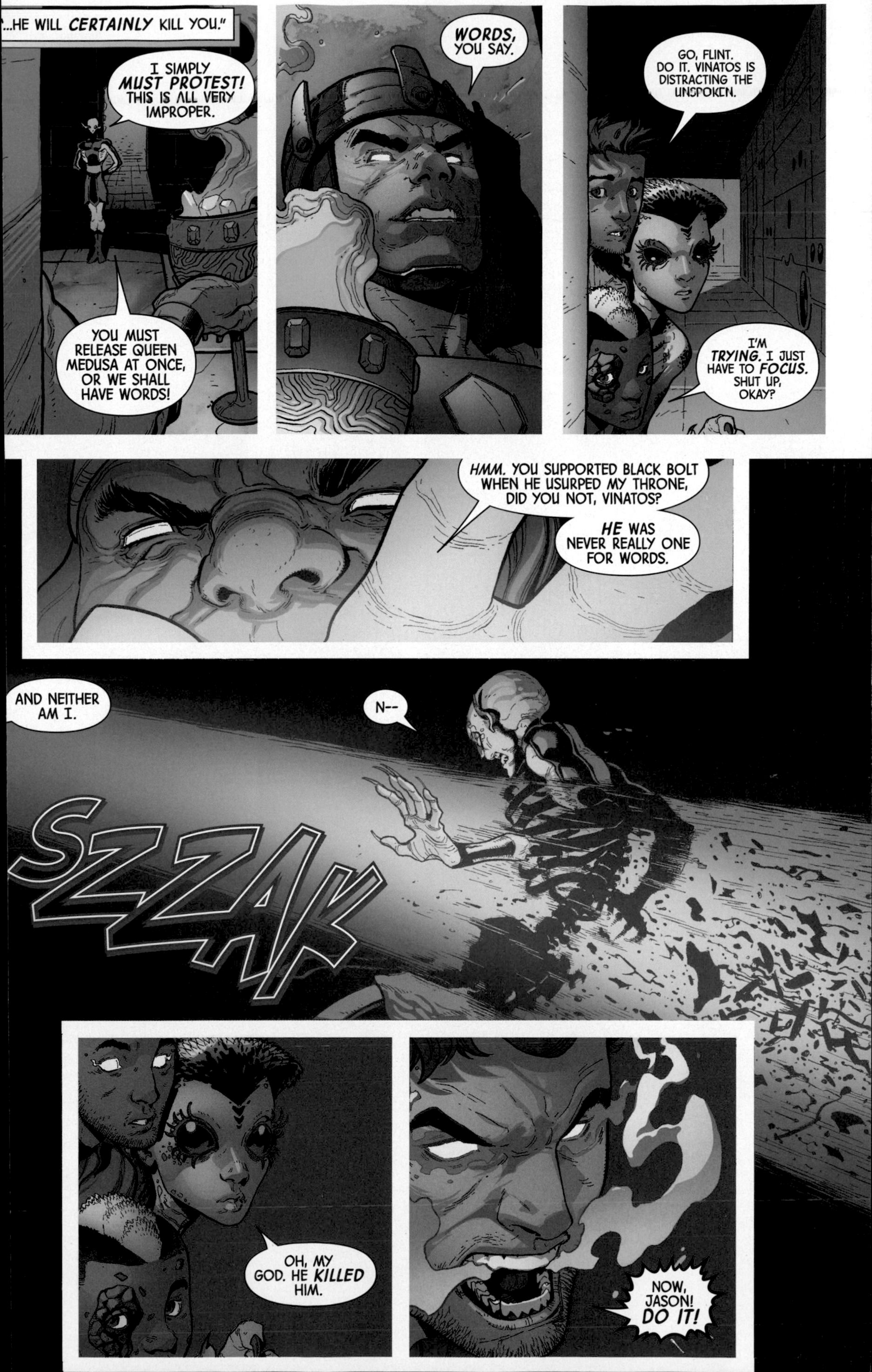
"...HE WILL CERTAINLY KILL YOU."
I SIMPLY MUST PROTEST! THIS IS ALL VERY IMPROPER.
YOU MUST RELEASE QUEEN MEDUSA AT ONCE, OR WE SHALL HAVE WORDS!
WORDS, YOU SAY.
GO, FLINT. DO IT. VINATOS IS DISTRACTING THE UNSPOKEN.
I'M TRYING. I JUST HAVE TO FOCUS. SHUT UP, OKAY?
HMM. YOU SUPPORTED BLACK BOLT WHEN HE USURPED MY THRONE, DID YOU NOT, VINATOS?
HE WAS NEVER REALLY ONE FOR WORDS.
AND NEITHER AM I.
N--
SZZAK
OH, MY GOD. HE KILLED HIM.
NOW, JASON! DO IT!

YOU'RE DONE, MAN.

OH, REALLY?

AND WHAT ARE *YOU?*

DANTE, *NO!* HE'S TOO STRONG!

I'M *INFERNO.*

HA! *CANDLE* WOULD SUIT YO BETTER.

I THINK I'LL *BLOW* YOU OUT.

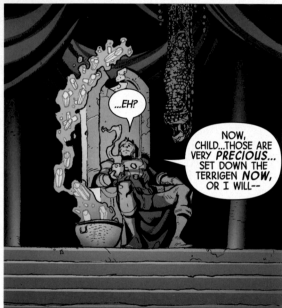

...EH?

NOW, CHILD...THOSE ARE VERY *PRECIOUS...* SET DOWN THE TERRIGEN *NOW,* OR I WILL--

YOU WANNA KNOW SOMETHING?

I *LIKED* THAT DOCTOR GUY.

SMASH

NOOOO!

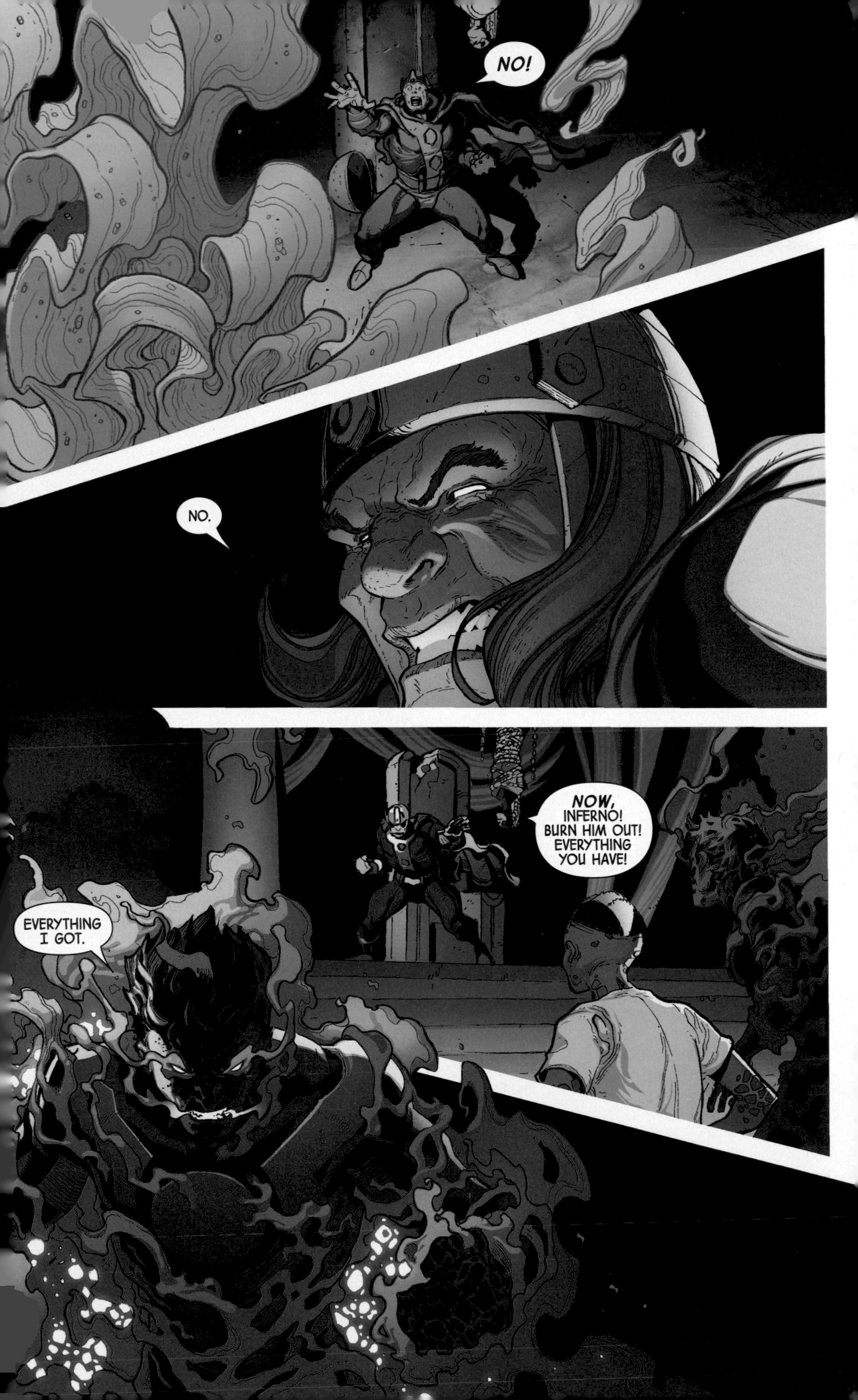
NO!
NO.
NOW, INFERNO! BURN HIM OUT! EVERYTHING YOU HAVE!
EVERYTHING I GOT.

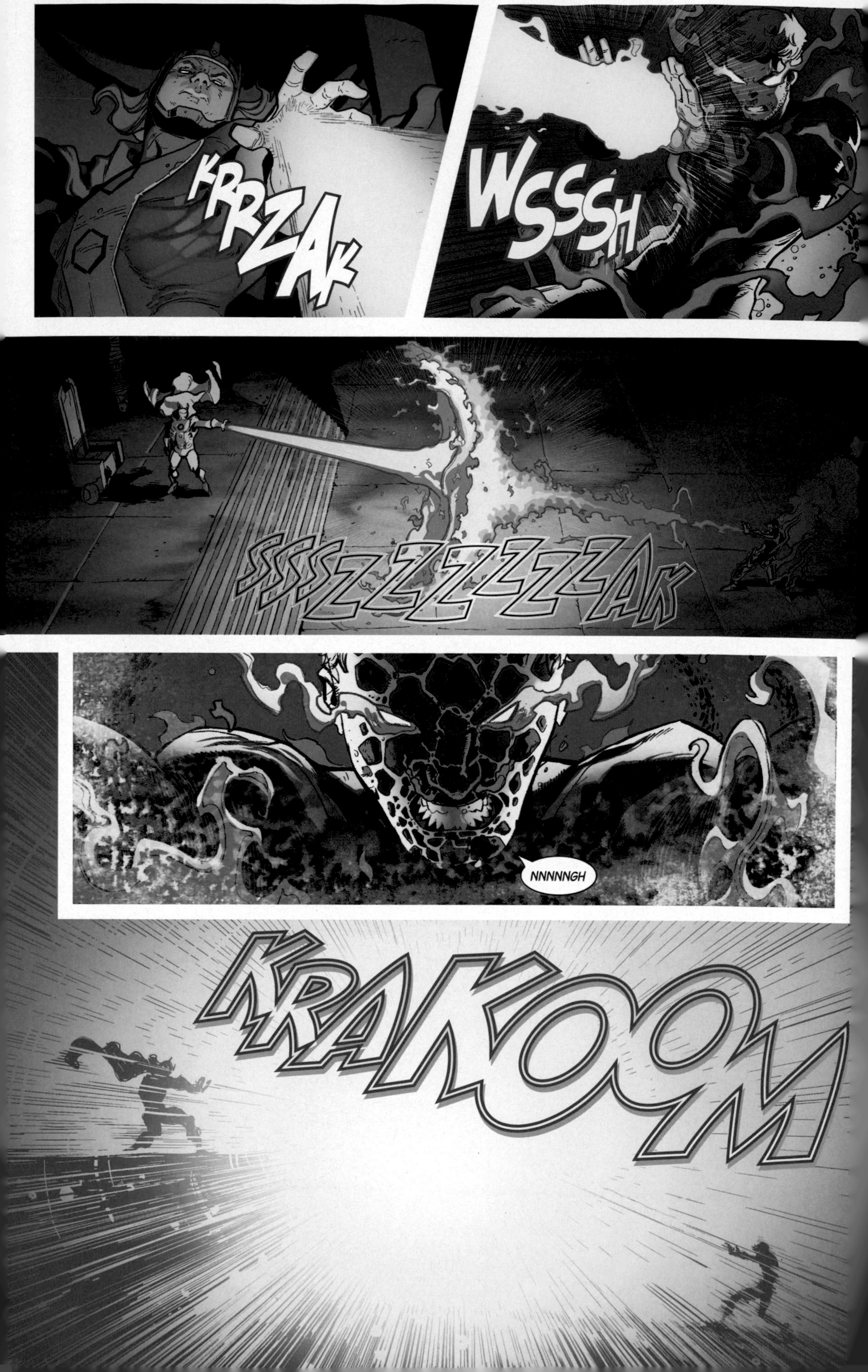
KRRZAK
WSSSH
SSSZZZZZZZAK
NNNNNGH
KRAKOOM

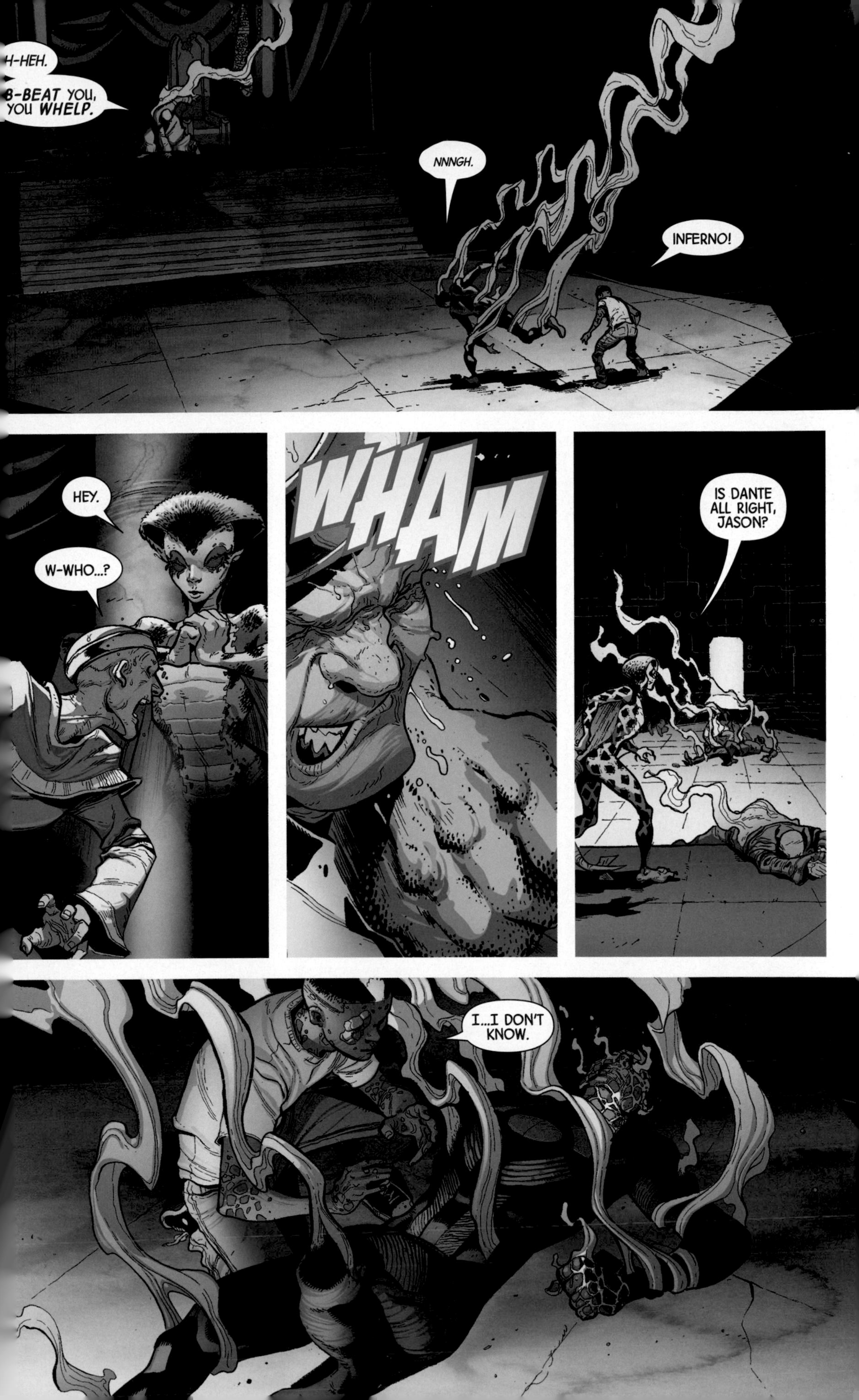
H-HEH.
B-BEAT YOU, YOU WHELP.
NNNGH.
INFERNO!
HEY.
W-WHO...?
WHAM
IS DANTE ALL RIGHT, JASON?
I...I DON'T KNOW.

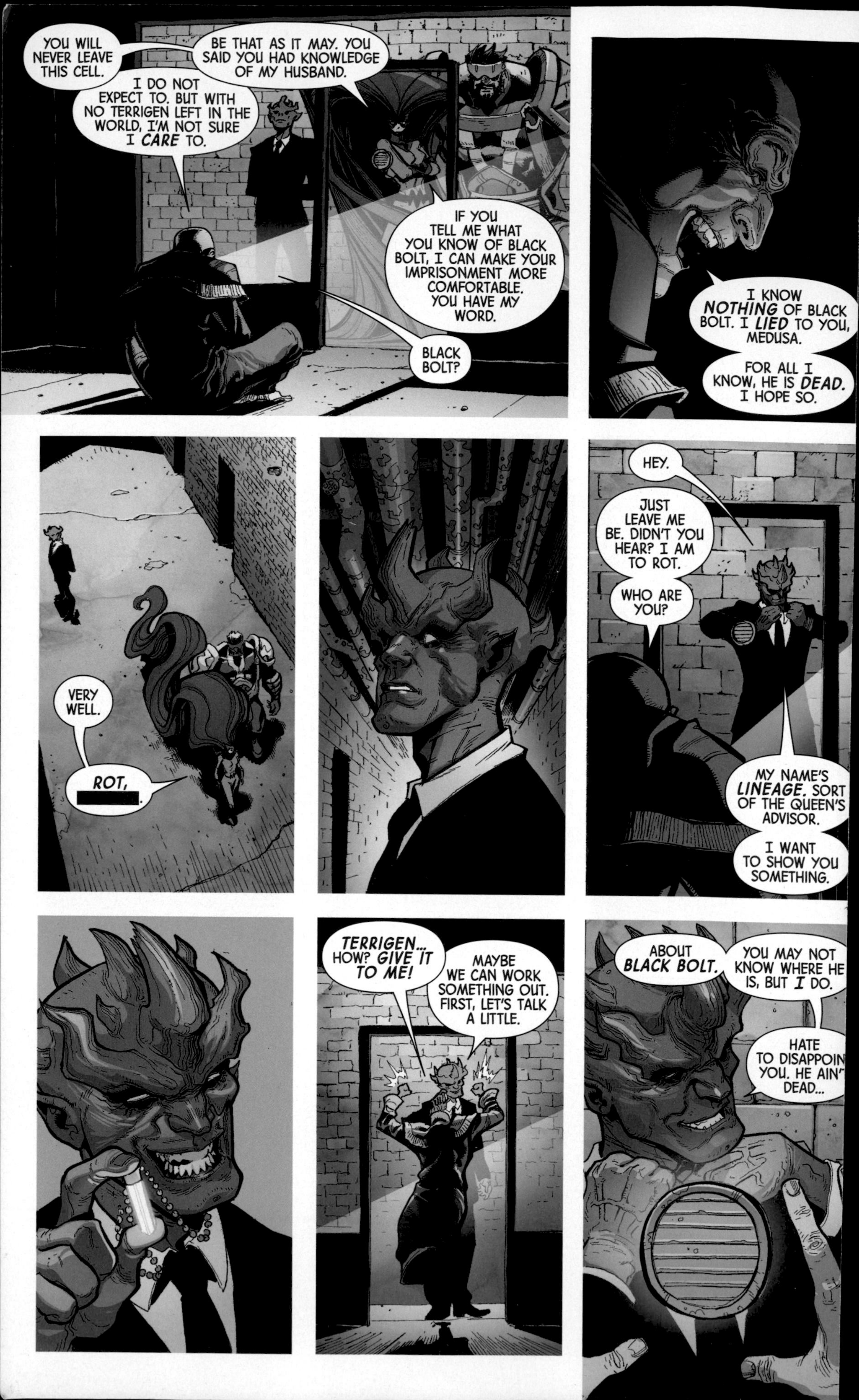

YOU WILL NEVER LEAVE THIS CELL.
I DO NOT EXPECT TO. BUT WITH NO TERRIGEN LEFT IN THE WORLD, I'M NOT SURE I *CARE* TO.
BE THAT AS IT MAY. YOU SAID YOU HAD KNOWLEDGE OF MY HUSBAND.
IF YOU TELL ME WHAT YOU KNOW OF BLACK BOLT, I CAN MAKE YOUR IMPRISONMENT MORE COMFORTABLE. YOU HAVE MY WORD.
BLACK BOLT?
I KNOW *NOTHING* OF BLACK BOLT. I *LIED* TO YOU, MEDUSA.
FOR ALL I KNOW, HE IS *DEAD*. I HOPE SO.
VERY WELL.
ROT, [redacted].
HEY.
JUST LEAVE ME BE. DIDN'T YOU HEAR? I AM TO ROT.
WHO ARE YOU?
MY NAME'S *LINEAGE.* SORT OF THE QUEEN'S ADVISOR.
I WANT TO SHOW YOU SOMETHING.
TERRIGEN... HOW? *GIVE IT TO ME!*
MAYBE WE CAN WORK SOMETHING OUT. FIRST, LET'S TALK A LITTLE.
ABOUT *BLACK BOLT.*
YOU MAY NOT KNOW WHERE HE IS, BUT *I* DO.
HATE TO DISAPPOIN YOU. HE AIN' DEAD...

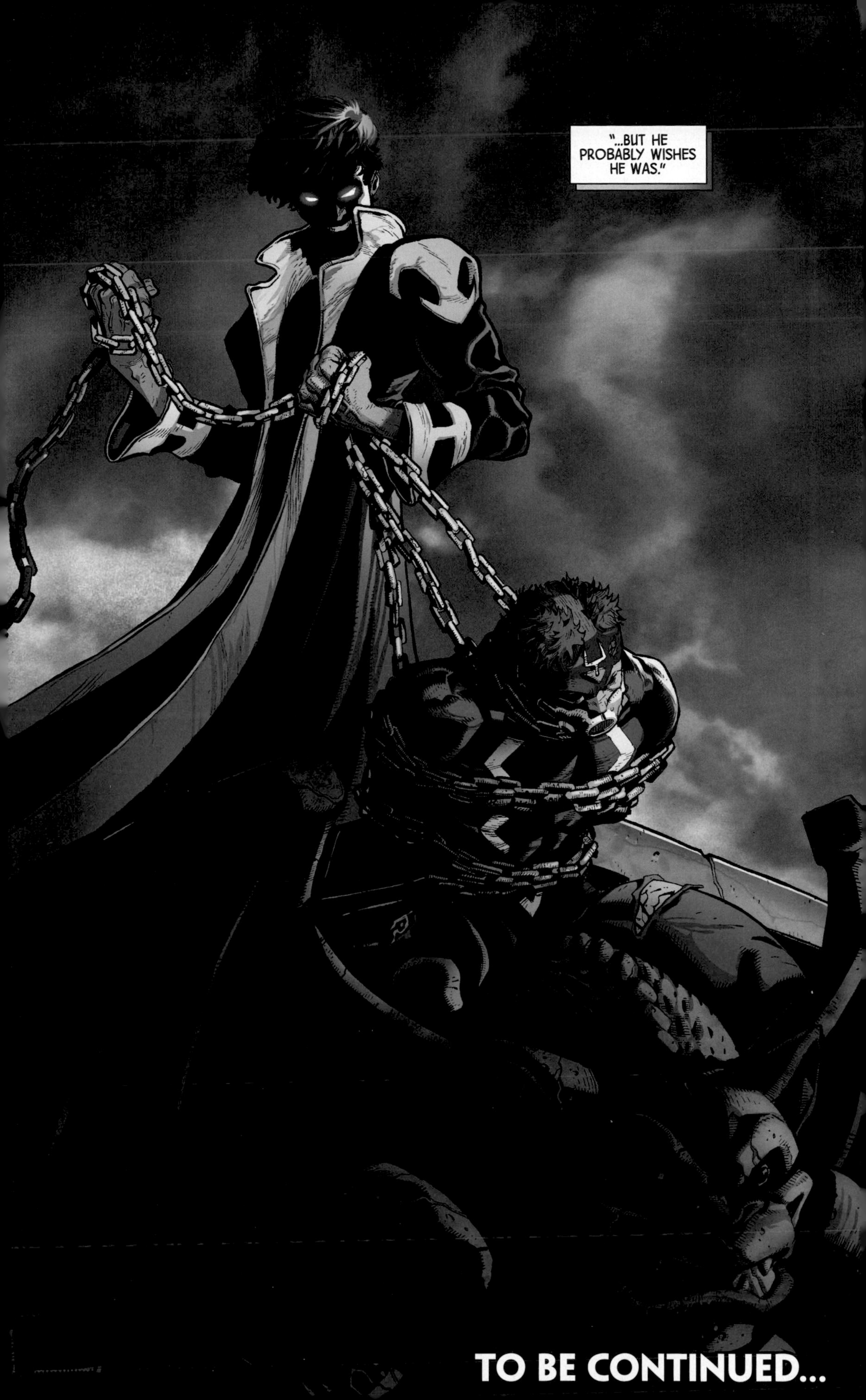
"...BUT HE PROBABLY WISHES HE WAS."
TO BE CONTINUED...

STARK TECH S.H.I.E.L.D. DATA MODULE

3/7/2014

SHIELD DATA FILE 095634.1

AFTER THE FALL OF THE INHUMAN CITY OF ATTILAN, IT APPEARS THAT AN UNKNOWN AMOUNT OF TERRIGEN GAS WAS RELEASED INTO EARTH'S ATMOSPHERE.

THE INCLUDED METEOROLOGICAL DATA TRACES THE MIST'S PATH ACROSS THE SURFACE OF THE PLANET. IT IS EVIDENT HOW NATURAL WIND CYCLES INFLUCENED THE SPREAD OF THE MIST.

TERRIGE

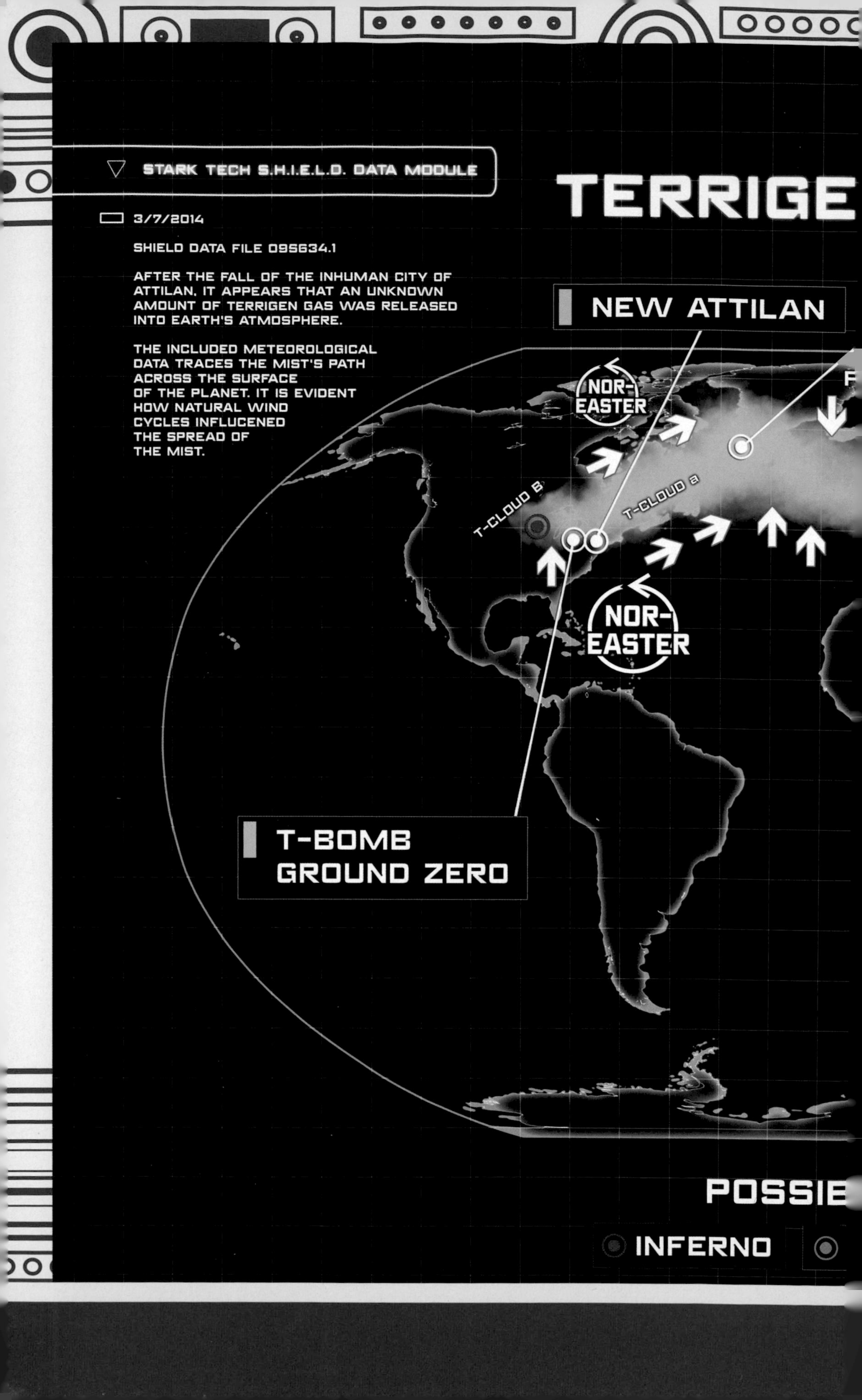
NEW ATTILAN
NOR-EASTER
T-CLOUD B
T-CLOUD a
NOR-EASTER
T-BOMB GROUND ZERO

POSSIE

INFERNO

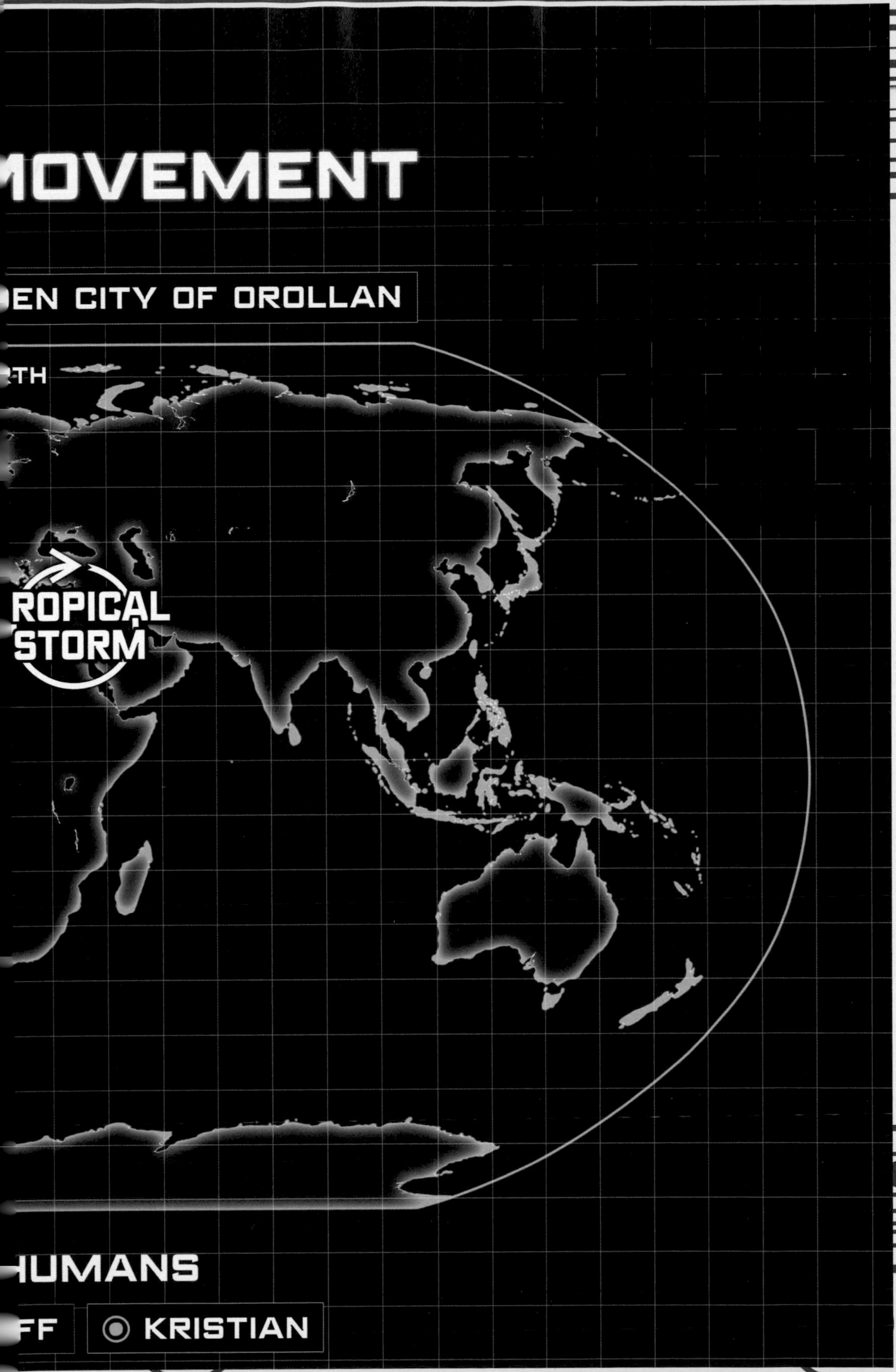
OVEMENT
EN CITY OF OROLLAN
TH
ROPICAL
STORM
UMANS
FF
KRISTIAN

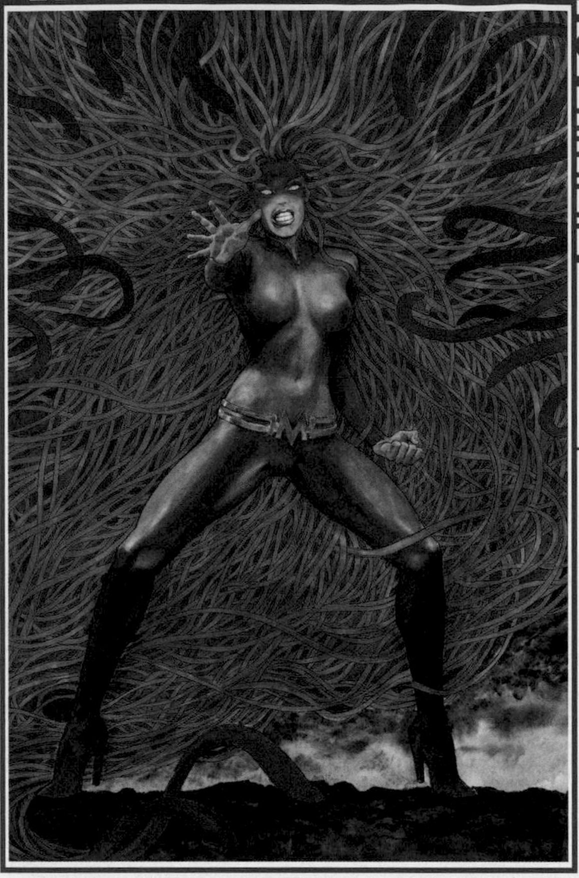

#1 VARIANT BY MILO MANARA

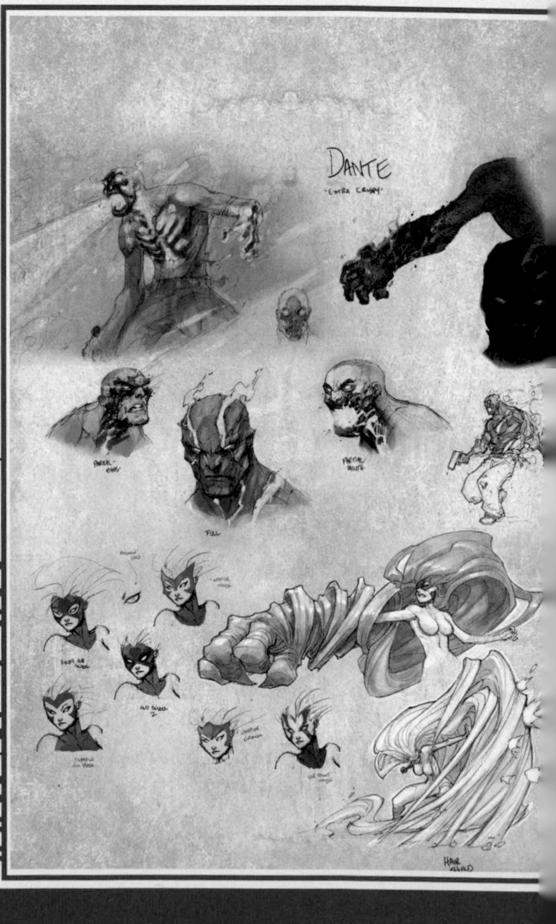
DANTE

#1 DESIGN VARIANT BY
JOE MADUREIRA

#1 VARIANT BY J. SCOTT CAMPBELL & NEI RUFFINO

#1 VARIANT BY HUMBERTO RAMOS & EDGAR DELGADO

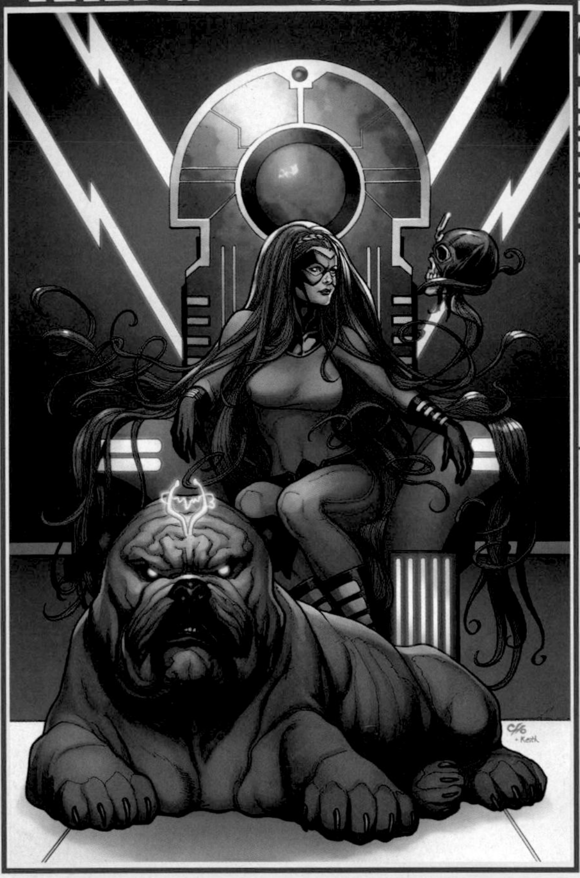

#2 VARIANT BY FRANK CHO & JASON KEITH

#3 VARIANT BY ED MCGUINNESS & ISRAEL SILVA

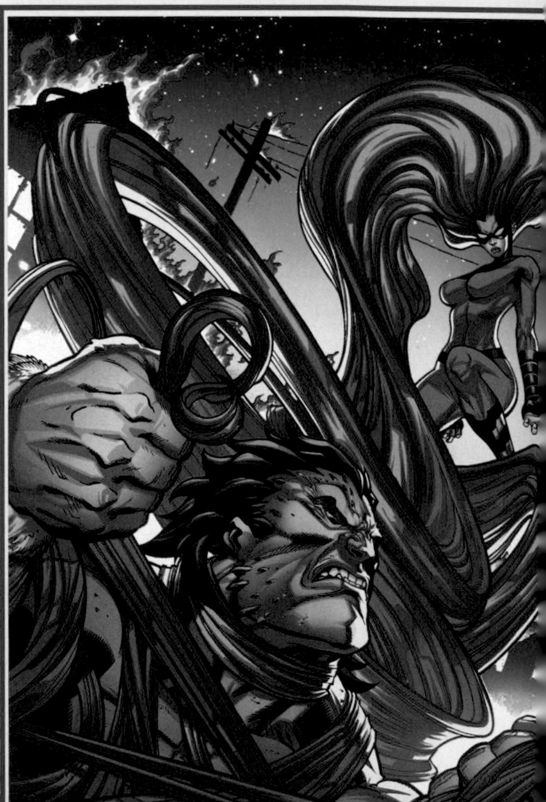

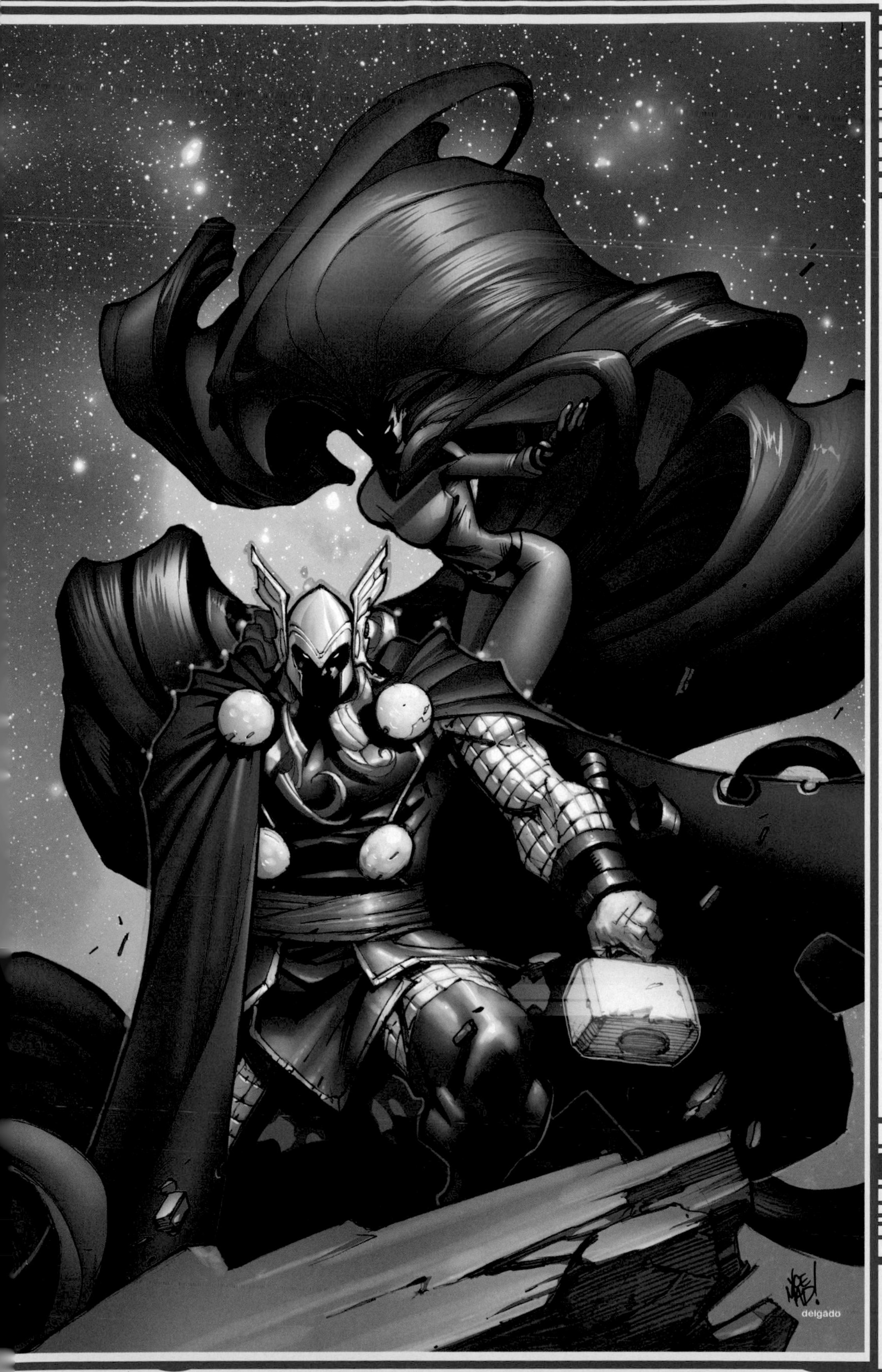
JOE MAD!
delgado

4

VARIANT BY JOE MADUREIRA
& EDGAR DELGADO

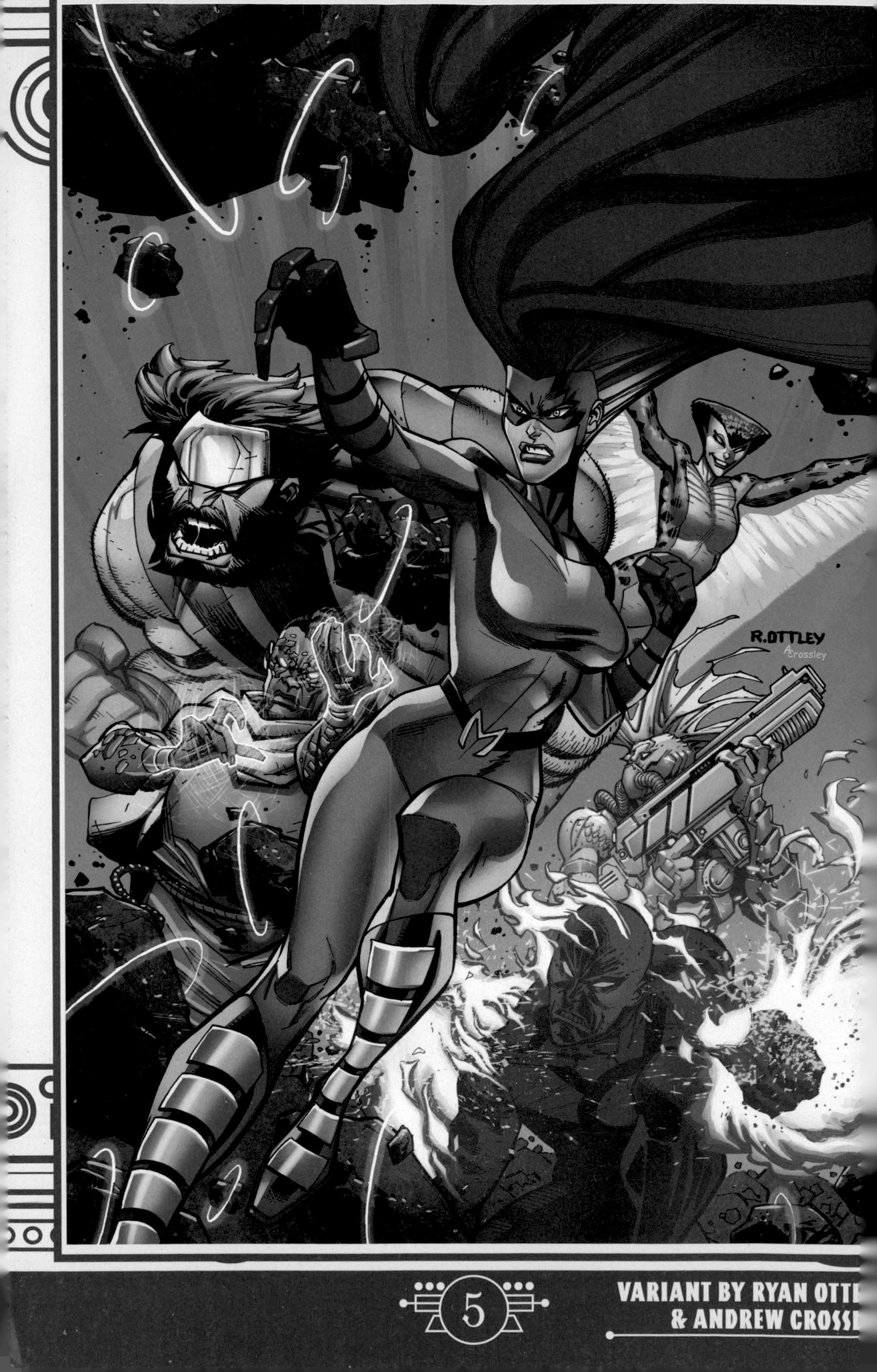
R.OTTLEY
A Crossley

5

VARIANT BY RYAN OTT
& ANDREW CROSS